MARVEL
GUARDIANS OF THE GALAXY

BASED ON THE TV SERIES WRITTEN BY

MAIRGHREAD SCOTT, ERIC KARTEN, MARSHA GRIFFIN, MARTY ISENBERG & HENRY GILROY

DIRECTED BY

JAMES YANG, JEFF WAMESTER & LEO RILEY

ANIMATION ART PRODUCED BY

MARVEL ANIMATION STUDIOS

ADAPTED BY

JOE CARAMAGNA

SPECIAL THANKS TO

HANNAH MACDONALD & PRODUCT FACTORY

EDITORS

CHRISTINA HARRINGTON, SEBASTIAN GIRNER & JON MOISAN

SENIOR EDITOR

MARK PANICCIA

COLLECTION EDITOR: **JENNIFER GRÜNWALD**
ASSISTANT EDITOR: **CAITLIN O'CONNELL**
ASSOCIATE MANAGING EDITOR: **KATERI WOODY**
EDITOR, SPECIAL PROJECTS: **MARK D. BEAZLEY**
VP PRODUCTION & SPECIAL PROJECTS: **JEFF YOUNGQUIST**
SVP PRINT, SALES & MARKETING: **DAVID GABRIEL**
HEAD OF MARVEL TELEVISION: **JEPH LOEB**

EDITOR IN CHIEF: **AXEL ALONSO**
CHIEF CREATIVE OFFICER: **JOE QUESADA**
PRESIDENT: **DAN BUCKLEY**
EXECUTIVE PRODUCER: **ALAN FINE**

MARVEL UNIVERSE GUARDIANS OF THE GALAXY, VOL. 5. Contains material originally published in magazine form as MARVEL UNIVERSE GUARDIANS OF THE GALAXY (2015A) #1-4 and (2015B) #17-19. First printing 2017. ISBN# 978-1-302-90510-1. Published by MARVEL WORLDWIDE, INC., a subsidiary of MARVEL ENTERTAINMENT, LLC. OFFICE OF PUBLICATION: 135 West 50th Street, New York, NY 10020. Copyright © 2017 MARVEL No similarity between any of the names, characters, persons, and/or institutions in this magazine with those of any living or dead person or institution is intended, and any such similarity which may exist is purely coincidental. **Printed in the U.S.A.** DAN BUCKLEY, President, Marvel Entertainment; JOE QUESADA, Chief Creative Officer; TOM BREVOORT, SVP of Publishing; DAVID BOGART, SVP of Business Affairs & Operations, Publishing & Partnership; C.B. CEBULSKI, VP of Brand Management & Development, Asia; DAVID GABRIEL, SVP of Sales & Marketing, Publishing; JEFF YOUNGQUIST, VP of Production & Special Projects; DAN CARR, Executive Director of Publishing Technology; ALEX MORALES; Director of Publishing Operations; SUSAN CRESPI, Production Manager; STAN LEE, Chairman Emeritus. For information regarding advertising in Marvel Comics or on Marvel.com, please contact Vit DeBellis, Integrated Sales Manager, at vdebellis@marvel.com. For Marvel subscription inquiries, please call 868-511-5480. **Manufactured between 3/10/2017 and 4/11/2017 by SHERIDAN, CHELSEA, MI, USA.**
10 9 8 7 6 5 4 3 2 1

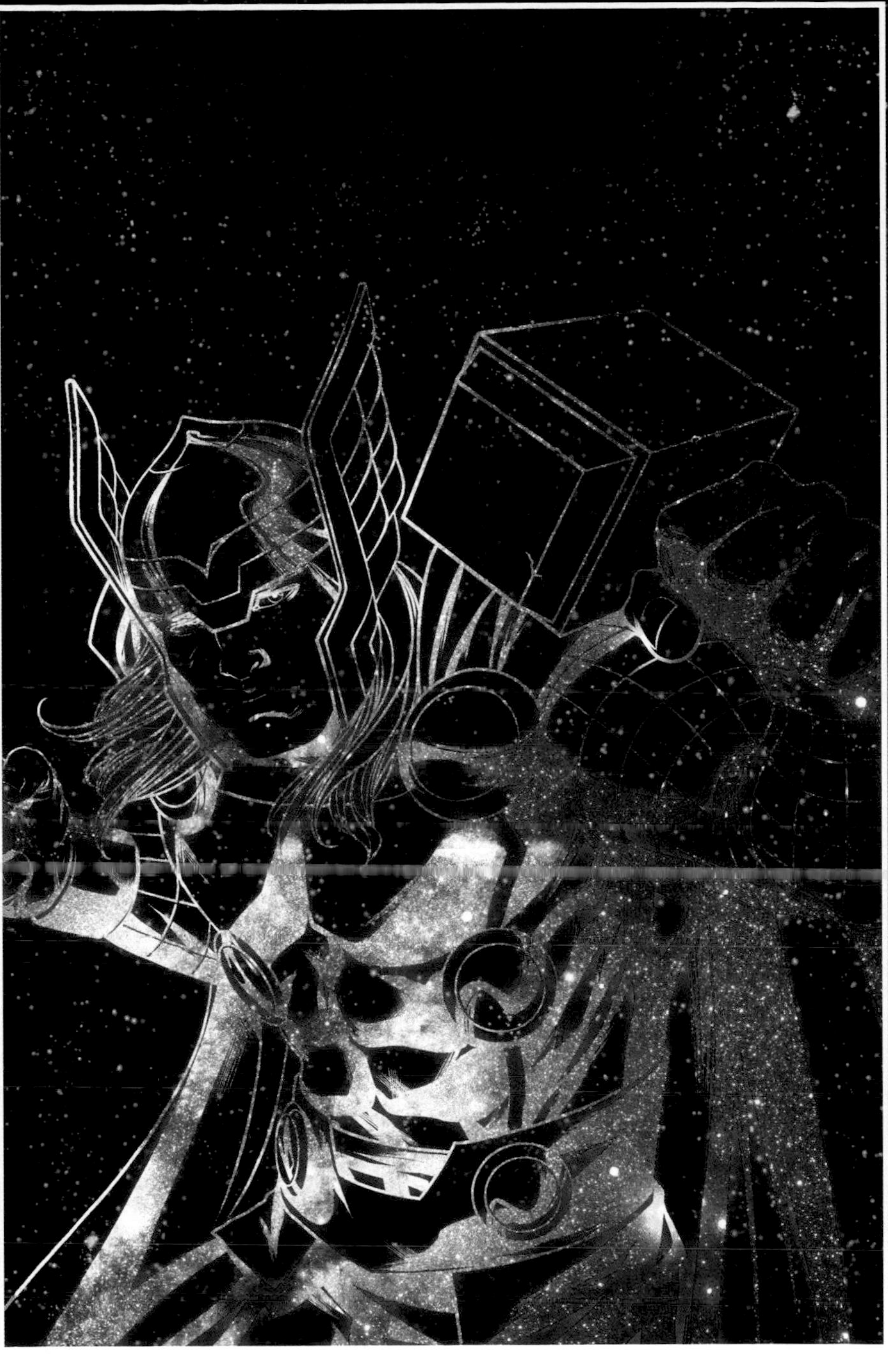

17 BASED ON **"WE ARE THE WORLD TREE"**

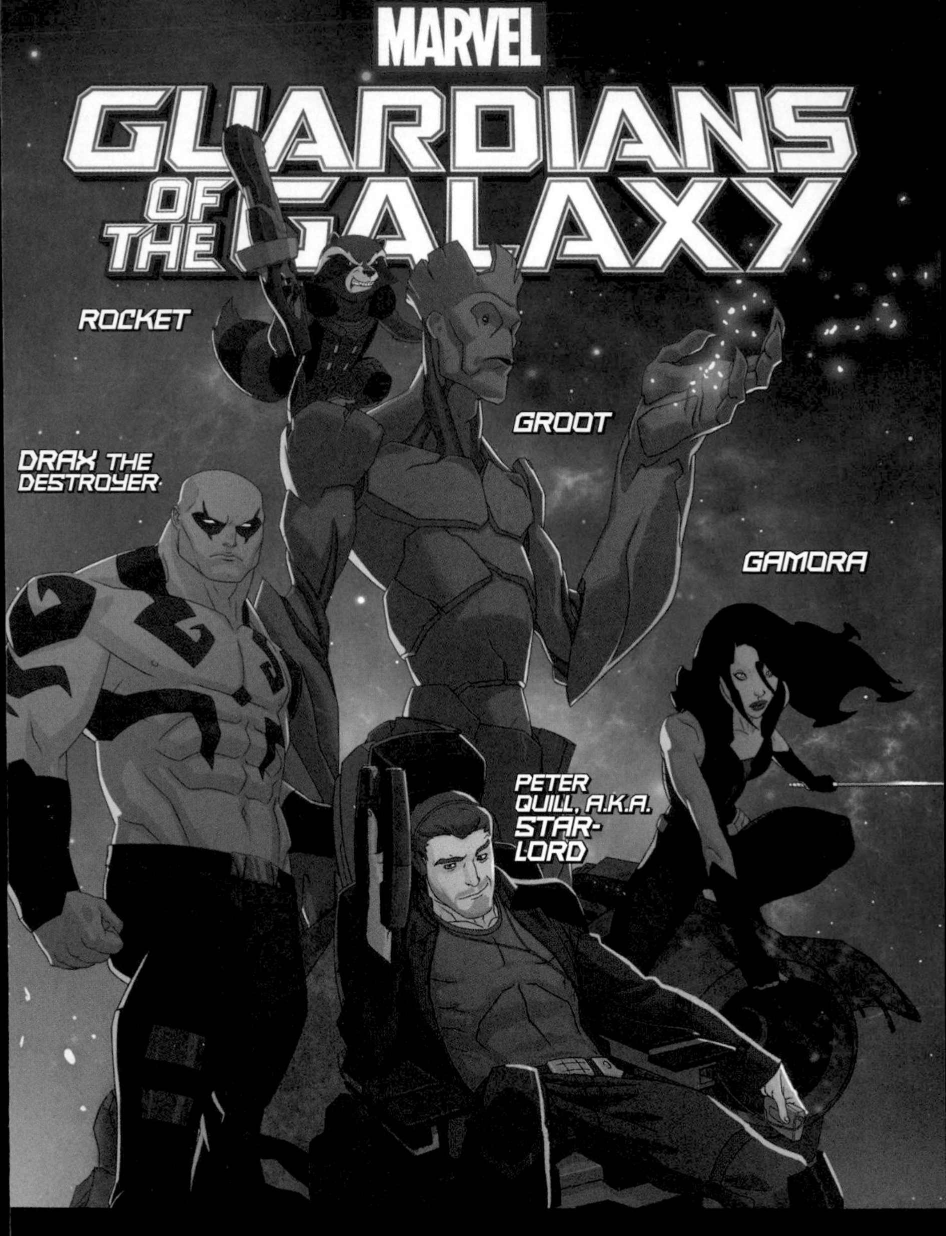
MARVEL
GUARDIANS OF THE GALAXY
ROCKET
GROOT
DRAX THE DESTROYER
GAMORA
PETER QUILL, A.K.A. STAR-LORD

PREVIOUSLY:

The Guardians came into possession of a mysterious Spartaxan cube that holds a map to an object of immense power called the Cosmic Seed. The Guardians traveled to Spartax to find out why Star-Lord is the only one able to access the map, and discovered that he is actually the heir to the Spartax Empire and King J'Son!

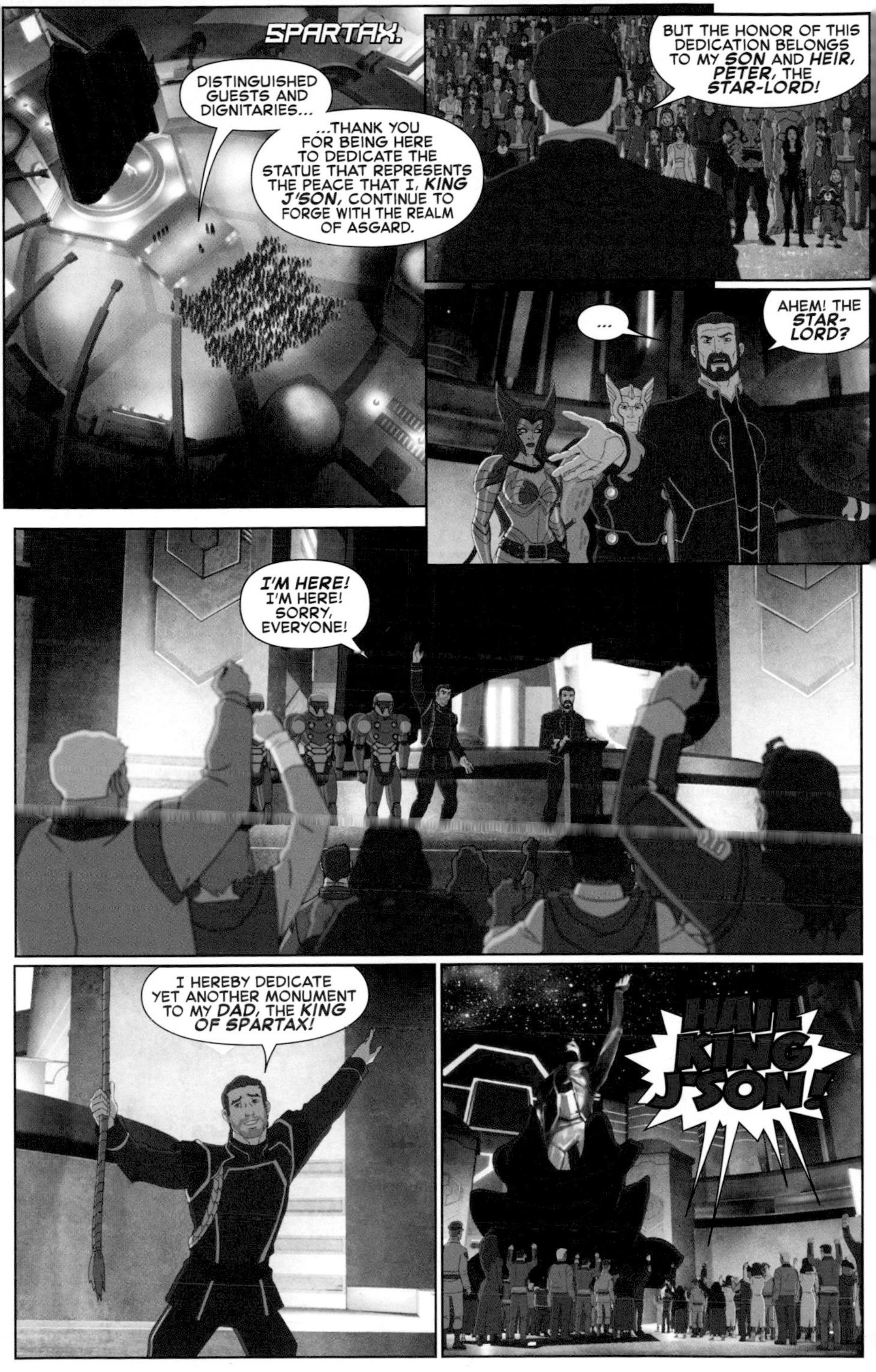
SPARTAX.
DISTINGUISHED GUESTS AND DIGNITARIES...
...THANK YOU FOR BEING HERE TO DEDICATE THE STATUE THAT REPRESENTS THE PEACE THAT I, KING J'SON, CONTINUE TO FORGE WITH THE REALM OF ASGARD.
BUT THE HONOR OF THIS DEDICATION BELONGS TO MY SON AND HEIR, PETER, THE STAR-LORD!
...
AHEM! THE STAR-LORD?
I'M HERE! I'M HERE! SORRY, EVERYONE!
I HEREBY DEDICATE YET ANOTHER MONUMENT TO MY DAD, THE KING OF SPARTAX!
HAIL KING J'SON!

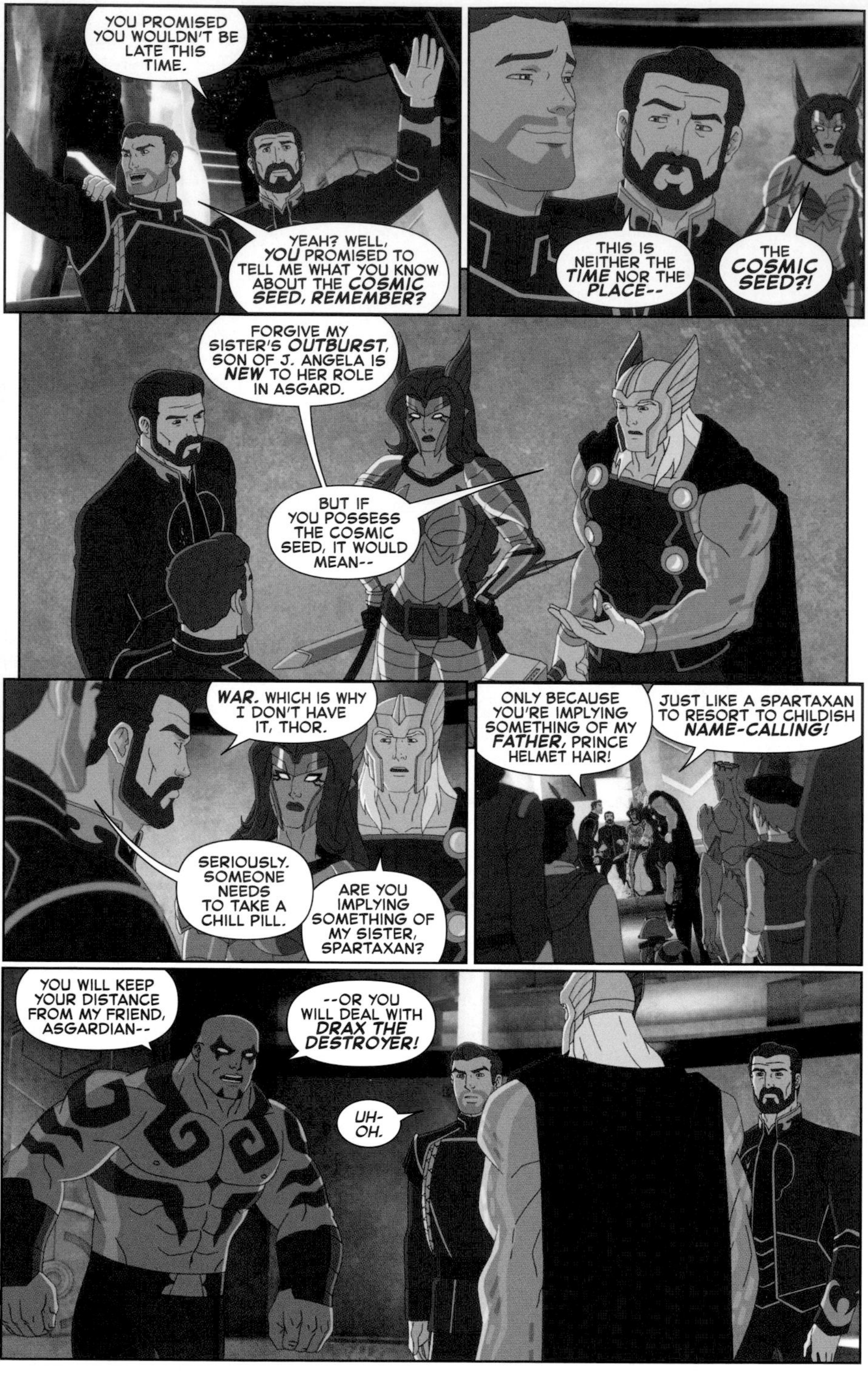
YOU PROMISED YOU WOULDN'T BE LATE THIS TIME.
YEAH? WELL, YOU PROMISED TO TELL ME WHAT YOU KNOW ABOUT THE COSMIC SEED, REMEMBER?
THIS IS NEITHER THE TIME NOR THE PLACE--
THE COSMIC SEED?!
FORGIVE MY SISTER'S OUTBURST, SON OF J. ANGELA IS NEW TO HER ROLE IN ASGARD.
BUT IF YOU POSSESS THE COSMIC SEED, IT WOULD MEAN--
WAR. WHICH IS WHY I DON'T HAVE IT, THOR.
SERIOUSLY. SOMEONE NEEDS TO TAKE A CHILL PILL.
ARE YOU IMPLYING SOMETHING OF MY SISTER, SPARTAXAN?
ONLY BECAUSE YOU'RE IMPLYING SOMETHING OF MY FATHER, PRINCE HELMET HAIR!
JUST LIKE A SPARTAXAN TO RESORT TO CHILDISH NAME-CALLING!
YOU WILL KEEP YOUR DISTANCE FROM MY FRIEND, ASGARDIAN--
--OR YOU WILL DEAL WITH DRAX THE DESTROYER!
UH-OH.

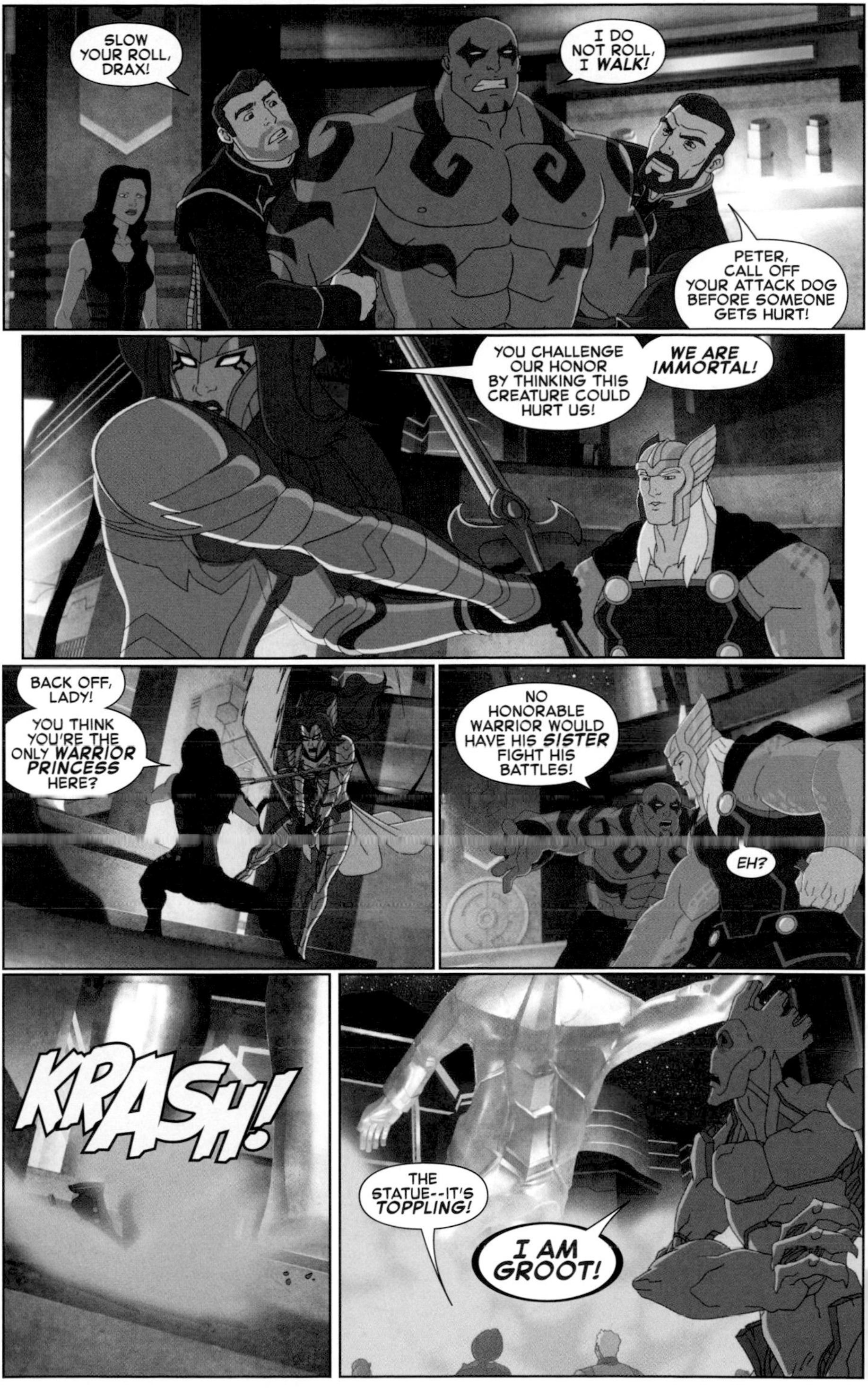
SLOW YOUR ROLL, DRAX!
I DO NOT ROLL, I *WALK!*
PETER, CALL OFF YOUR ATTACK DOG BEFORE SOMEONE GETS HURT!
YOU CHALLENGE OUR HONOR BY THINKING THIS CREATURE COULD HURT US!
WE ARE IMMORTAL!
BACK OFF, LADY!
YOU THINK YOU'RE THE ONLY *WARRIOR PRINCESS* HERE?
NO HONORABLE WARRIOR WOULD HAVE HIS *SISTER* FIGHT HIS BATTLES!
EH?
KRASH!
THE STATUE--IT'S *TOPPLING!*
I AM GROOT!

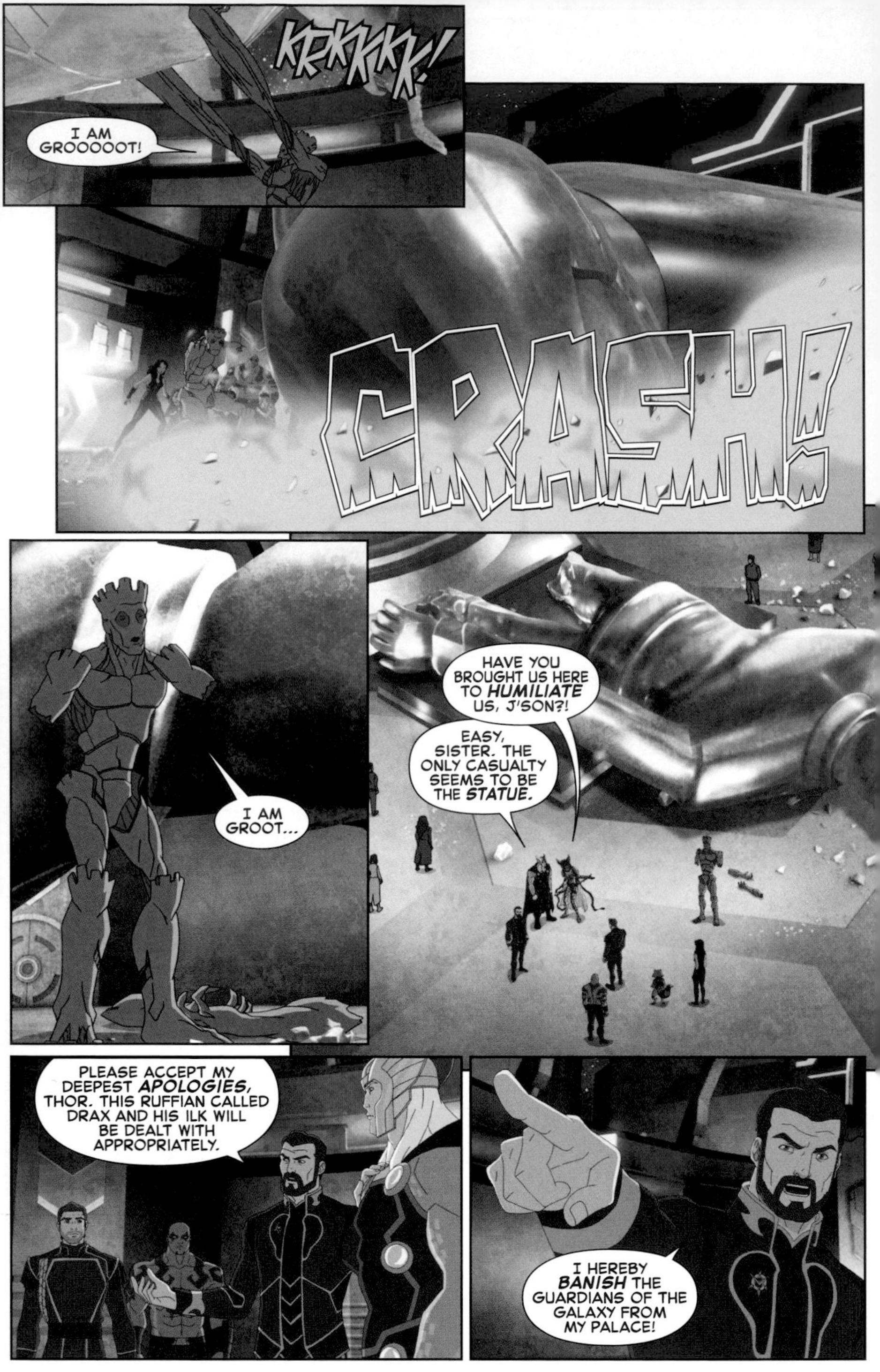
KRKKKKK!
I AM GROOOOOT!
CRASH!
I AM GROOT...
HAVE YOU BROUGHT US HERE TO *HUMILIATE* US, J'SON?!
EASY, SISTER. THE ONLY CASUALTY SEEMS TO BE THE *STATUE.*
PLEASE ACCEPT MY DEEPEST *APOLOGIES,* THOR. THIS RUFFIAN CALLED DRAX AND HIS ILK WILL BE DEALT WITH APPROPRIATELY.
I HEREBY *BANISH* THE GUARDIANS OF THE GALAXY FROM MY PALACE!

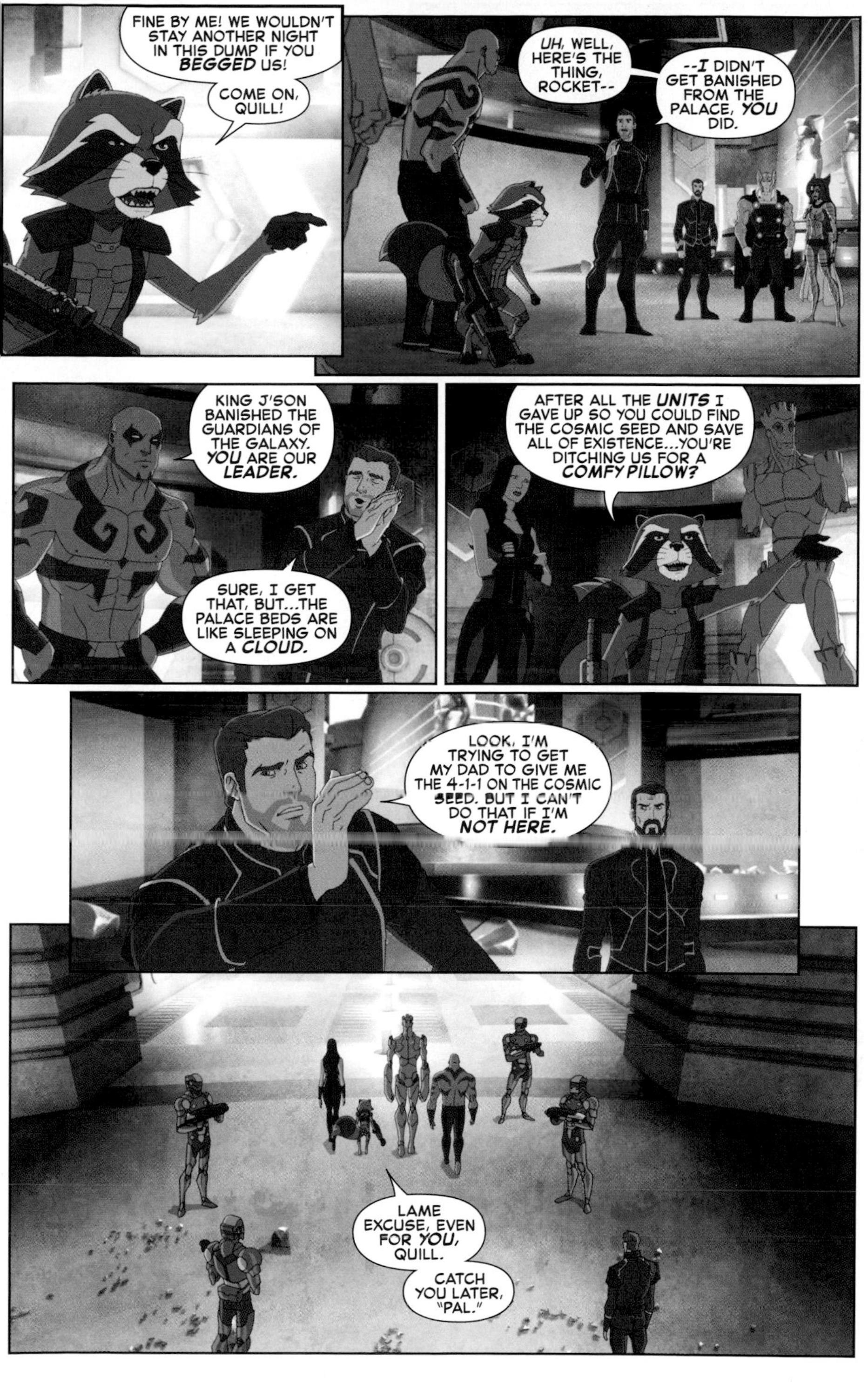
FINE BY ME! WE WOULDN'T STAY ANOTHER NIGHT IN THIS DUMP IF YOU BEGGED US!
COME ON, QUILL!
UH, WELL, HERE'S THE THING, ROCKET--
--I DIDN'T GET BANISHED FROM THE PALACE, YOU DID.
KING J'SON BANISHED THE GUARDIANS OF THE GALAXY. YOU ARE OUR LEADER.
SURE, I GET THAT, BUT...THE PALACE BEDS ARE LIKE SLEEPING ON A CLOUD.
AFTER ALL THE UNITS I GAVE UP SO YOU COULD FIND THE COSMIC SEED AND SAVE ALL OF EXISTENCE...YOU'RE DITCHING US FOR A COMFY PILLOW?
LOOK, I'M TRYING TO GET MY DAD TO GIVE ME THE 4-1-1 ON THE COSMIC SEED. BUT I CAN'T DO THAT IF I'M NOT HERE.
LAME EXCUSE, EVEN FOR YOU, QUILL.
CATCH YOU LATER, "PAL."

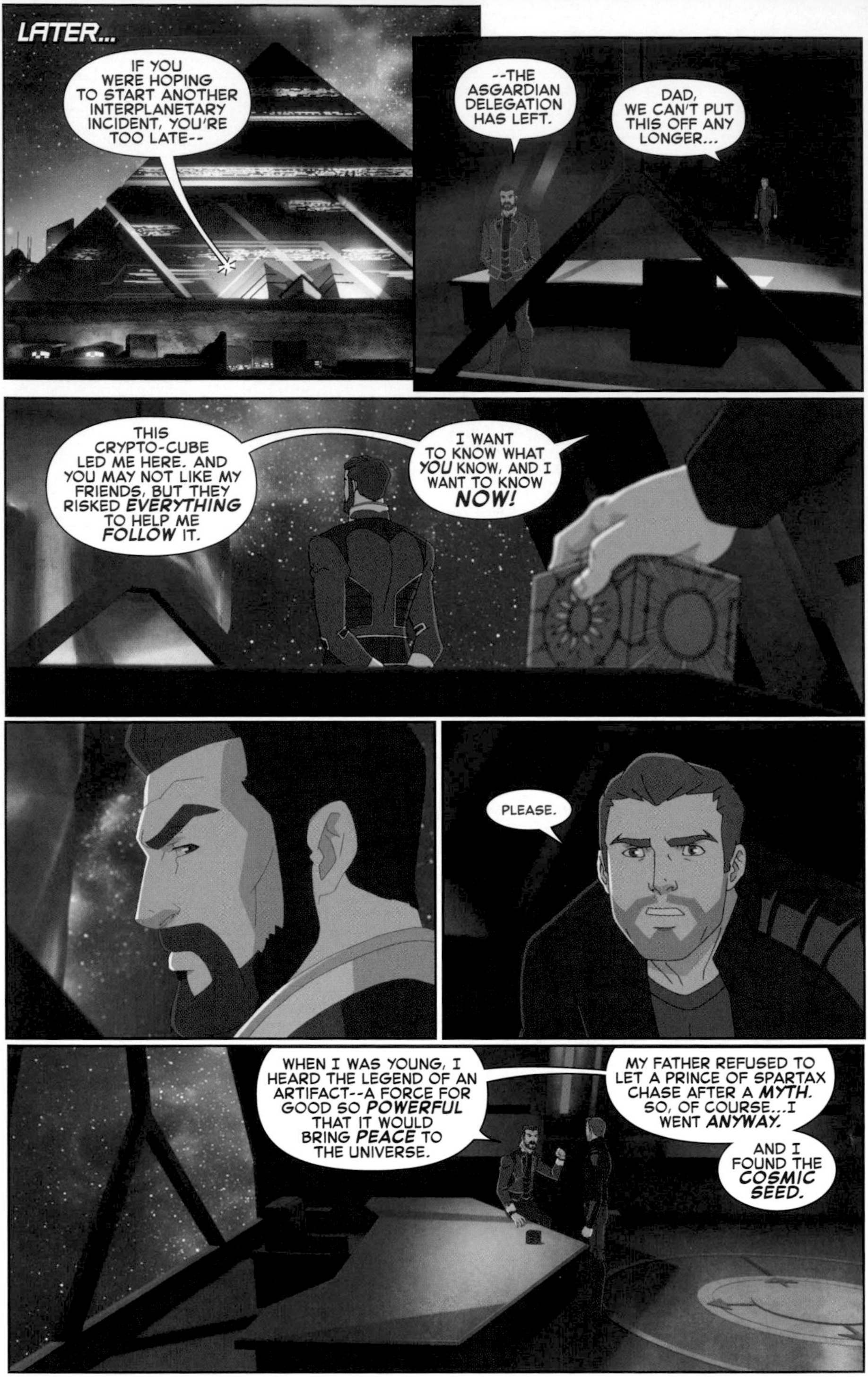
LATER...
IF YOU WERE HOPING TO START ANOTHER INTERPLANETARY INCIDENT, YOU'RE TOO LATE--
--THE ASGARDIAN DELEGATION HAS LEFT.
DAD, WE CAN'T PUT THIS OFF ANY LONGER...
THIS CRYPTO-CUBE LED ME HERE. AND YOU MAY NOT LIKE MY FRIENDS, BUT THEY RISKED EVERYTHING TO HELP ME FOLLOW IT.
I WANT TO KNOW WHAT YOU KNOW, AND I WANT TO KNOW NOW!
PLEASE.
WHEN I WAS YOUNG, I HEARD THE LEGEND OF AN ARTIFACT--A FORCE FOR GOOD SO POWERFUL THAT IT WOULD BRING PEACE TO THE UNIVERSE.
MY FATHER REFUSED TO LET A PRINCE OF SPARTAX CHASE AFTER A MYTH. SO, OF COURSE...I WENT ANYWAY.
AND I FOUND THE COSMIC SEED.

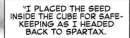

"I PLACED THE SEED INSIDE THE CUBE FOR SAFE-KEEPING AS I HEADED BACK TO SPARTAX.

"THE CUBE MUST'VE EMITTED SOME OF THE SEED'S *ENERGY* EVERYWHERE I STOPPED, WHICH IS HOW YOU *TRACKED* IT.

"UNFORTUNATELY, THE SEED WAS TAKEN FROM ME BY FORCE BEFORE I MADE IT HOME. MY SHIP WAS DAMAGED IN THE ALTERCATION...

"...AND I *CRASH-LANDED* ON EARTH.

"YOUR MOTHER MEREDITH FOUND ME IN A FIELD, VERY BADLY WOUNDED.

"SHE SINGLEHANDEDLY NURSED ME BACK TO HEALTH--SHE WAS AN AMAZING WOMAN.

"SUFFICE IT TO SAY, OUR ROMANCE WAS *BRIEF.* I WAS CALLED BACK TO SPARTAX BECAUSE WAR WAS COMING AND I HAD TO PROTECT THE EMPIRE.

"I GAVE MEREDITH MY *ELEMENT BLASTER--*

"--AND KEYED THE CRYPTO-CUBE TO *BOTH* OF OUR DNA PATTERNS AS A PROMISE TO RETURN."

I HEARD LATER THAT THE *RAVAGERS* FOUND YOU BOTH--OBVIOUSLY THAT DIDN'T HAPPEN. BUT AT THE TIME, IN MY ANGER, I HURLED THE CUBE INTO SPACE, NEVER TO BE SEEN AGAIN.

AND I *FOUND* IT.

DON'T YOU SEE? IT'S *DESTINY!*

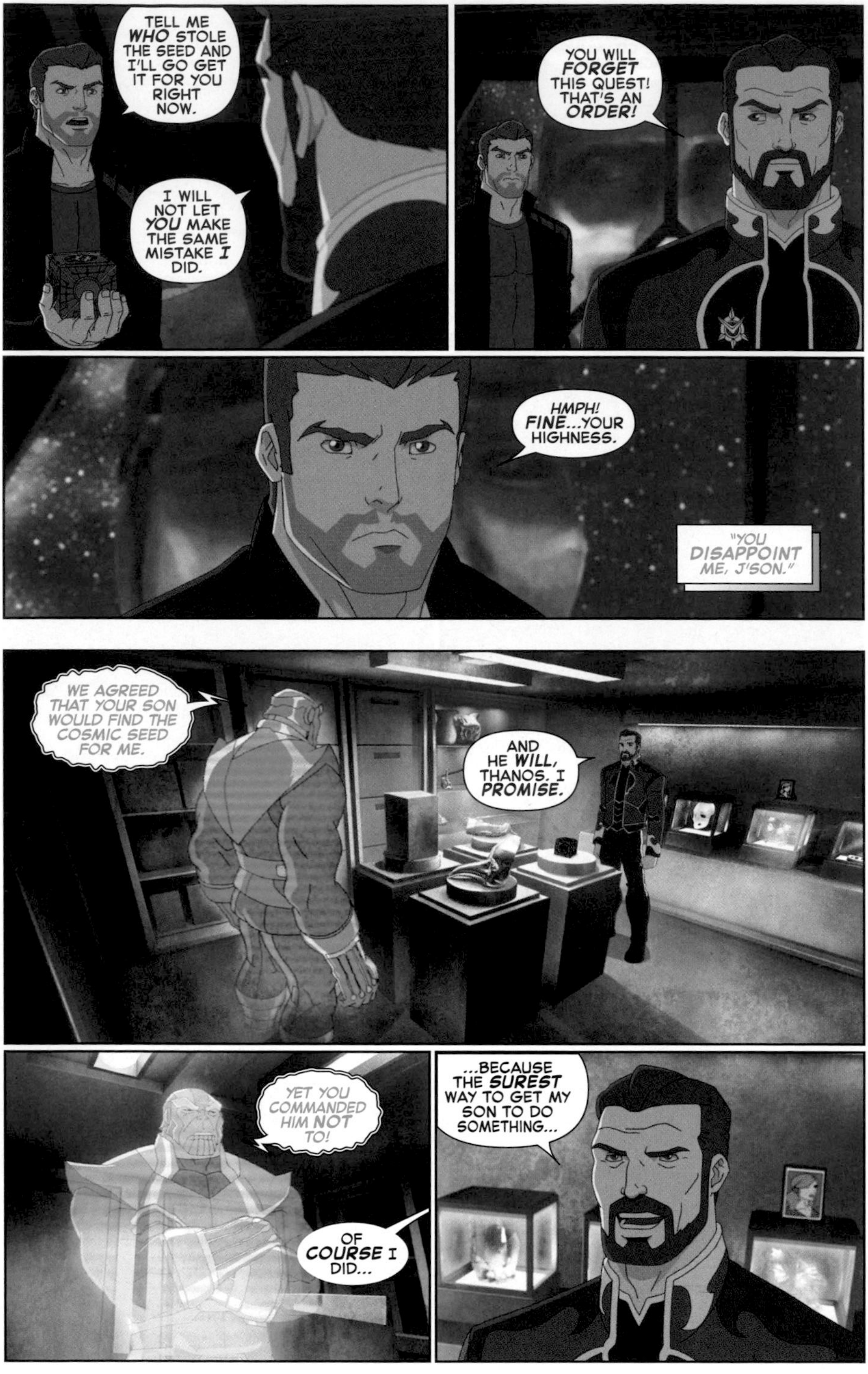
TELL ME WHO STOLE THE SEED AND I'LL GO GET IT FOR YOU RIGHT NOW.
I WILL NOT LET YOU MAKE THE SAME MISTAKE I DID.
YOU WILL FORGET THIS QUEST! THAT'S AN ORDER!
HMPH! FINE...YOUR HIGHNESS.
"YOU DISAPPOINT ME, J'SON."
WE AGREED THAT YOUR SON WOULD FIND THE COSMIC SEED FOR ME.
AND HE WILL, THANOS. I PROMISE.
YET YOU COMMANDED HIM NOT TO!
OF COURSE I DID...
...BECAUSE THE SUREST WAY TO GET MY SON TO DO SOMETHING...

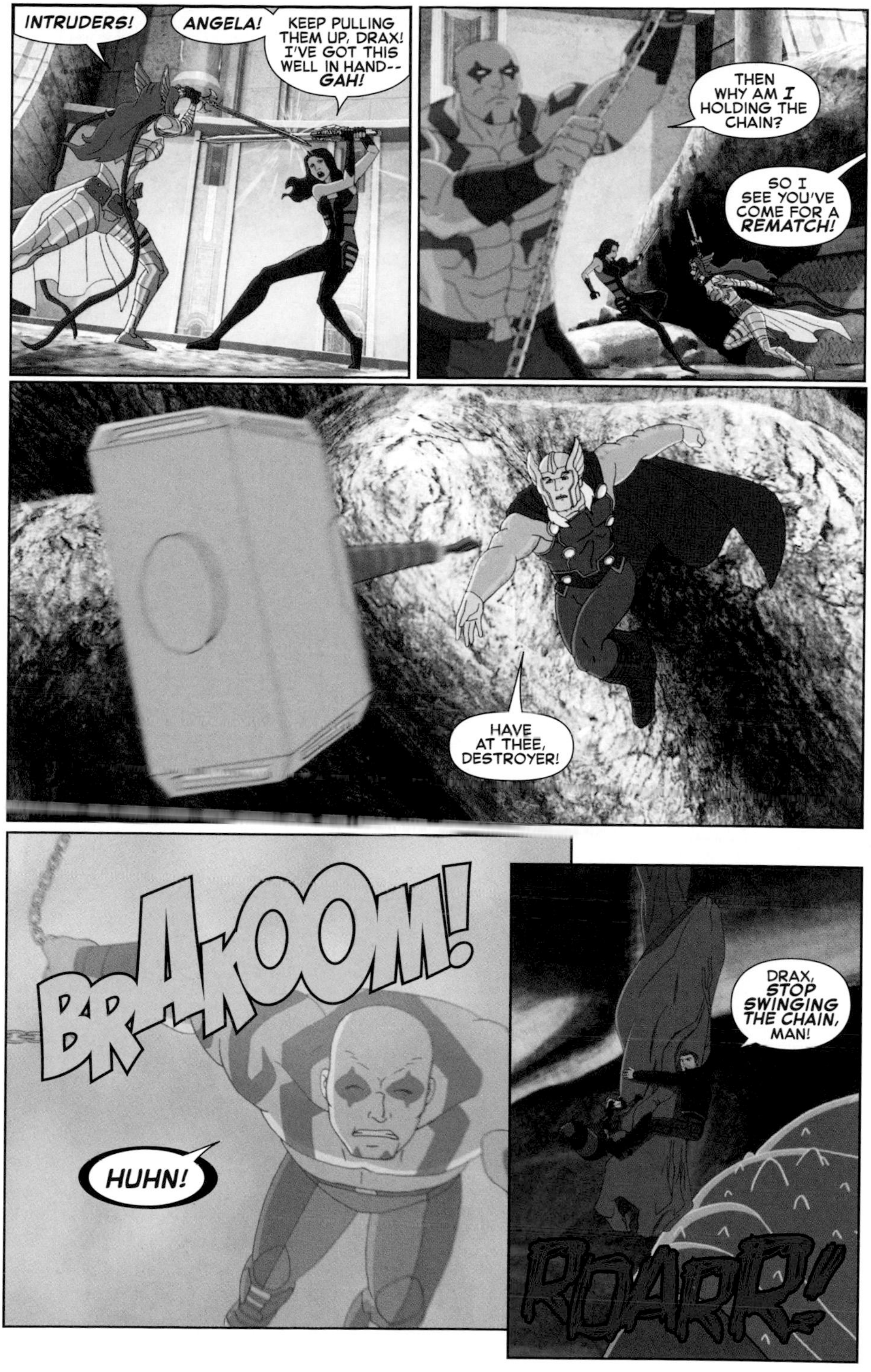
INTRUDERS!
ANGELA!
KEEP PULLING THEM UP, DRAX! I'VE GOT THIS WELL IN HAND-- GAH!
THEN WHY AM I HOLDING THE CHAIN?
SO I SEE YOU'VE COME FOR A REMATCH!
HAVE AT THEE, DESTROYER!
BRAKOOM!
HUHN!
DRAX, STOP SWINGING THE CHAIN, MAN!
ROARR!

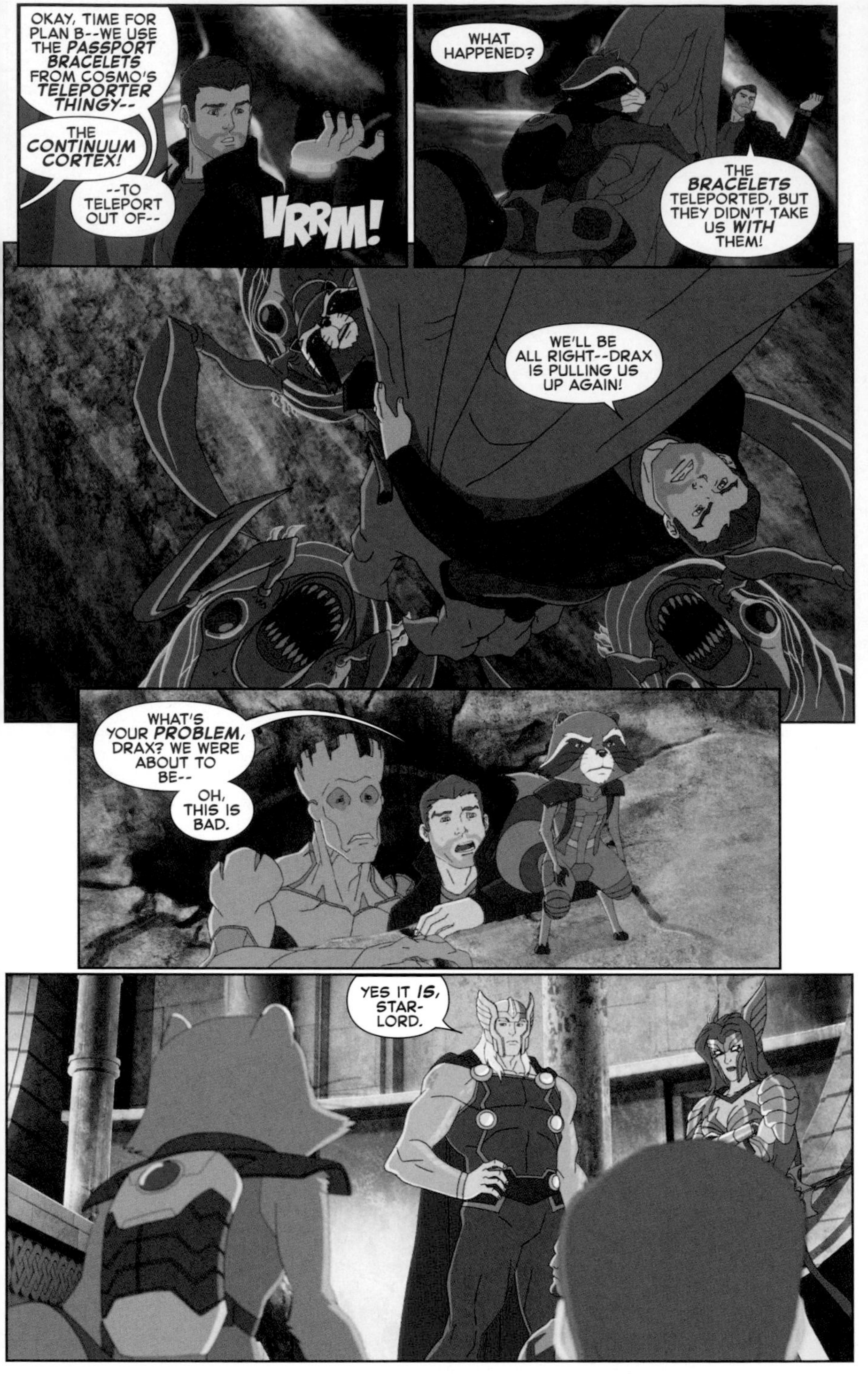
OKAY, TIME FOR PLAN B--WE USE THE PASSPORT BRACELETS FROM COSMO'S TELEPORTER THINGY--
THE CONTINUUM CORTEX!
--TO TELEPORT OUT OF--
VRRM!
WHAT HAPPENED?
THE BRACELETS TELEPORTED, BUT THEY DIDN'T TAKE US WITH THEM!
WE'LL BE ALL RIGHT--DRAX IS PULLING US UP AGAIN!
WHAT'S YOUR PROBLEM, DRAX? WE WERE ABOUT TO BE--
OH, THIS IS BAD.
YES IT IS, STAR-LORD.

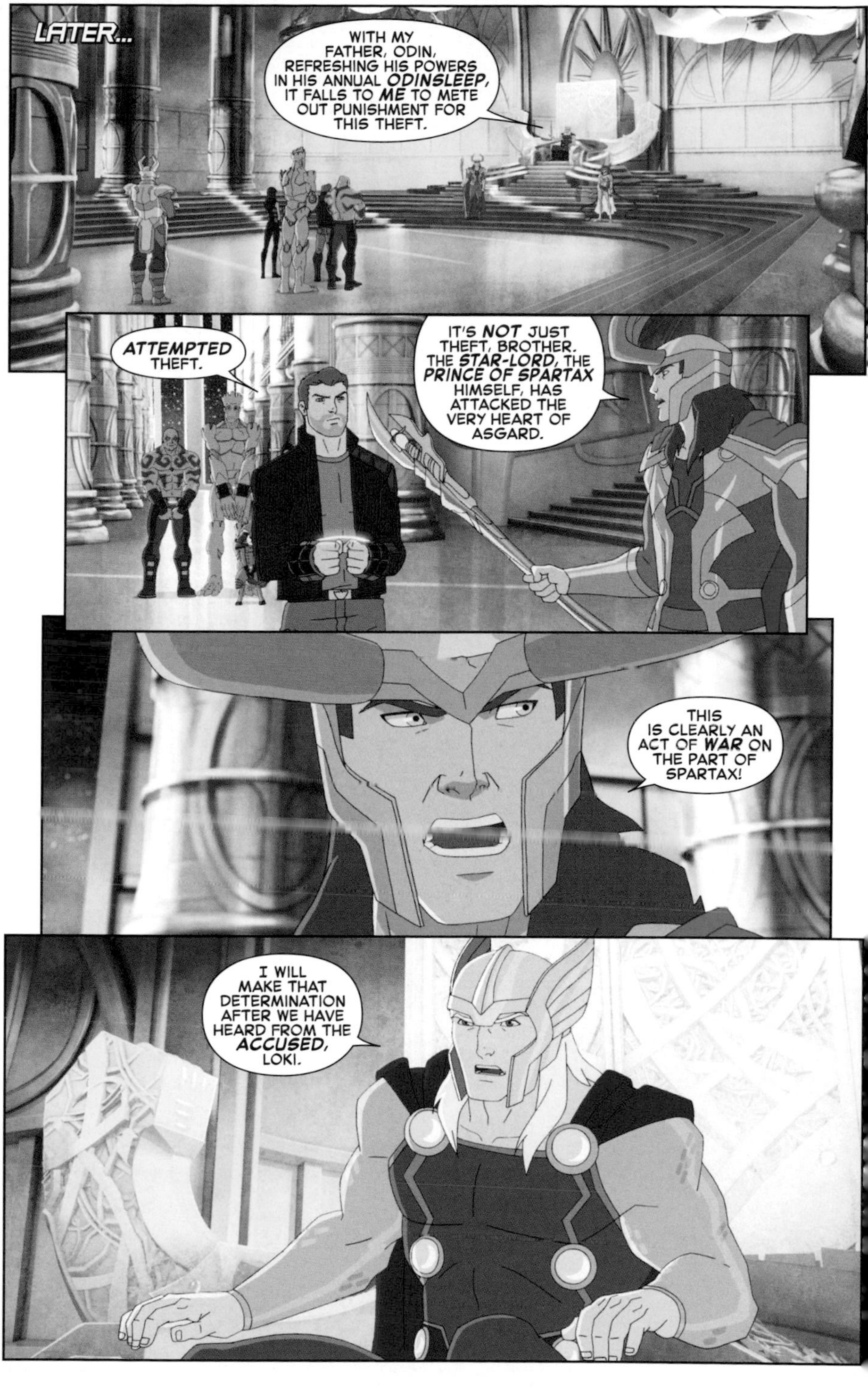
LATER...
WITH MY FATHER, ODIN, REFRESHING HIS POWERS IN HIS ANNUAL ODINSLEEP, IT FALLS TO ME TO METE OUT PUNISHMENT FOR THIS THEFT.
ATTEMPTED THEFT.
IT'S NOT JUST THEFT, BROTHER. THE STAR-LORD, THE PRINCE OF SPARTAX HIMSELF, HAS ATTACKED THE VERY HEART OF ASGARD.
THIS IS CLEARLY AN ACT OF WAR ON THE PART OF SPARTAX!
I WILL MAKE THAT DETERMINATION AFTER WE HAVE HEARD FROM THE ACCUSED, LOKI.

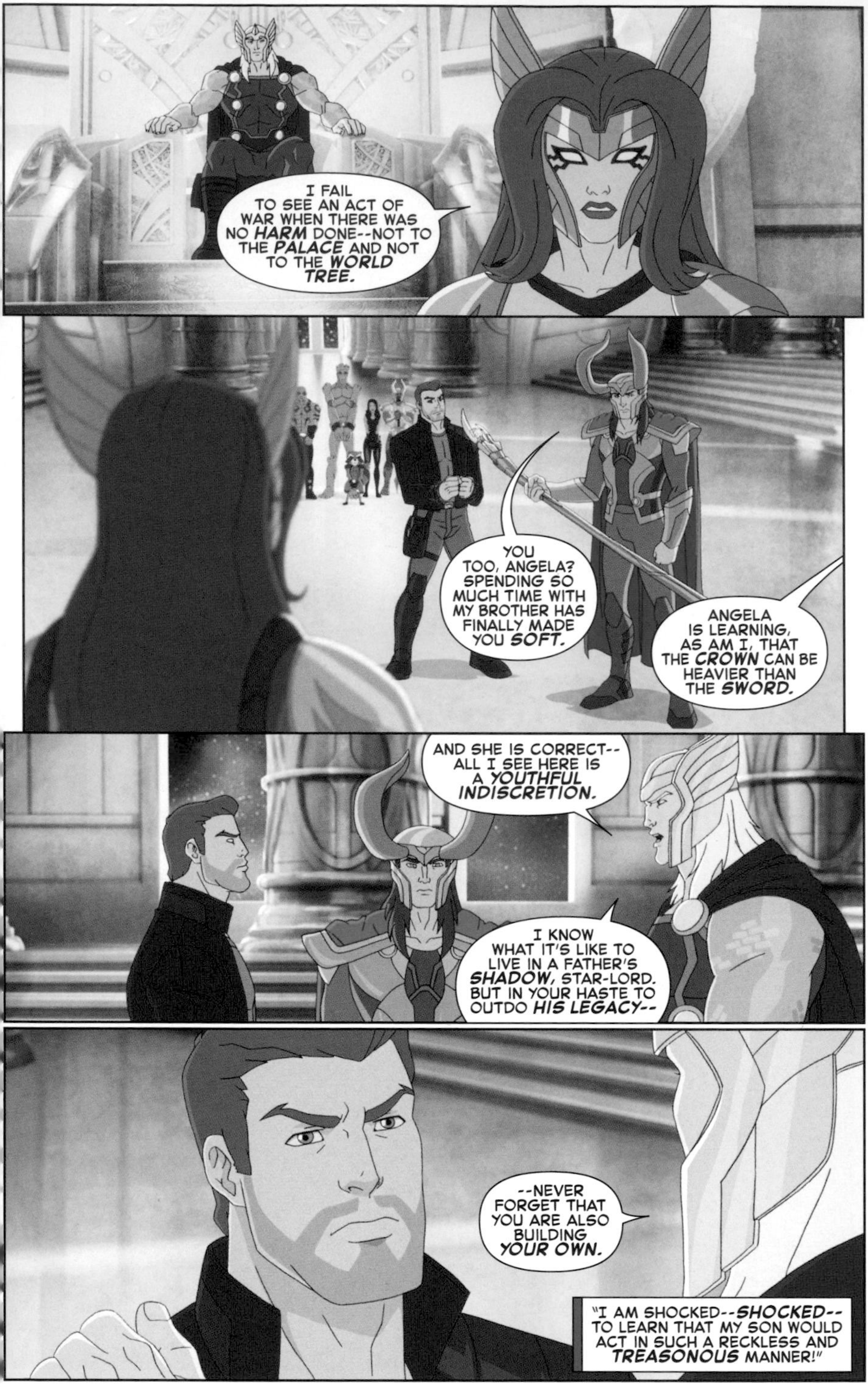
I FAIL TO SEE AN ACT OF WAR WHEN THERE WAS NO HARM DONE--NOT TO THE PALACE AND NOT TO THE WORLD TREE.
YOU TOO, ANGELA? SPENDING SO MUCH TIME WITH MY BROTHER HAS FINALLY MADE YOU SOFT.
ANGELA IS LEARNING, AS AM I, THAT THE CROWN CAN BE HEAVIER THAN THE SWORD.
AND SHE IS CORRECT-- ALL I SEE HERE IS A YOUTHFUL INDISCRETION.
I KNOW WHAT IT'S LIKE TO LIVE IN A FATHER'S SHADOW, STAR-LORD. BUT IN YOUR HASTE TO OUTDO HIS LEGACY--
--NEVER FORGET THAT YOU ARE ALSO BUILDING YOUR OWN.
"I AM SHOCKED--SHOCKED-- TO LEARN THAT MY SON WOULD ACT IN SUCH A RECKLESS AND TREASONOUS MANNER!"

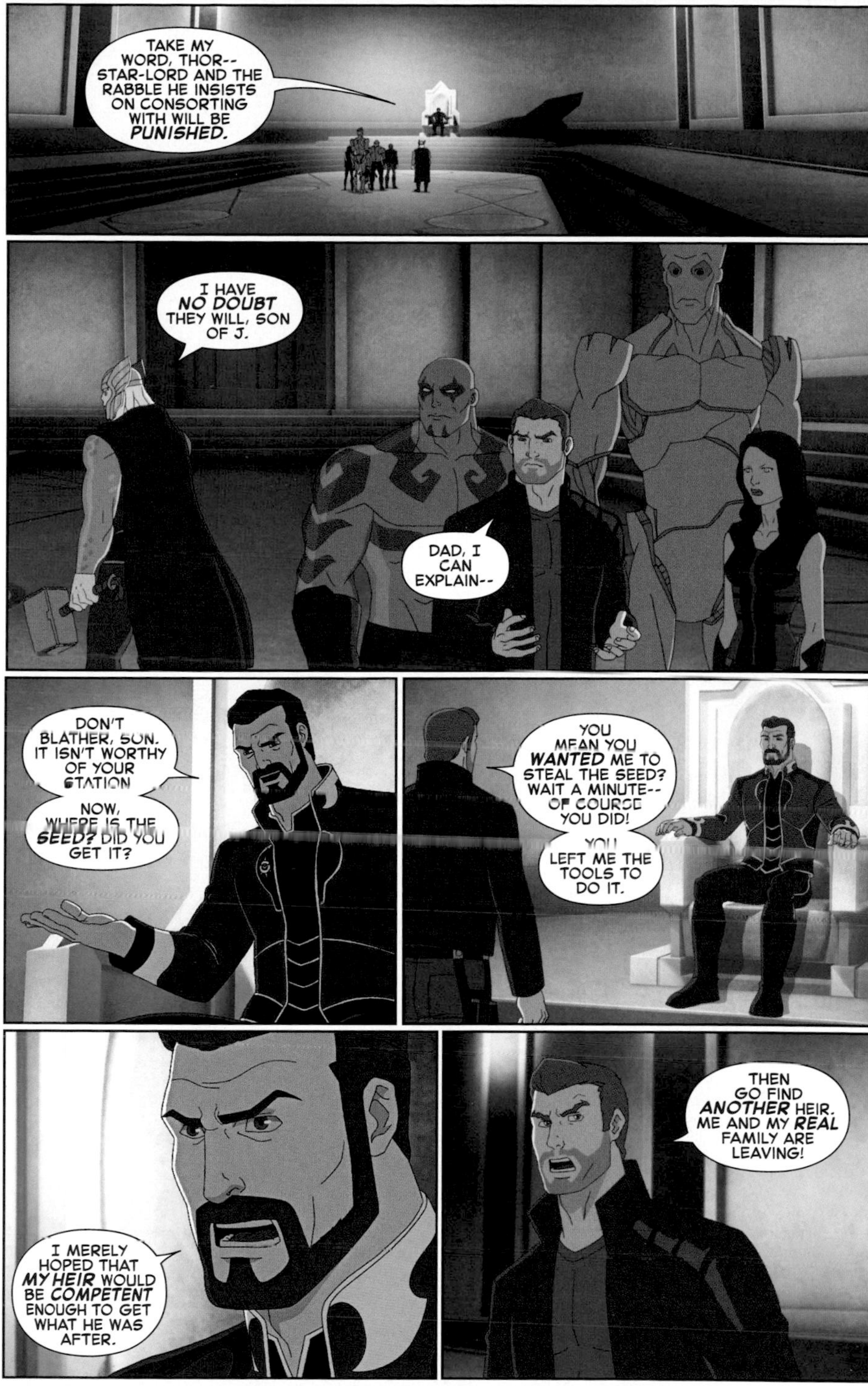
TAKE MY WORD, THOR-- STAR-LORD AND THE RABBLE HE INSISTS ON CONSORTING WITH WILL BE PUNISHED.
I HAVE NO DOUBT THEY WILL, SON OF J.
DAD, I CAN EXPLAIN--
DON'T BLATHER, SON. IT ISN'T WORTHY OF YOUR STATION.
NOW, WHERE IS THE SEED? DID YOU GET IT?
YOU MEAN YOU WANTED ME TO STEAL THE SEED? WAIT A MINUTE-- OF COURSE YOU DID!
YOU LEFT ME THE TOOLS TO DO IT.
I MERELY HOPED THAT MY HEIR WOULD BE COMPETENT ENOUGH TO GET WHAT HE WAS AFTER.
THEN GO FIND ANOTHER HEIR. ME AND MY REAL FAMILY ARE LEAVING!

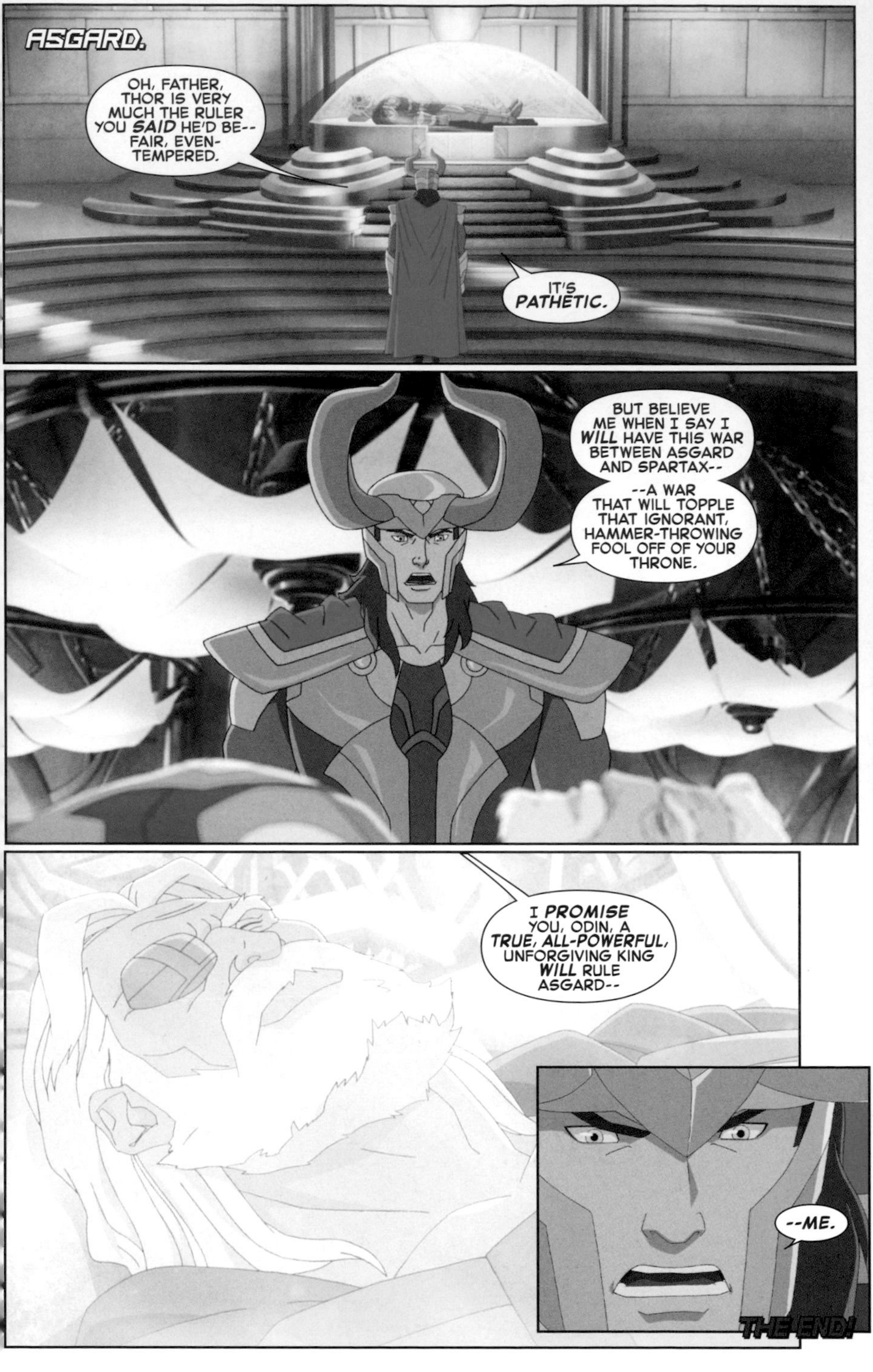
ASGARD.
OH, FATHER, THOR IS VERY MUCH THE RULER YOU SAID HE'D BE-- FAIR, EVEN-TEMPERED.
IT'S PATHETIC.
BUT BELIEVE ME WHEN I SAY I WILL HAVE THIS WAR BETWEEN ASGARD AND SPARTAX--
--A WAR THAT WILL TOPPLE THAT IGNORANT, HAMMER-THROWING FOOL OFF OF YOUR THRONE.
I PROMISE YOU, ODIN, A TRUE, ALL-POWERFUL, UNFORGIVING KING WILL RULE ASGARD--
--ME.
THE END!

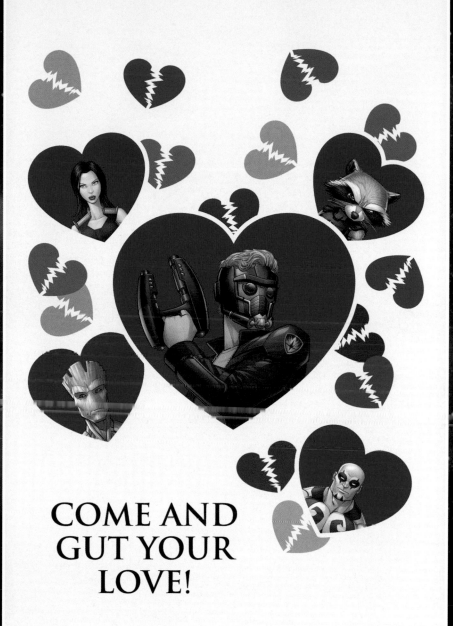

COME AND
GUT YOUR
LOVE!

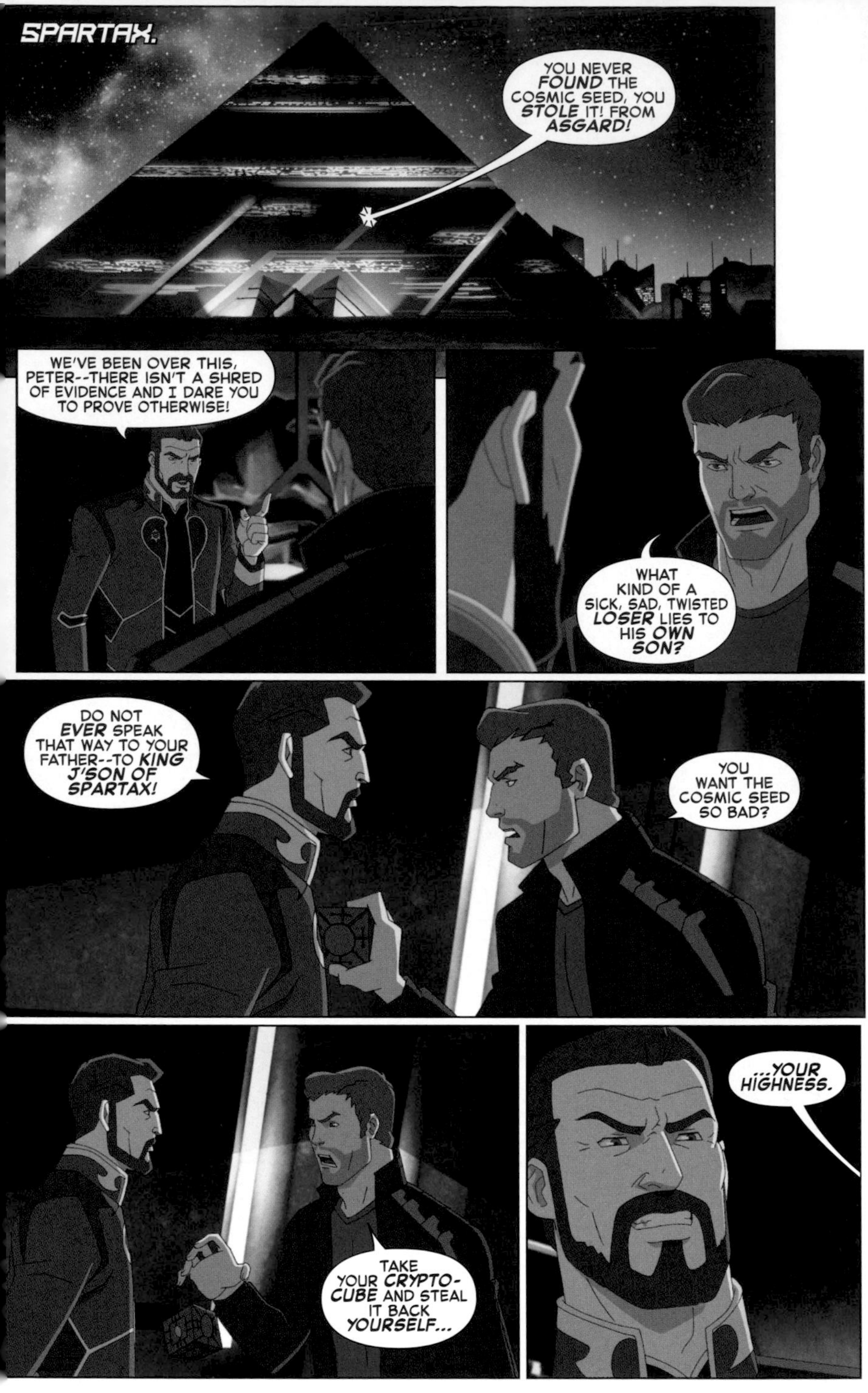
SPARTAX.
YOU NEVER FOUND THE COSMIC SEED, YOU STOLE IT! FROM ASGARD!
WE'VE BEEN OVER THIS, PETER--THERE ISN'T A SHRED OF EVIDENCE AND I DARE YOU TO PROVE OTHERWISE!
WHAT KIND OF A SICK, SAD, TWISTED LOSER LIES TO HIS OWN SON?
DO NOT EVER SPEAK THAT WAY TO YOUR FATHER--TO KING J'SON OF SPARTAX!
YOU WANT THE COSMIC SEED SO BAD?
TAKE YOUR CRYPTO-CUBE AND STEAL IT BACK YOURSELF...
...YOUR HIGHNESS.

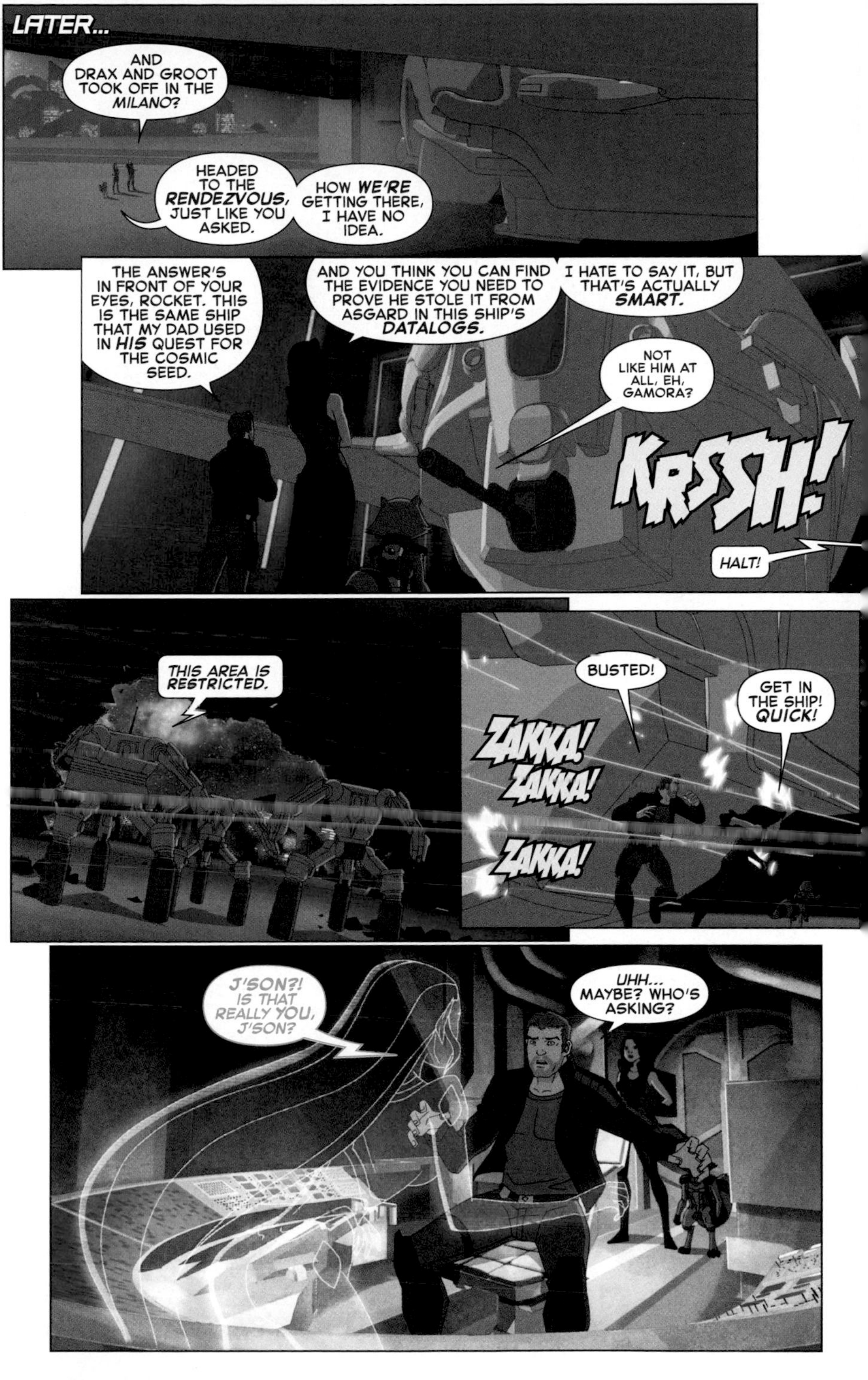
LATER...
AND DRAX AND GROOT TOOK OFF IN THE MILANO?
HEADED TO THE RENDEZVOUS, JUST LIKE YOU ASKED.
HOW WE'RE GETTING THERE, I HAVE NO IDEA.
THE ANSWER'S IN FRONT OF YOUR EYES, ROCKET. THIS IS THE SAME SHIP THAT MY DAD USED IN HIS QUEST FOR THE COSMIC SEED.
AND YOU THINK YOU CAN FIND THE EVIDENCE YOU NEED TO PROVE HE STOLE IT FROM ASGARD IN THIS SHIP'S DATALOGS.
I HATE TO SAY IT, BUT THAT'S ACTUALLY SMART.
NOT LIKE HIM AT ALL, EH, GAMORA?
KRSSH!
HALT!
THIS AREA IS RESTRICTED.
BUSTED!
GET IN THE SHIP! QUICK!
ZAKKA! ZAKKA!
ZAKKA!
J'SON?! IS THAT REALLY YOU, J'SON?
UHH... MAYBE? WHO'S ASKING?

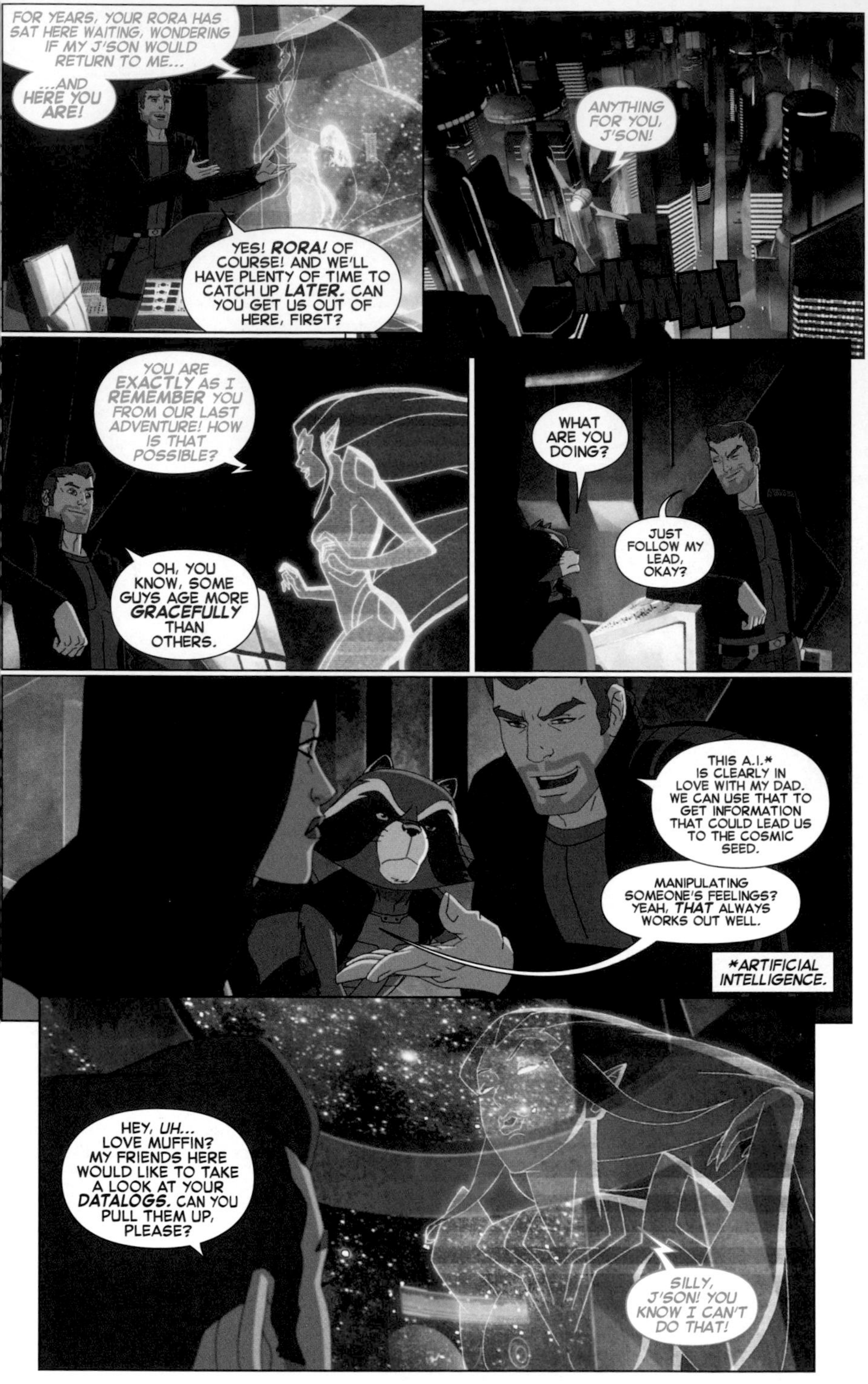
FOR YEARS, YOUR RORA HAS SAT HERE WAITING, WONDERING IF MY J'SON WOULD RETURN TO ME...
...AND HERE YOU ARE!
YES! RORA! OF COURSE! AND WE'LL HAVE PLENTY OF TIME TO CATCH UP LATER. CAN YOU GET US OUT OF HERE, FIRST?
ANYTHING FOR YOU, J'SON!
YOU ARE EXACTLY AS I REMEMBER YOU FROM OUR LAST ADVENTURE! HOW IS THAT POSSIBLE?
OH, YOU KNOW, SOME GUYS AGE MORE GRACEFULLY THAN OTHERS.
WHAT ARE YOU DOING?
JUST FOLLOW MY LEAD, OKAY?
THIS A.I.* IS CLEARLY IN LOVE WITH MY DAD. WE CAN USE THAT TO GET INFORMATION THAT COULD LEAD US TO THE COSMIC SEED.
MANIPULATING SOMEONE'S FEELINGS? YEAH, THAT ALWAYS WORKS OUT WELL.
*ARTIFICIAL INTELLIGENCE.
HEY, UH... LOVE MUFFIN? MY FRIENDS HERE WOULD LIKE TO TAKE A LOOK AT YOUR DATALOGS. CAN YOU PULL THEM UP, PLEASE?
SILLY, J'SON! YOU KNOW I CAN'T DO THAT!

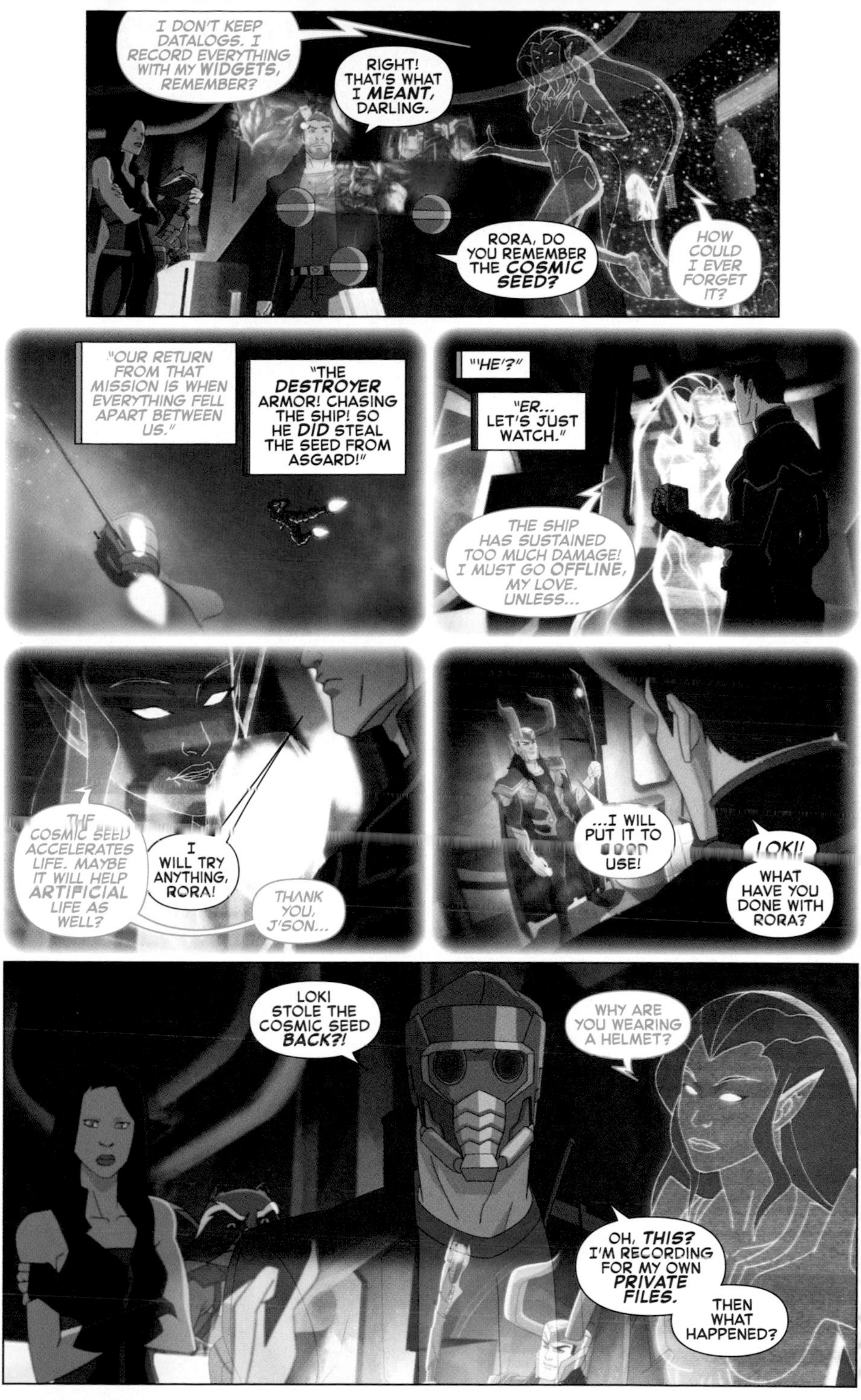
I DON'T KEEP DATALOGS. I RECORD EVERYTHING WITH MY WIDGETS, REMEMBER?
RIGHT! THAT'S WHAT I MEANT, DARLING.
RORA, DO YOU REMEMBER THE COSMIC SEED?
HOW COULD I EVER FORGET IT?
"OUR RETURN FROM THAT MISSION IS WHEN EVERYTHING FELL APART BETWEEN US."
"THE DESTROYER ARMOR! CHASING THE SHIP! SO HE DID STEAL THE SEED FROM ASGARD!"
"'HE'?"
"ER... LET'S JUST WATCH."
THE SHIP HAS SUSTAINED TOO MUCH DAMAGE! I MUST GO OFFLINE, MY LOVE. UNLESS...
THE COSMIC SEED ACCELERATES LIFE. MAYBE IT WILL HELP ARTIFICIAL LIFE AS WELL?
I WILL TRY ANYTHING, RORA!
THANK YOU, J'SON...
...I WILL PUT IT TO USE!
LOKI! WHAT HAVE YOU DONE WITH RORA?
LOKI STOLE THE COSMIC SEED BACK?!
WHY ARE YOU WEARING A HELMET?
OH, THIS? I'M RECORDING FOR MY OWN PRIVATE FILES.
THEN WHAT HAPPENED?

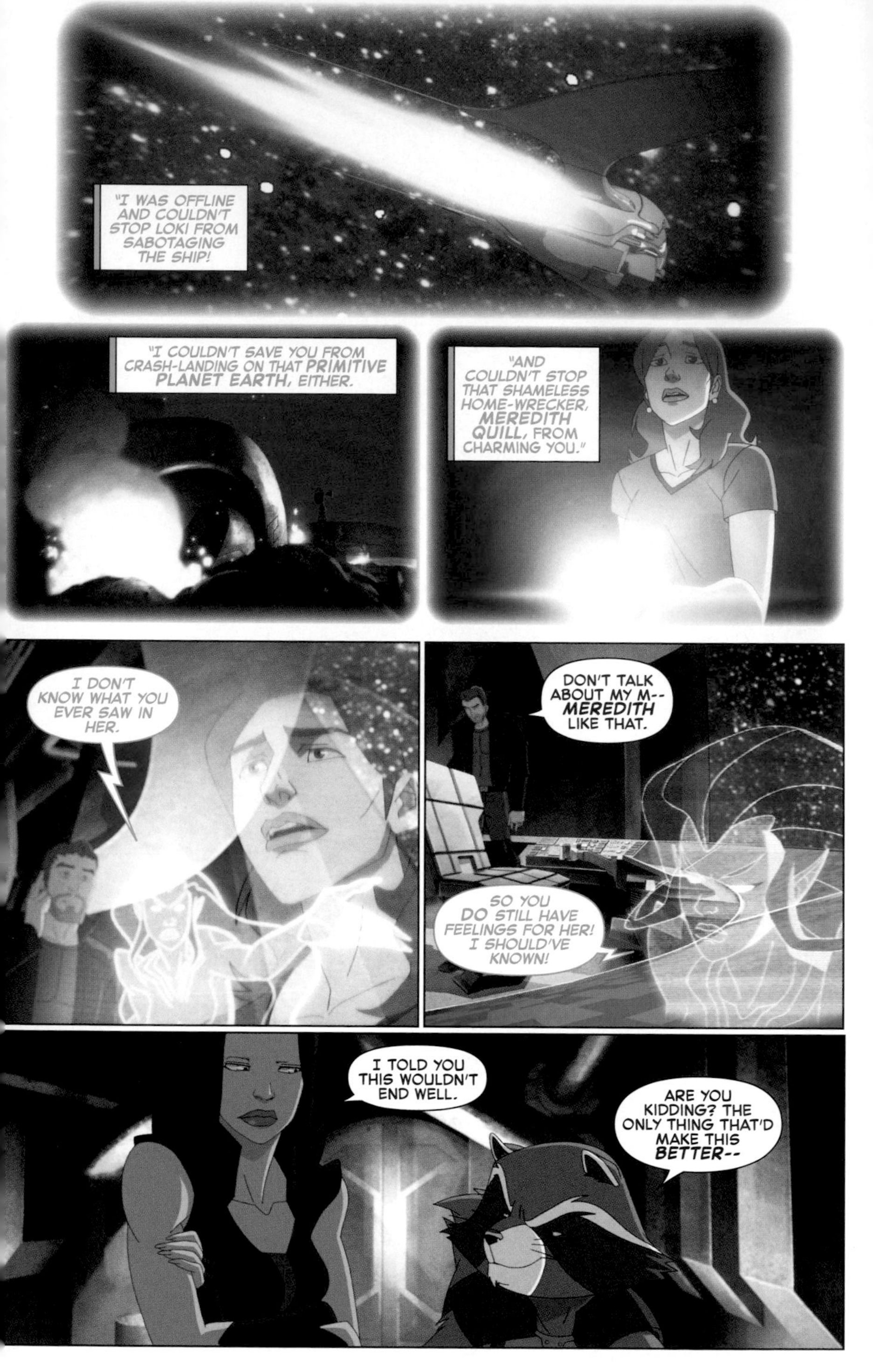
"I WAS OFFLINE AND COULDN'T STOP LOKI FROM SABOTAGING THE SHIP!
"I COULDN'T SAVE YOU FROM CRASH-LANDING ON THAT PRIMITIVE PLANET EARTH, EITHER.
"AND COULDN'T STOP THAT SHAMELESS HOME-WRECKER, MEREDITH QUILL, FROM CHARMING YOU."
I DON'T KNOW WHAT YOU EVER SAW IN HER.
DON'T TALK ABOUT MY M-- MEREDITH LIKE THAT.
SO YOU DO STILL HAVE FEELINGS FOR HER! I SHOULD'VE KNOWN!
I TOLD YOU THIS WOULDN'T END WELL.
ARE YOU KIDDING? THE ONLY THING THAT'D MAKE THIS BETTER--

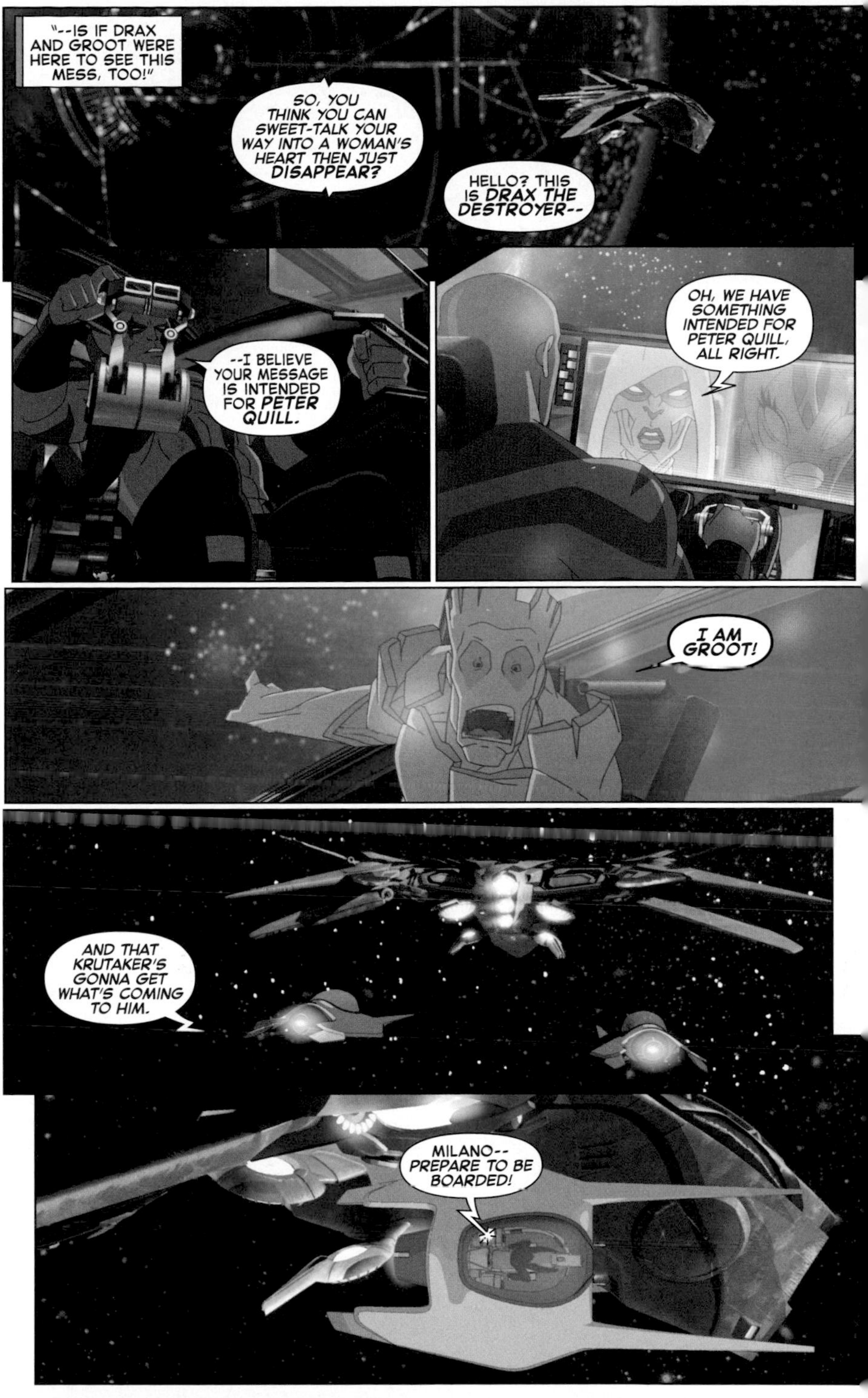
"--IS IF DRAX AND GROOT WERE HERE TO SEE THIS MESS, TOO!"
SO, YOU THINK YOU CAN SWEET-TALK YOUR WAY INTO A WOMAN'S HEART THEN JUST DISAPPEAR?
HELLO? THIS IS DRAX THE DESTROYER--
--I BELIEVE YOUR MESSAGE IS INTENDED FOR PETER QUILL.
OH, WE HAVE SOMETHING INTENDED FOR PETER QUILL, ALL RIGHT.
I AM GROOT!
AND THAT KRUTAKER'S GONNA GET WHAT'S COMING TO HIM.
MILANO-- PREPARE TO BE BOARDED!

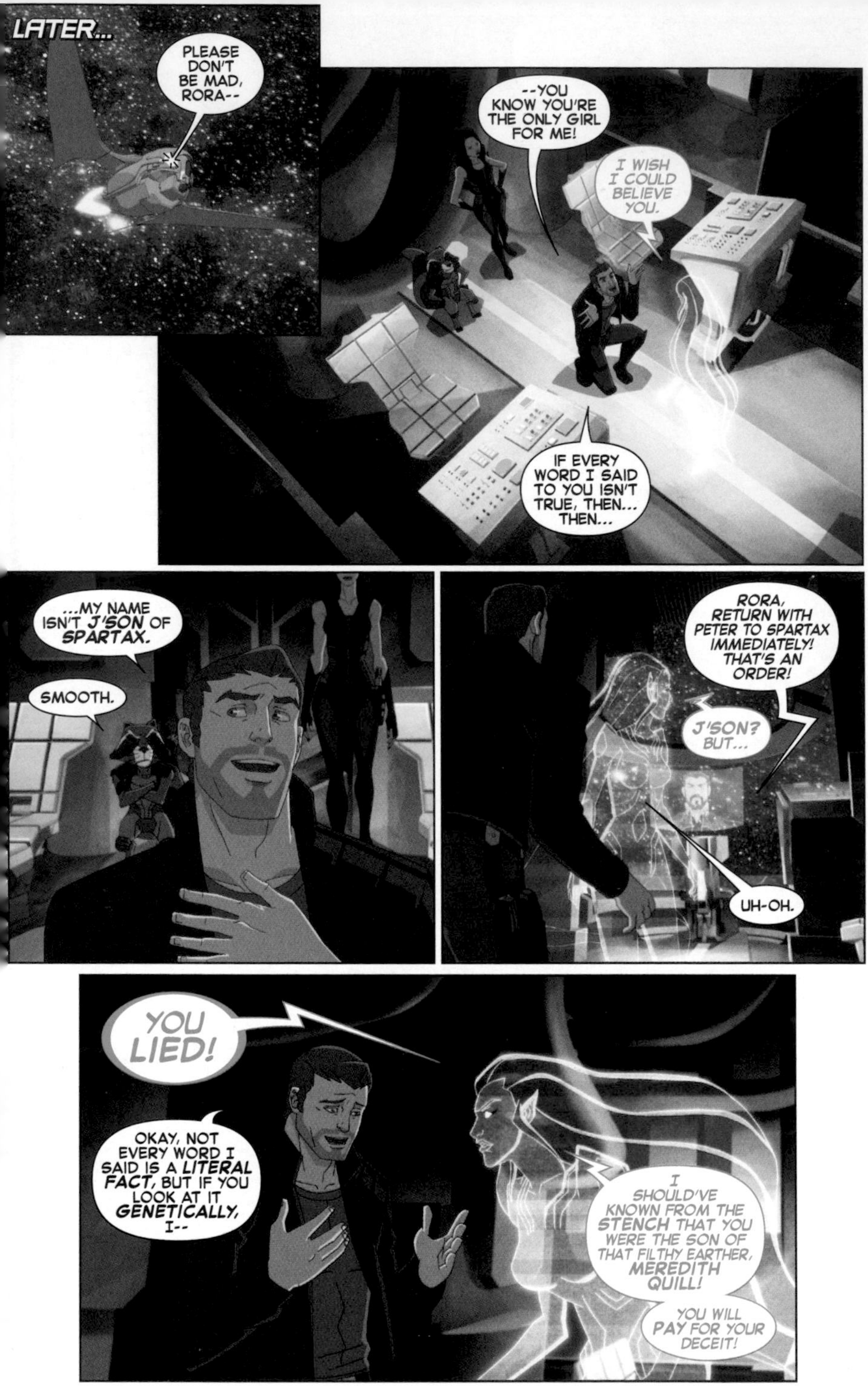
LATER...
PLEASE DON'T BE MAD, RORA--
--YOU KNOW YOU'RE THE ONLY GIRL FOR ME!
I WISH I COULD BELIEVE YOU.
IF EVERY WORD I SAID TO YOU ISN'T TRUE, THEN... THEN...
...MY NAME ISN'T J'SON OF SPARTAX.
SMOOTH.
RORA, RETURN WITH PETER TO SPARTAX IMMEDIATELY! THAT'S AN ORDER!
J'SON? BUT...
UH-OH.
YOU LIED!
OKAY, NOT EVERY WORD I SAID IS A LITERAL FACT, BUT IF YOU LOOK AT IT GENETICALLY, I--
I SHOULD'VE KNOWN FROM THE STENCH THAT YOU WERE THE SON OF THAT FILTHY EARTHER, MEREDITH QUILL!
YOU WILL PAY FOR YOUR DECEIT!

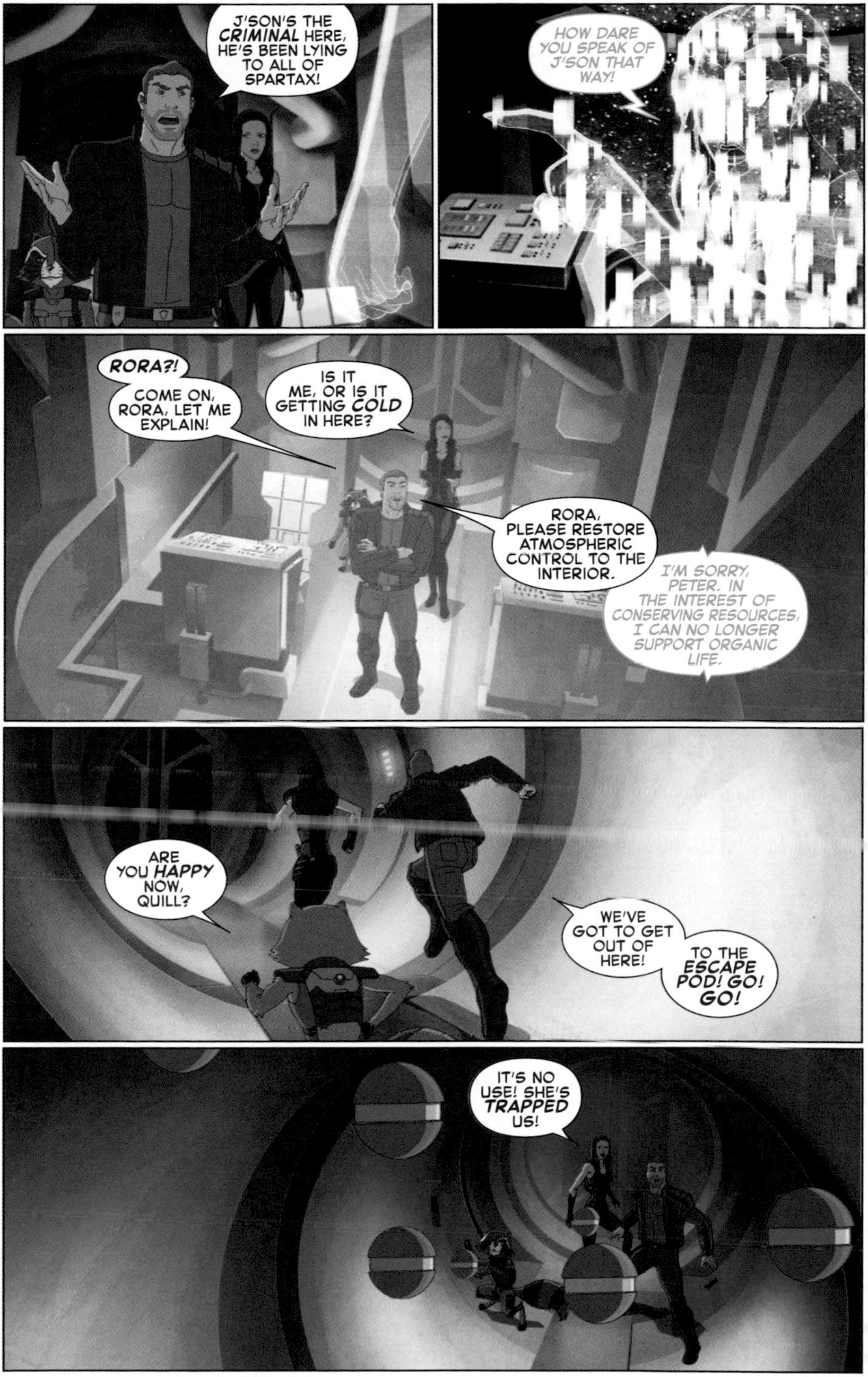
J'SON'S THE CRIMINAL HERE, HE'S BEEN LYING TO ALL OF SPARTAX!
HOW DARE YOU SPEAK OF J'SON THAT WAY!
RORA?!
COME ON, RORA, LET ME EXPLAIN!
IS IT ME, OR IS IT GETTING COLD IN HERE?
RORA, PLEASE RESTORE ATMOSPHERIC CONTROL TO THE INTERIOR.
I'M SORRY, PETER. IN THE INTEREST OF CONSERVING RESOURCES, I CAN NO LONGER SUPPORT ORGANIC LIFE.
ARE YOU HAPPY NOW, QUILL?
WE'VE GOT TO GET OUT OF HERE!
TO THE ESCAPE POD! GO! GO!
IT'S NO USE! SHE'S TRAPPED US!

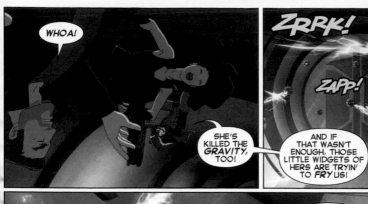

WHOA!

SHE'S KILLED THE *GRAVITY*, TOO!

ZRRK!

ZAPP!

AND IF THAT WASN'T ENOUGH, THOSE LITTLE WIDGETS OF HERS ARE TRYIN' TO *FRY* US!

ZRRK!

THEIR *LASERS* SHORTED OUT MY *ELEMENT BLASTER!*

IF THEY'RE DISABLING *OUR* TECH--

--WE'LL JUST MAKE USE OF *THEIRS.*

SSS

WHAT DO YOU MEAN?

JUST GIMME COVER!

HMM. THIS HERE LOOKS LIKE SOMETHING...

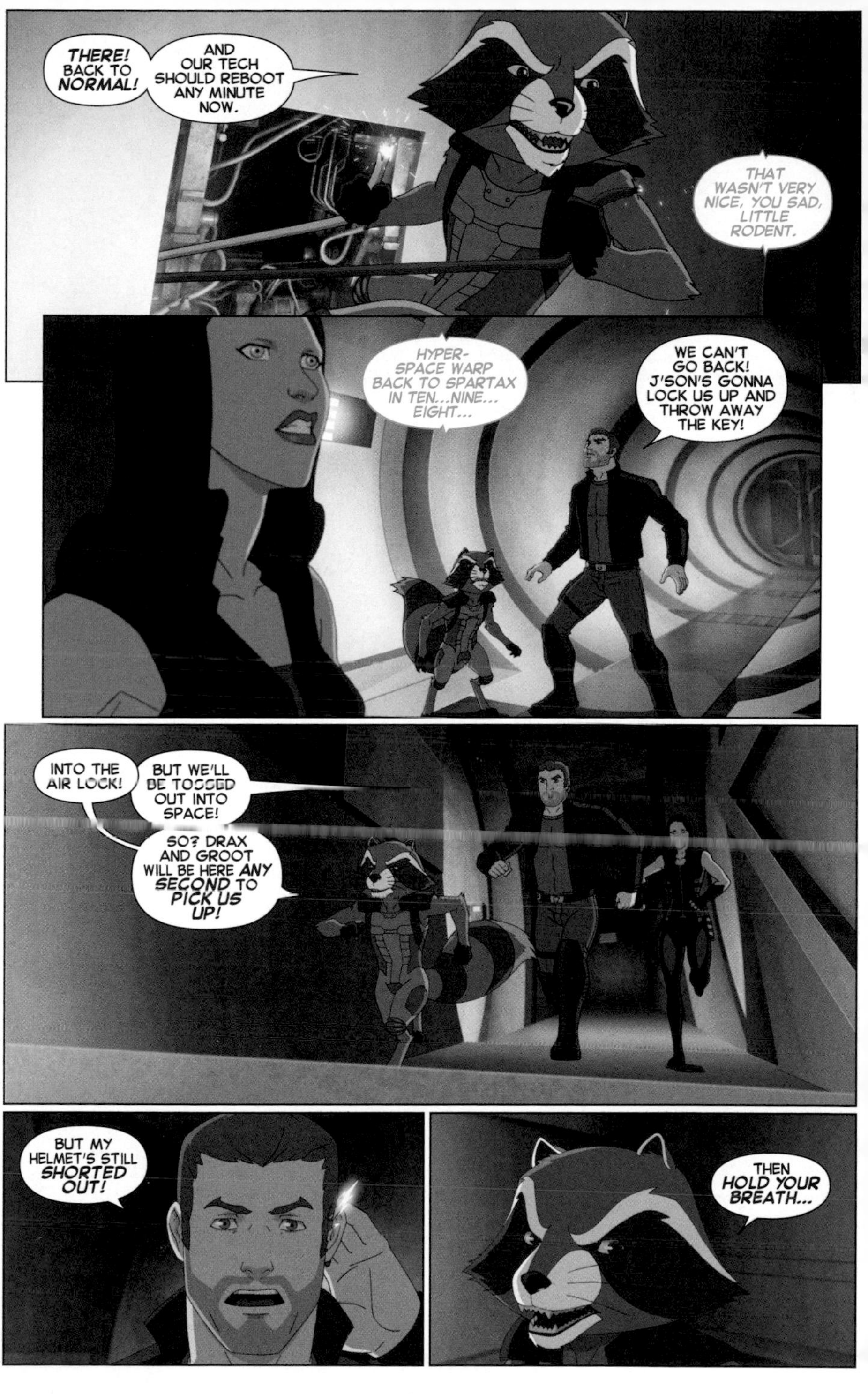
THERE! BACK TO NORMAL!
AND OUR TECH SHOULD REBOOT ANY MINUTE NOW.
THAT WASN'T VERY NICE, YOU SAD, LITTLE RODENT.
HYPER-SPACE WARP BACK TO SPARTAX IN TEN...NINE... EIGHT...
WE CAN'T GO BACK! J'SON'S GONNA LOCK US UP AND THROW AWAY THE KEY!
INTO THE AIR LOCK!
BUT WE'LL BE TOSSED OUT INTO SPACE!
SO? DRAX AND GROOT WILL BE HERE ANY SECOND TO PICK US UP!
BUT MY HELMET'S STILL SHORTED OUT!
THEN HOLD YOUR BREATH...

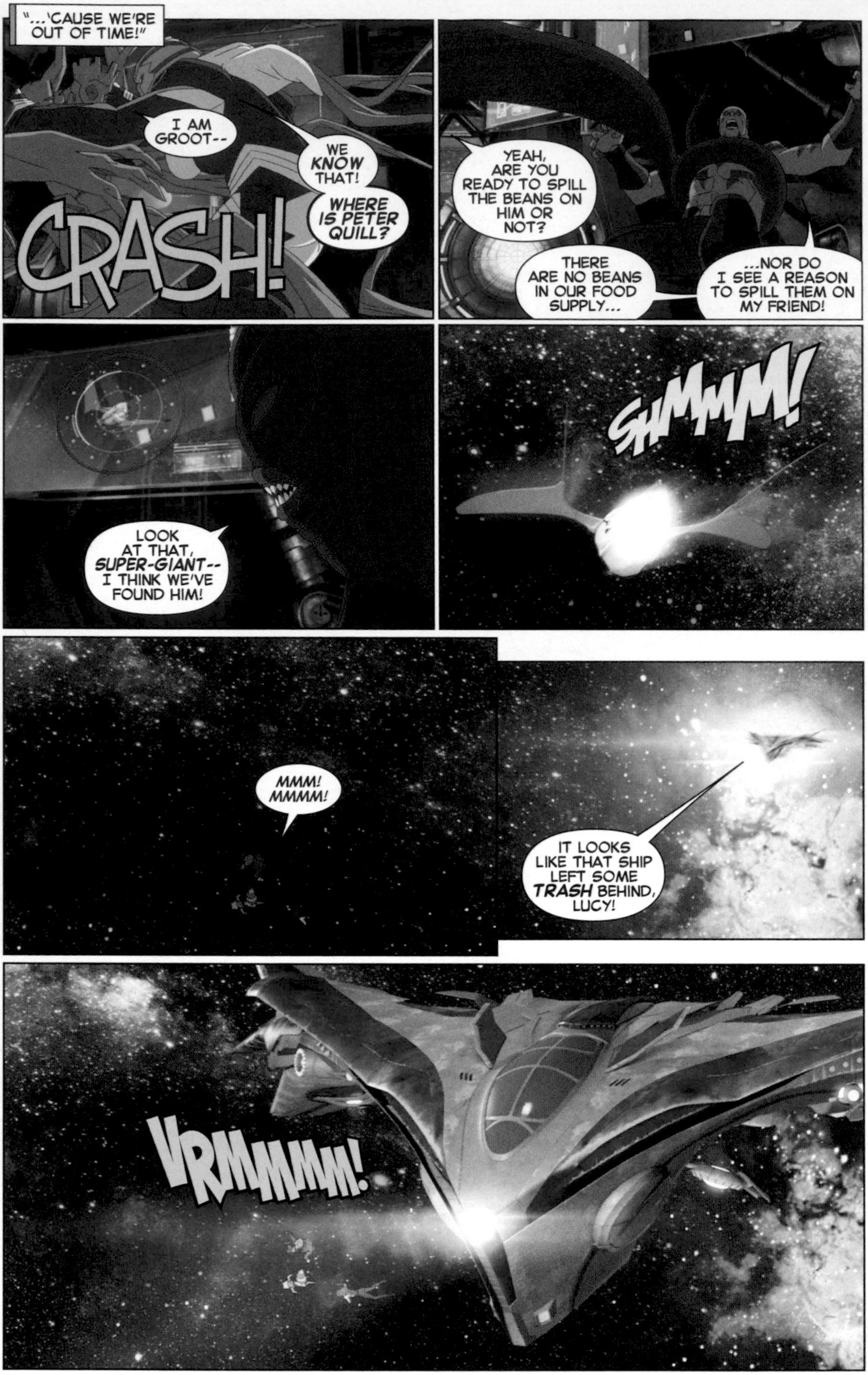
"...'CAUSE WE'RE OUT OF TIME!"
I AM GROOT--
CRASH!
WE KNOW THAT! WHERE IS PETER QUILL?
YEAH, ARE YOU READY TO SPILL THE BEANS ON HIM OR NOT?
THERE ARE NO BEANS IN OUR FOOD SUPPLY...
...NOR DO I SEE A REASON TO SPILL THEM ON MY FRIEND!
LOOK AT THAT, SUPER-GIANT-- I THINK WE'VE FOUND HIM!
SHMMM!
MMM! MMMM!
IT LOOKS LIKE THAT SHIP LEFT SOME TRASH BEHIND, LUCY!
VRMMMM!

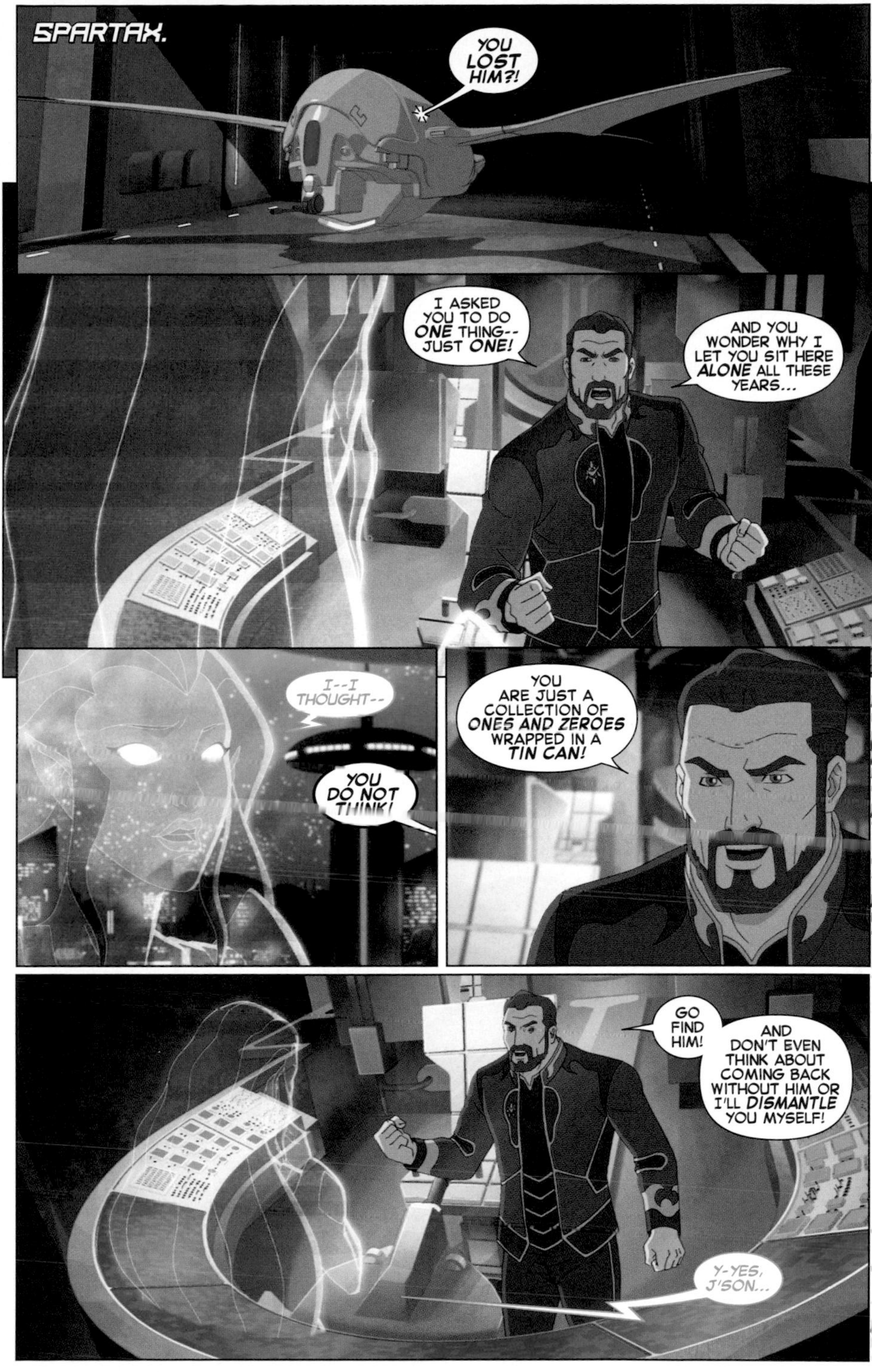
SPARTAX.
YOU LOST HIM?!
I ASKED YOU TO DO ONE THING-- JUST ONE!
AND YOU WONDER WHY I LET YOU SIT HERE ALONE ALL THESE YEARS...
I--I THOUGHT--
YOU DO NOT THINK!
YOU ARE JUST A COLLECTION OF ONES AND ZEROES WRAPPED IN A TIN CAN!
GO FIND HIM!
AND DON'T EVEN THINK ABOUT COMING BACK WITHOUT HIM OR I'LL DISMANTLE YOU MYSELF!
Y-YES, J'SON...

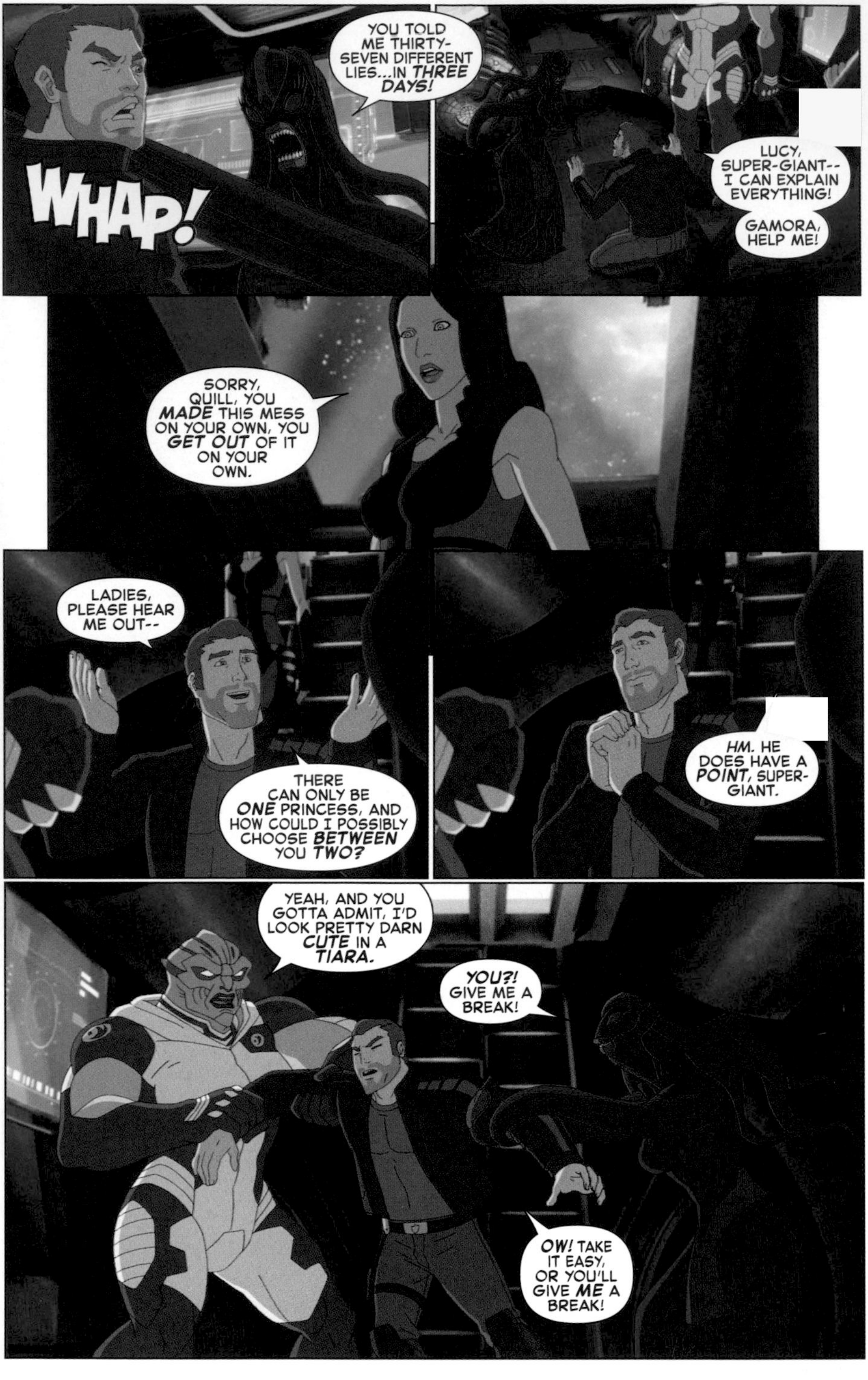
YOU TOLD ME THIRTY-SEVEN DIFFERENT LIES...IN THREE DAYS!
WHAP!
LUCY, SUPER-GIANT-- I CAN EXPLAIN EVERYTHING!
GAMORA, HELP ME!
SORRY, QUILL, YOU MADE THIS MESS ON YOUR OWN, YOU GET OUT OF IT ON YOUR OWN.
LADIES, PLEASE HEAR ME OUT--
THERE CAN ONLY BE ONE PRINCESS, AND HOW COULD I POSSIBLY CHOOSE BETWEEN YOU TWO?
HM. HE DOES HAVE A POINT, SUPER-GIANT.
YEAH, AND YOU GOTTA ADMIT, I'D LOOK PRETTY DARN CUTE IN A TIARA.
YOU?! GIVE ME A BREAK!
OW! TAKE IT EASY, OR YOU'LL GIVE ME A BREAK!

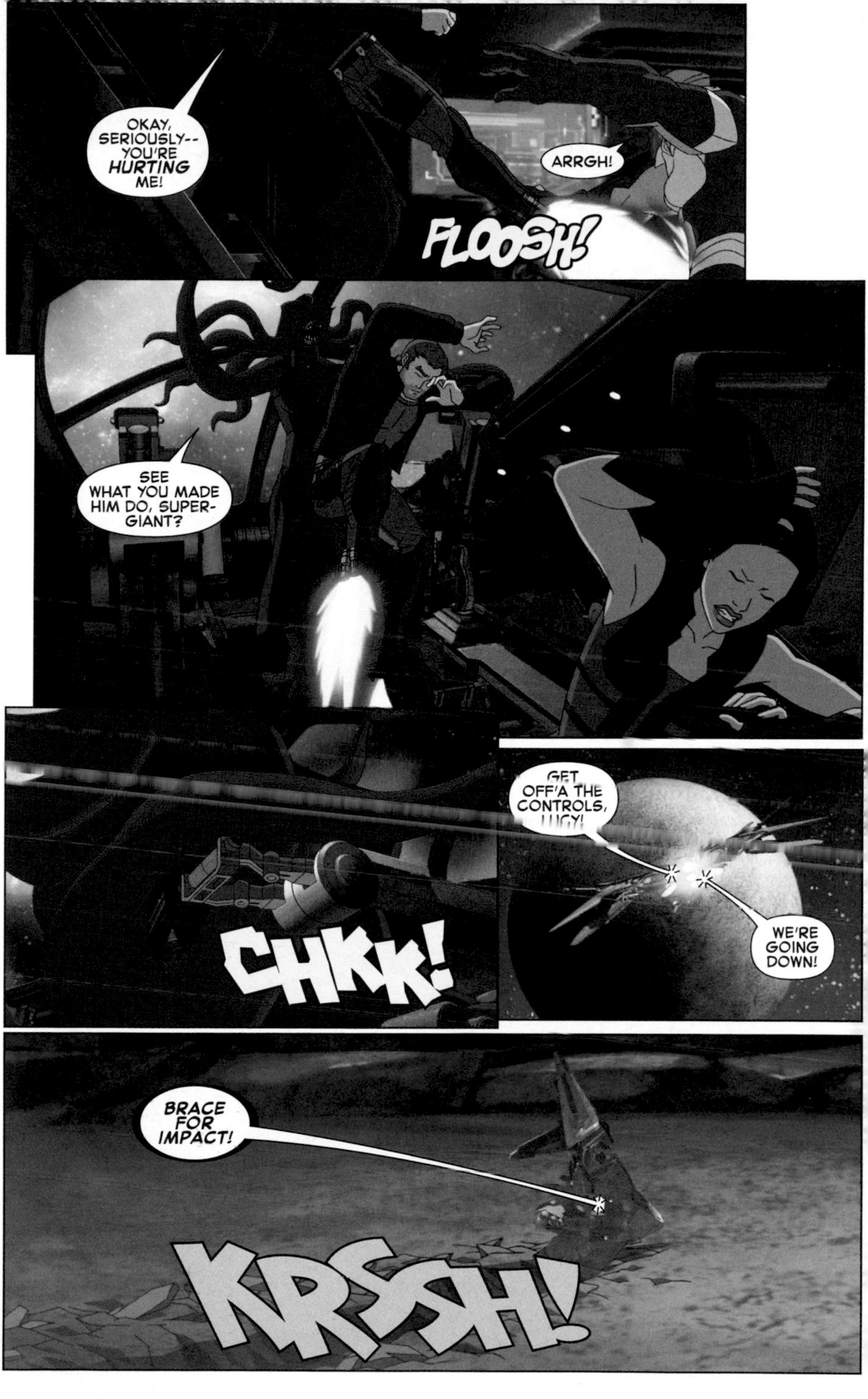

OKAY, SERIOUSLY-- YOU'RE *HURTING* ME!
ARRGH!
FLOOSH!
SEE WHAT YOU MADE HIM DO, SUPER-GIANT?
CHKK!
GET OFF'A THE CONTROLS, LUCY!
WE'RE GOING DOWN!
BRACE FOR IMPACT!
KRSSH!

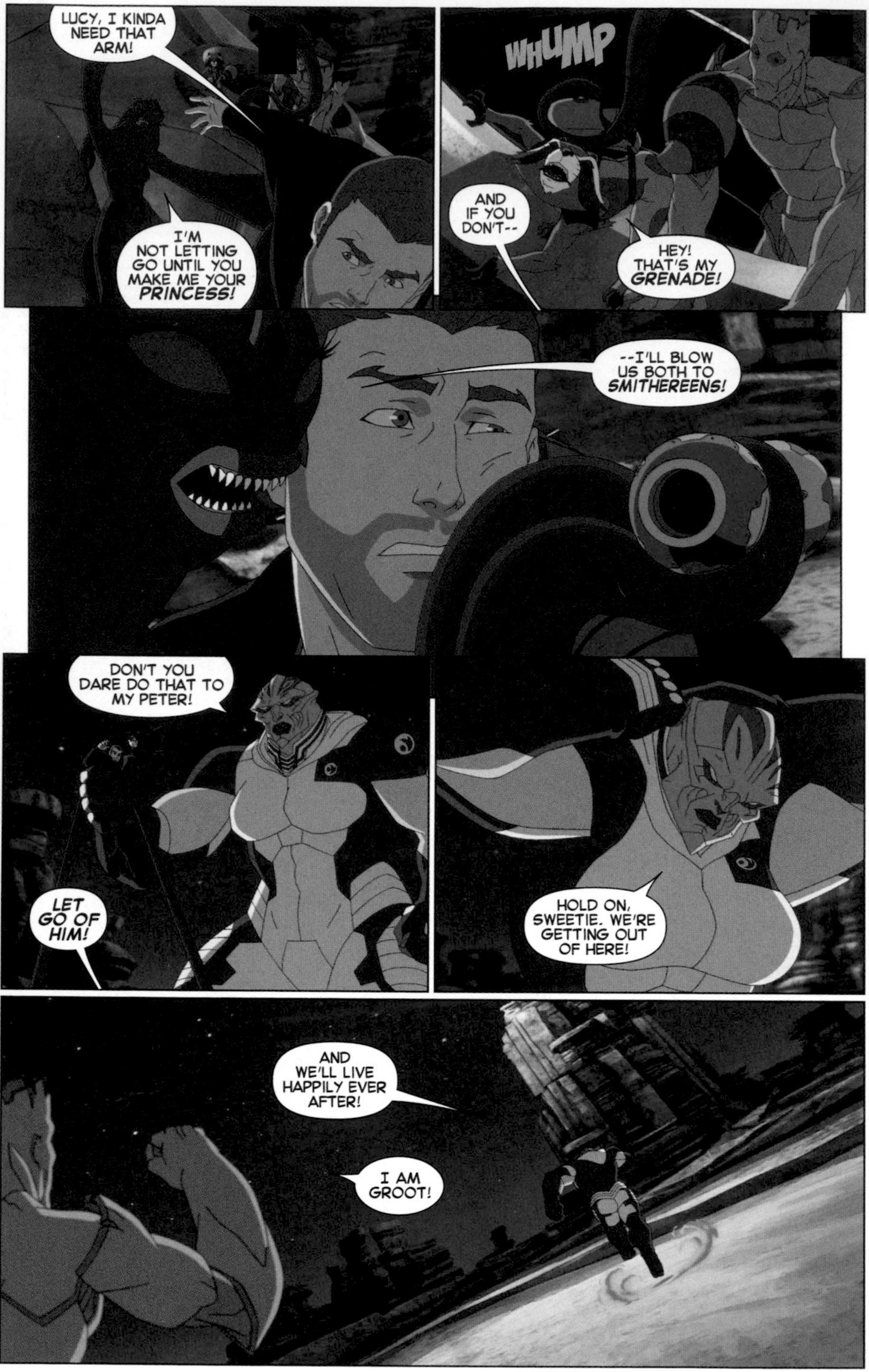
LUCY, I KINDA NEED THAT ARM!
I'M NOT LETTING GO UNTIL YOU MAKE ME YOUR *PRINCESS!*
WHUMP
AND IF YOU DON'T--
HEY! THAT'S MY *GRENADE!*
--I'LL BLOW US BOTH TO *SMITHEREENS!*
DON'T YOU DARE DO THAT TO MY PETER!
LET GO OF HIM!
HOLD ON, SWEETIE. WE'RE GETTING OUT OF HERE!
AND WE'LL LIVE HAPPILY EVER AFTER!
I AM GROOT!

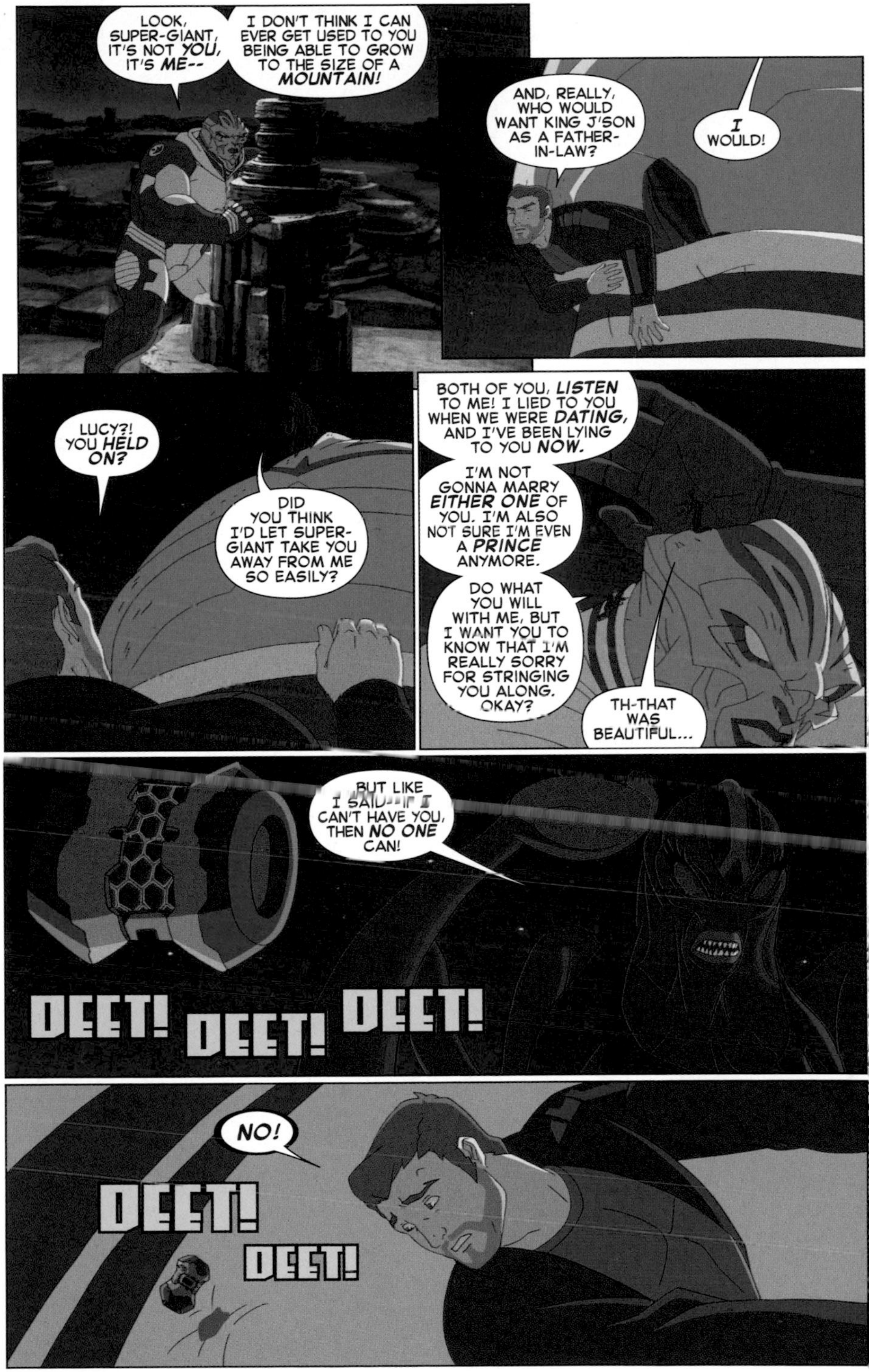
LOOK, SUPER-GIANT, IT'S NOT *YOU*, IT'S *ME*--
I DON'T THINK I CAN EVER GET USED TO YOU BEING ABLE TO GROW TO THE SIZE OF A *MOUNTAIN!*
AND, REALLY, WHO WOULD WANT KING J'SON AS A FATHER-IN-LAW?
I WOULD!
LUCY?! YOU *HELD ON?*
DID YOU THINK I'D LET SUPER-GIANT TAKE YOU AWAY FROM ME SO EASILY?
BOTH OF YOU, *LISTEN* TO ME! I LIED TO YOU WHEN WE WERE *DATING,* AND I'VE BEEN LYING TO YOU *NOW.*
I'M NOT GONNA MARRY *EITHER ONE* OF YOU. I'M ALSO NOT SURE I'M EVEN A *PRINCE* ANYMORE.
DO WHAT YOU WILL WITH ME, BUT I WANT YOU TO KNOW THAT I'M REALLY SORRY FOR STRINGING YOU ALONG. OKAY?
TH-THAT WAS BEAUTIFUL...
BUT LIKE I SAID--IF I CAN'T HAVE YOU, THEN *NO ONE* CAN!
DEET! DEET! DEET!
NO!
DEET!
DEET!

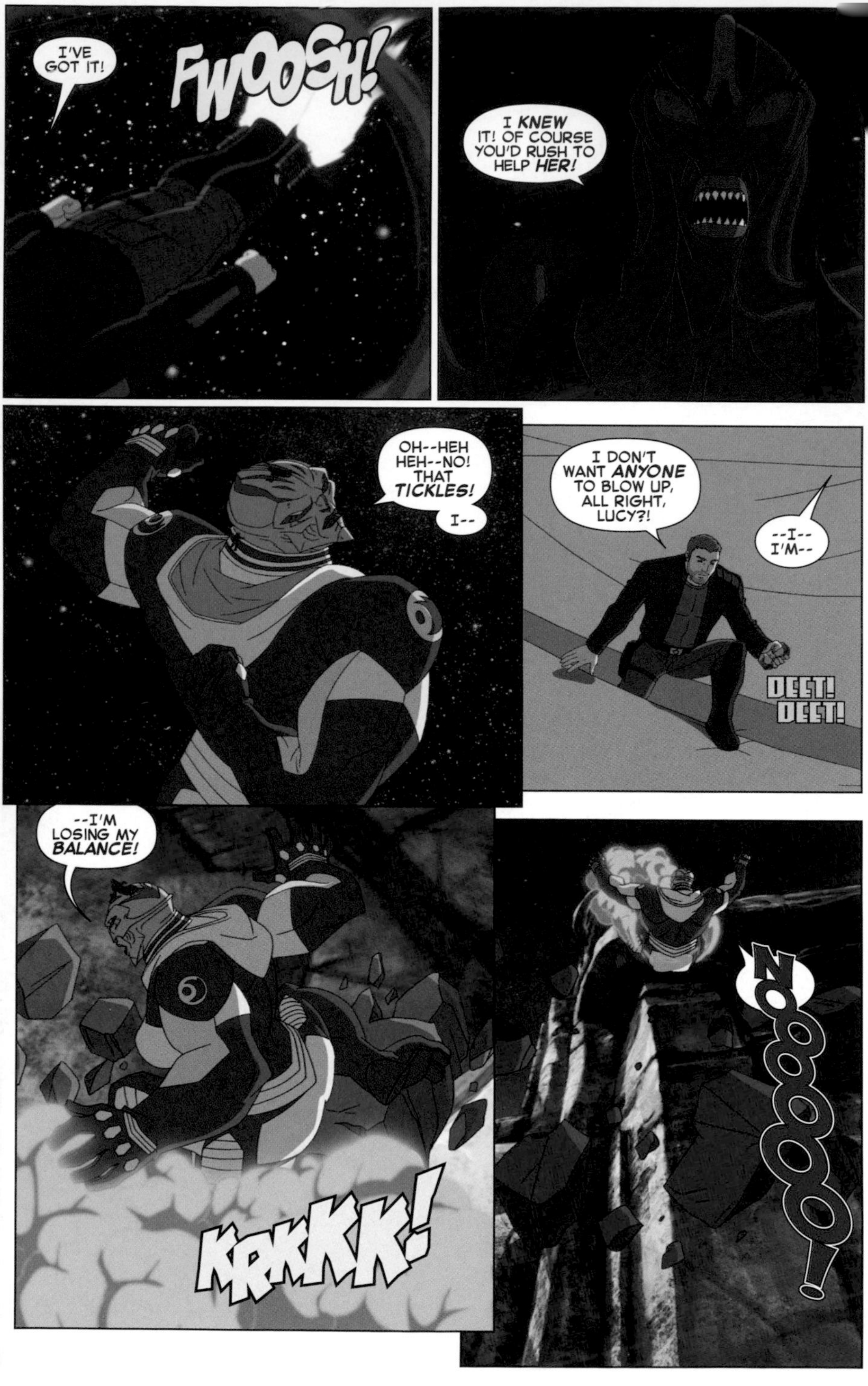
I'VE GOT IT!
FWOOSH!
I KNEW IT! OF COURSE YOU'D RUSH TO HELP HER!
OH--HEH HEH--NO! THAT TICKLES!
I--
I DON'T WANT ANYONE TO BLOW UP, ALL RIGHT, LUCY?!
--I-- I'M--
DEET! DEET!
--I'M LOSING MY BALANCE!
KRKKK!
NOOOOOO!

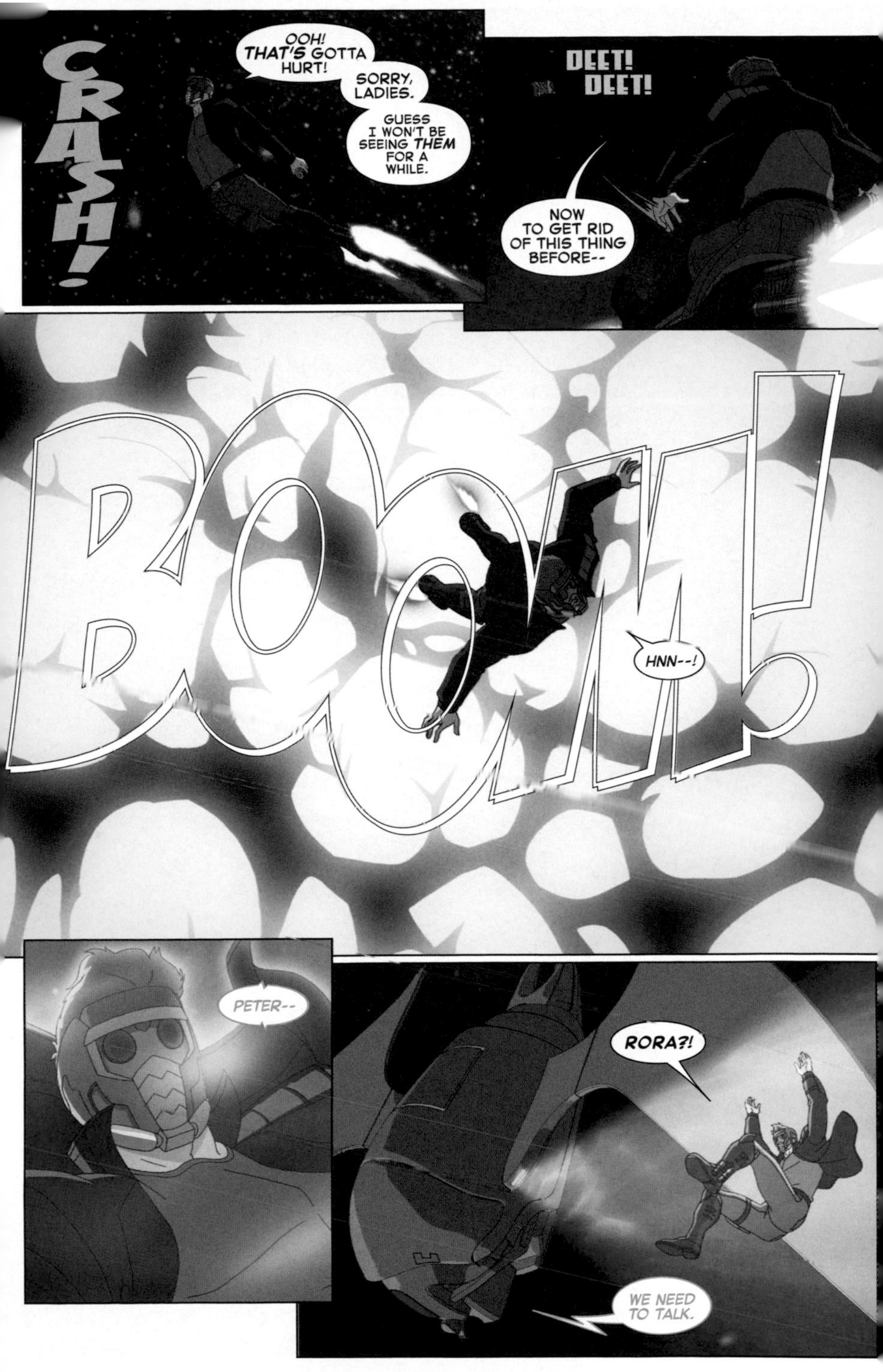
CRASH!
OOH! THAT'S GOTTA HURT!
SORRY, LADIES.
GUESS I WON'T BE SEEING THEM FOR A WHILE.
DEET! DEET!
NOW TO GET RID OF THIS THING BEFORE--
BOOM!
HNN--!
PETER--
RORA?!
WE NEED TO TALK.

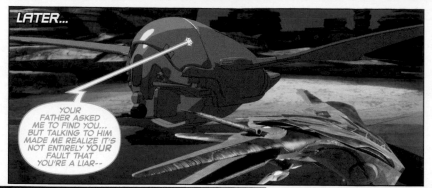

LATER...

YOUR FATHER ASKED ME TO FIND YOU... BUT TALKING TO HIM MADE ME REALIZE IT'S NOT ENTIRELY *YOUR* FAULT THAT YOU'RE A LIAR--

--YOU WERE *BORN* TO IT.

BUT THERE'S SOMETHING *ELSE* YOU NEED TO KNOW ABOUT YOUR FATHER, PETER.

LISTEN, YONDU--ALL PETER NEEDS TO KNOW IS THAT HE'S A NOTHING EARTHER WHO'S BEEN ABDUCTED BY *PIRATES.*

I DON'T WANT TO *SEE* HIM, I DON'T WANT TO *KNOW* ABOUT HIM UNTIL YOU'VE TURNED HIM INTO A PROPER *THIEF.*

WHY WOULD ANY MAN DO THAT TO HIS SON?

BECAUSE I'M THE ONE WHO COULD OPEN THE CRYPTO-CUBE. I'M THE ONLY ONE WHO COULD FINISH HIS QUEST.

EVEN THOUGH DECEPTION IS IN YOUR BLOOD, IT DOESN'T HAVE TO BE IN YOUR HEART.

I WAITED TWENTY-FIVE YEARS FOR THE LOVE AND APPROVAL OF A MAN WHO IS INCAPABALE OF CARING FOR ANYTHING BUT *HIMSELF.*

I HOPE THAT YOU DON'T DO THE SAME.

I HAVE *ANOTHER* VIDEO TO SHOW YOU--SOMETHING YOU'LL WANT TO RECORD WITH YOUR HELMET.

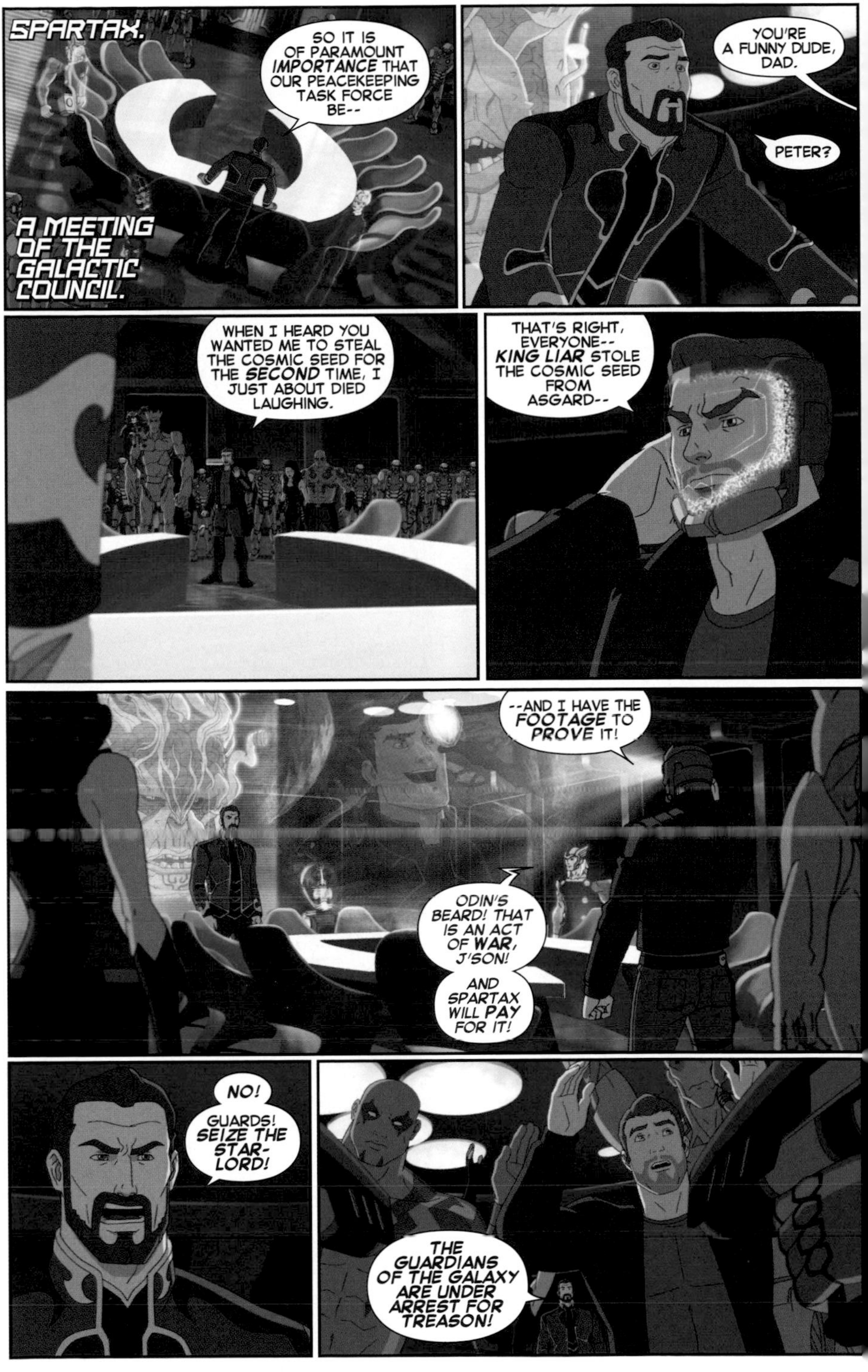
SPARTAX.
A MEETING OF THE GALACTIC COUNCIL.
SO IT IS OF PARAMOUNT IMPORTANCE THAT OUR PEACEKEEPING TASK FORCE BE--
YOU'RE A FUNNY DUDE, DAD.
PETER?
WHEN I HEARD YOU WANTED ME TO STEAL THE COSMIC SEED FOR THE SECOND TIME, I JUST ABOUT DIED LAUGHING.
THAT'S RIGHT, EVERYONE-- KING LIAR STOLE THE COSMIC SEED FROM ASGARD--
--AND I HAVE THE FOOTAGE TO PROVE IT!
ODIN'S BEARD! THAT IS AN ACT OF WAR, J'SON!
AND SPARTAX WILL PAY FOR IT!
NO!
GUARDS! SEIZE THE STAR-LORD!
THE GUARDIANS OF THE GALAXY ARE UNDER ARREST FOR TREASON!

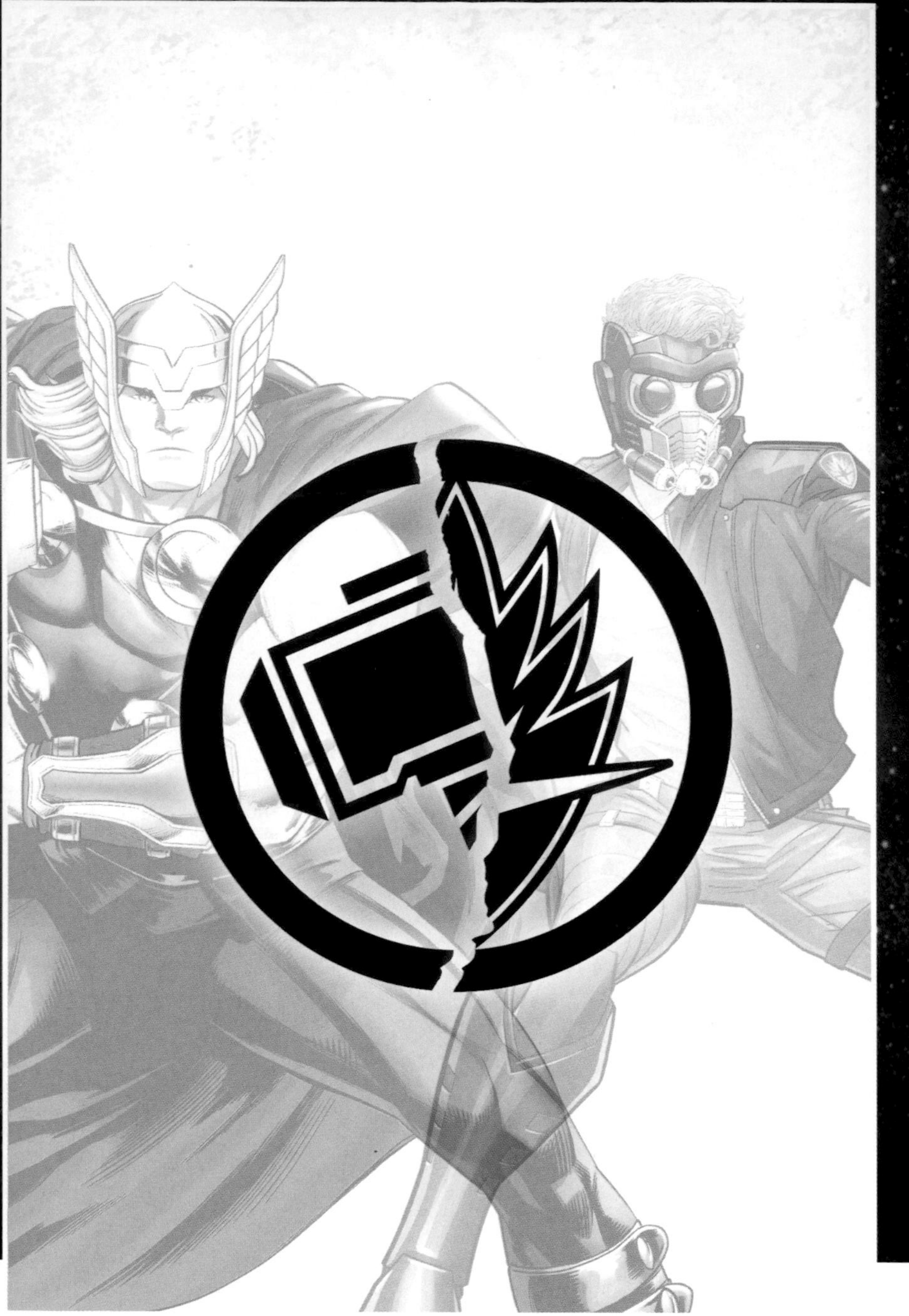

BASED ON **"LIGHTNIN' STRIKES"** **19**

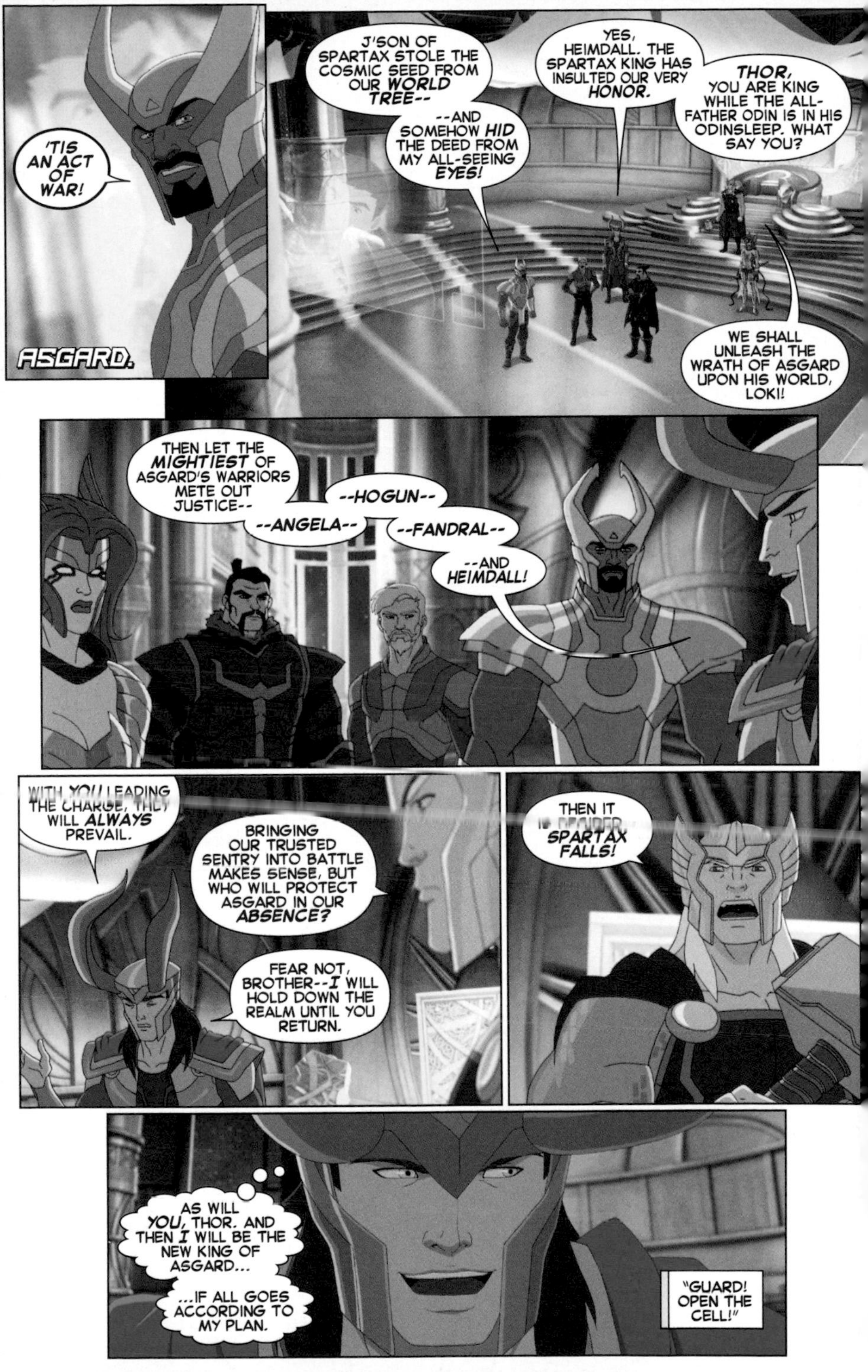
'TIS AN ACT OF WAR!
ASGARD.
J'SON OF SPARTAX STOLE THE COSMIC SEED FROM OUR WORLD TREE--
--AND SOMEHOW HID THE DEED FROM MY ALL-SEEING EYES!
YES, HEIMDALL. THE SPARTAX KING HAS INSULTED OUR VERY HONOR.
THOR, YOU ARE KING WHILE THE ALL-FATHER ODIN IS IN HIS ODINSLEEP. WHAT SAY YOU?
WE SHALL UNLEASH THE WRATH OF ASGARD UPON HIS WORLD, LOKI!
THEN LET THE MIGHTIEST OF ASGARD'S WARRIORS METE OUT JUSTICE--
--ANGELA--
--HOGUN--
--FANDRAL--
--AND HEIMDALL!
WITH YOU LEADING THE CHARGE, THEY WILL ALWAYS PREVAIL.
BRINGING OUR TRUSTED SENTRY INTO BATTLE MAKES SENSE, BUT WHO WILL PROTECT ASGARD IN OUR ABSENCE?
FEAR NOT, BROTHER--I WILL HOLD DOWN THE REALM UNTIL YOU RETURN.
THEN IT
SPARTAX FALLS!
AS WILL YOU, THOR. AND THEN I WILL BE THE NEW KING OF ASGARD...
...IF ALL GOES ACCORDING TO MY PLAN.
"GUARD! OPEN THE CELL!"

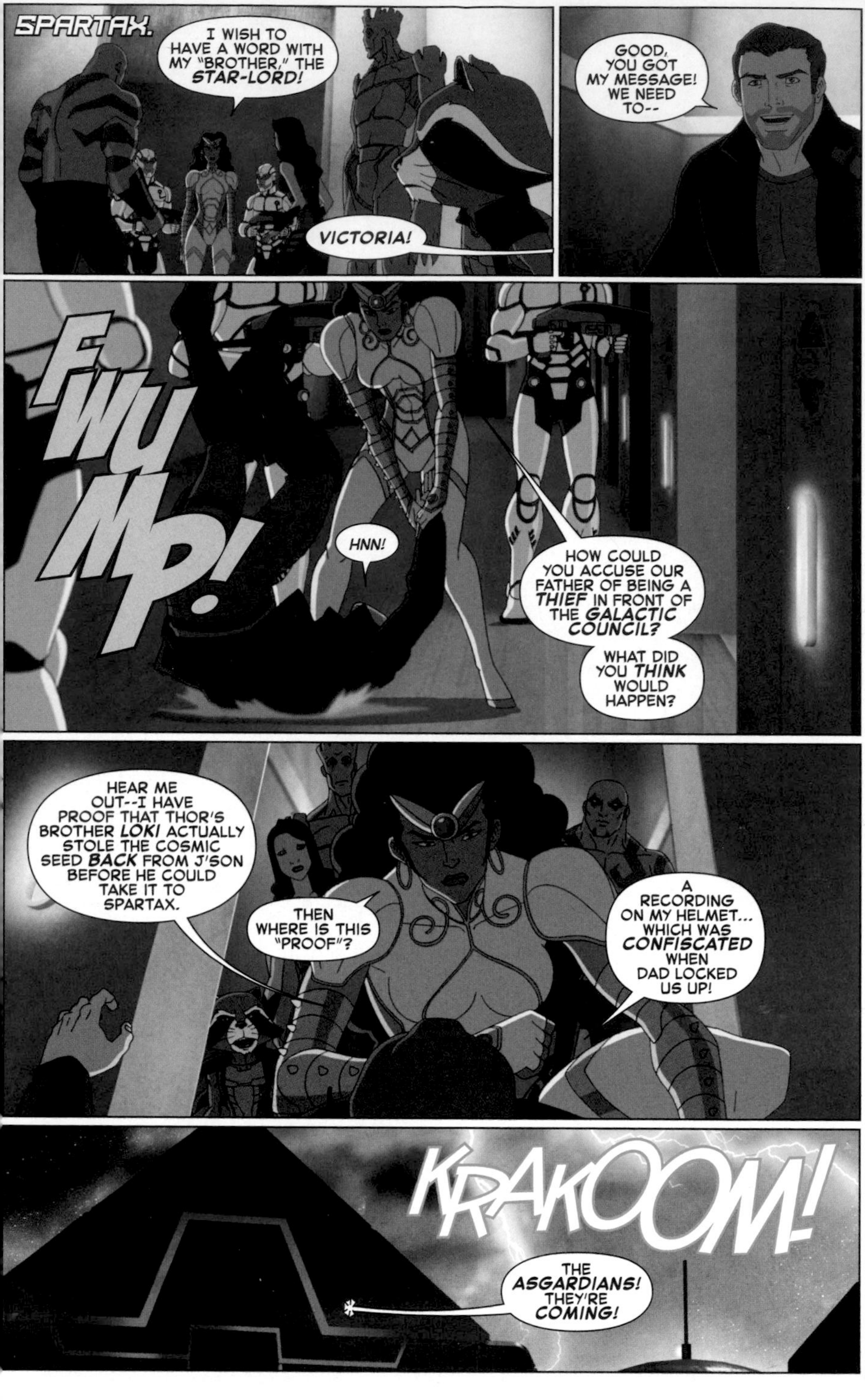
SPARTAX.
I WISH TO HAVE A WORD WITH MY "BROTHER," THE STAR-LORD!
VICTORIA!
GOOD, YOU GOT MY MESSAGE! WE NEED TO--
FWUMP!
HNN!
HOW COULD YOU ACCUSE OUR FATHER OF BEING A THIEF IN FRONT OF THE GALACTIC COUNCIL?
WHAT DID YOU THINK WOULD HAPPEN?
HEAR ME OUT--I HAVE PROOF THAT THOR'S BROTHER LOKI ACTUALLY STOLE THE COSMIC SEED BACK FROM J'SON BEFORE HE COULD TAKE IT TO SPARTAX.
THEN WHERE IS THIS "PROOF"?
A RECORDING ON MY HELMET... WHICH WAS CONFISCATED WHEN DAD LOCKED US UP!
KRAKOOM!
THE ASGARDIANS! THEY'RE COMING!

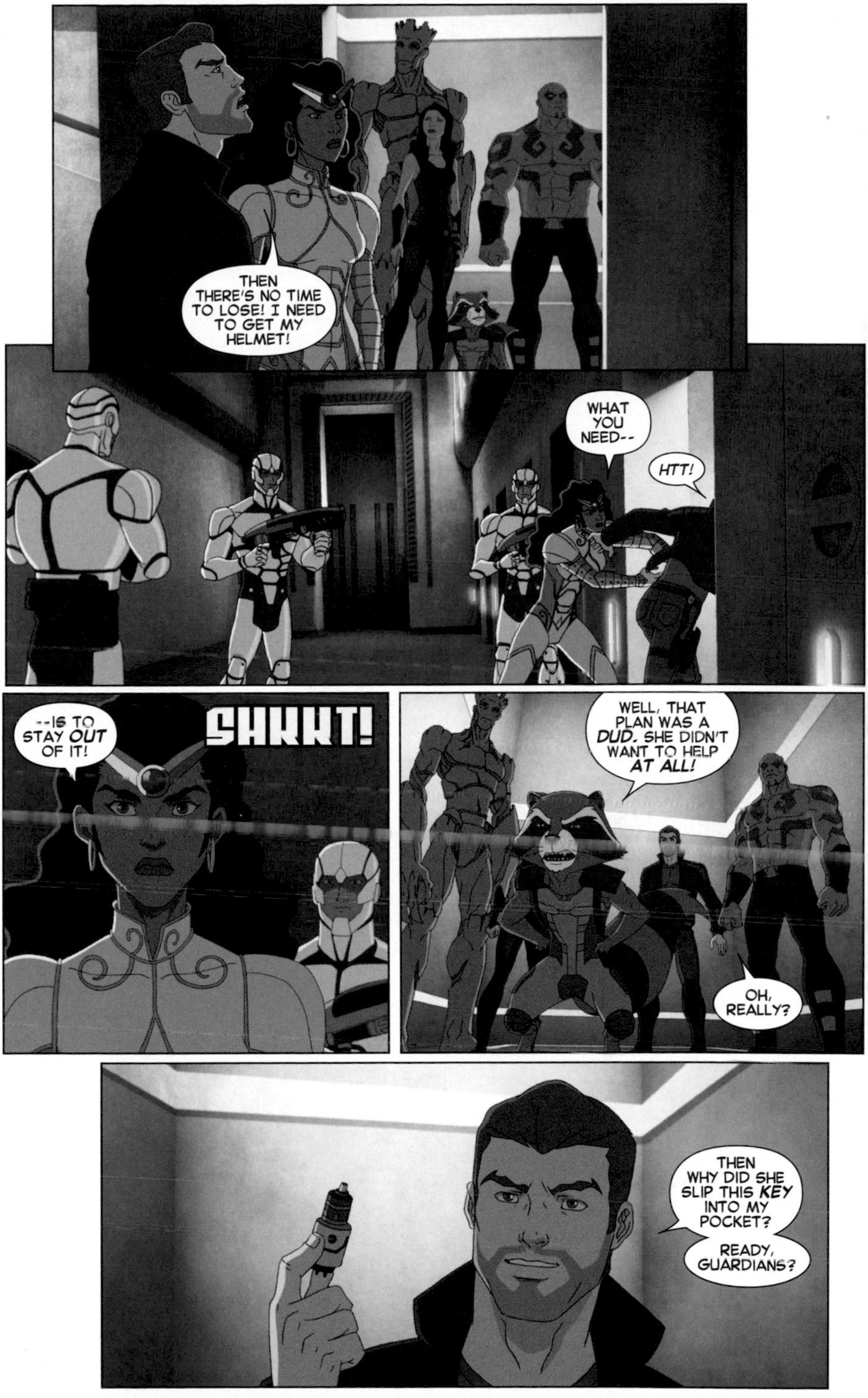
THEN THERE'S NO TIME TO LOSE! I NEED TO GET MY HELMET!
WHAT YOU NEED--
HTT!
--IS TO STAY OUT OF IT!
SHKKT!
WELL, THAT PLAN WAS A DUD. SHE DIDN'T WANT TO HELP AT ALL!
OH, REALLY?
THEN WHY DID SHE SLIP THIS KEY INTO MY POCKET?
READY, GUARDIANS?

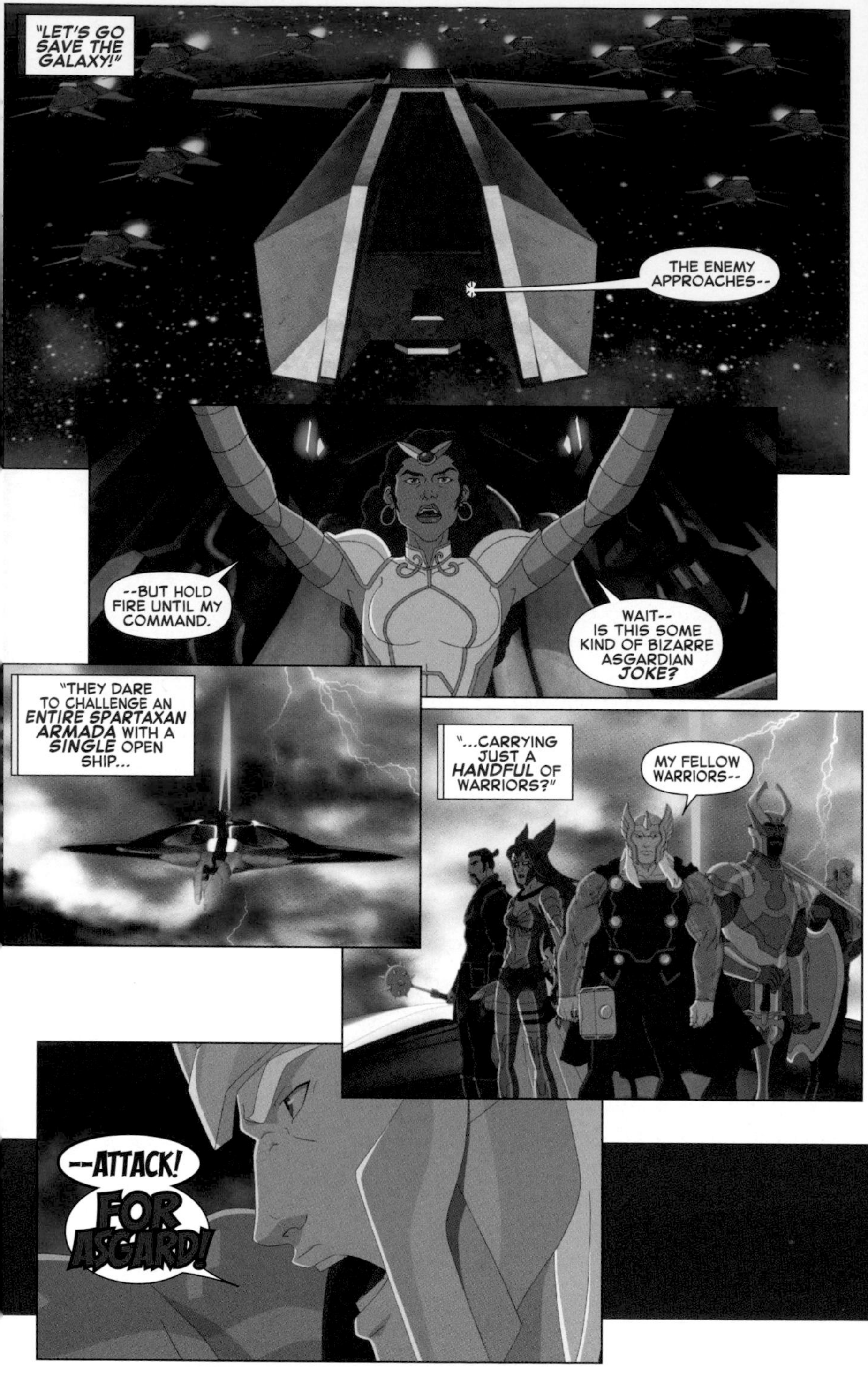
"LET'S GO SAVE THE GALAXY!"
THE ENEMY APPROACHES--
--BUT HOLD FIRE UNTIL MY COMMAND.
WAIT-- IS THIS SOME KIND OF BIZARRE ASGARDIAN JOKE?
"THEY DARE TO CHALLENGE AN ENTIRE SPARTAXAN ARMADA WITH A SINGLE OPEN SHIP...
"...CARRYING JUST A HANDFUL OF WARRIORS?"
MY FELLOW WARRIORS--
--ATTACK!
FOR ASGARD!

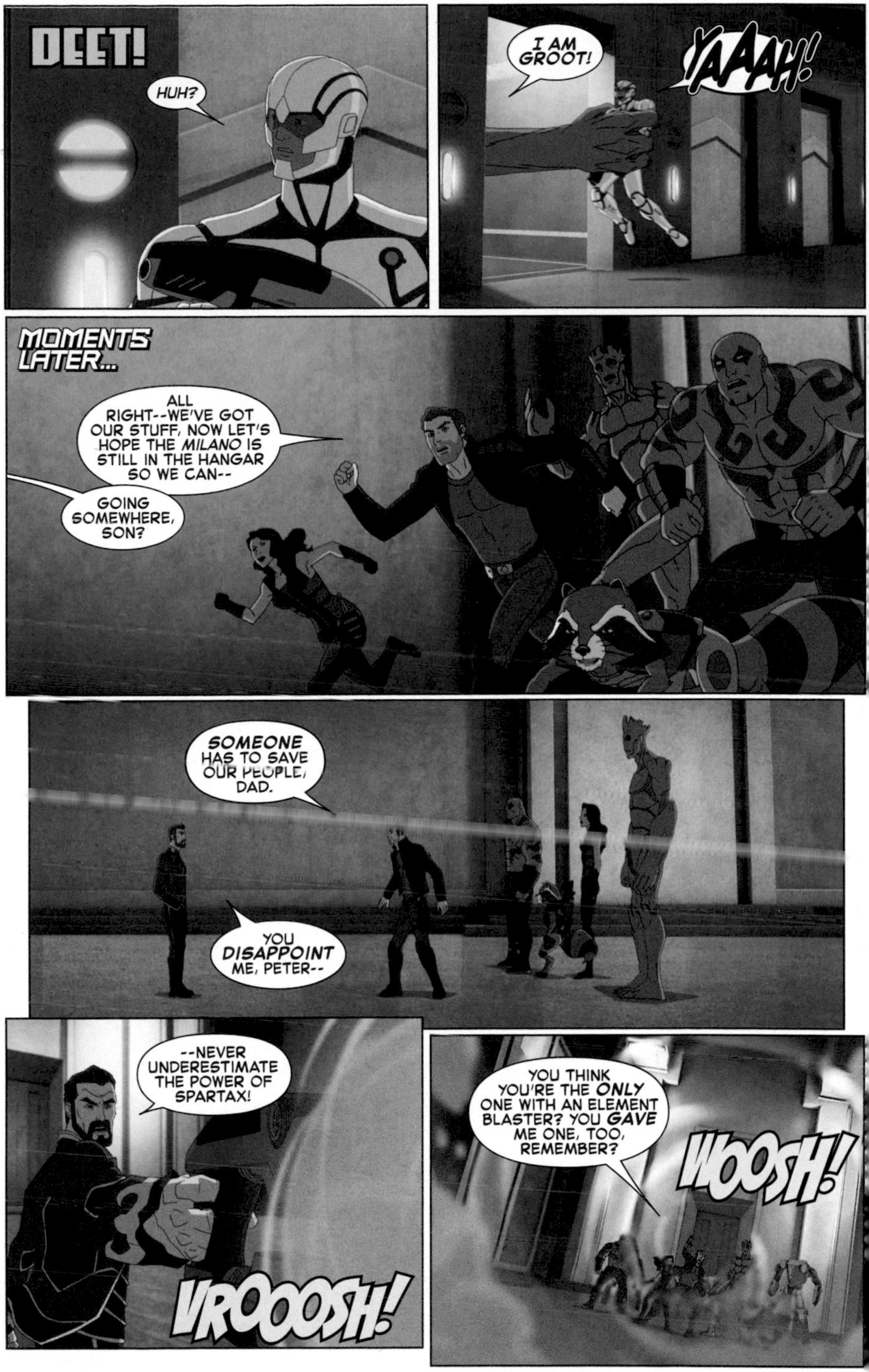
DEET!
HUH?
I AM GROOT!
YAAAH!
MOMENTS LATER...
ALL RIGHT--WE'VE GOT OUR STUFF, NOW LET'S HOPE THE *MILANO* IS STILL IN THE HANGAR SO WE CAN--
GOING SOMEWHERE, SON?
SOMEONE HAS TO SAVE OUR PEOPLE, DAD.
YOU *DISAPPOINT* ME, PETER--
--NEVER UNDERESTIMATE THE POWER OF SPARTAX!
VROOOSH!
YOU THINK YOU'RE THE *ONLY* ONE WITH AN ELEMENT BLASTER? YOU *GAVE* ME ONE, TOO, REMEMBER?
WOOSH!

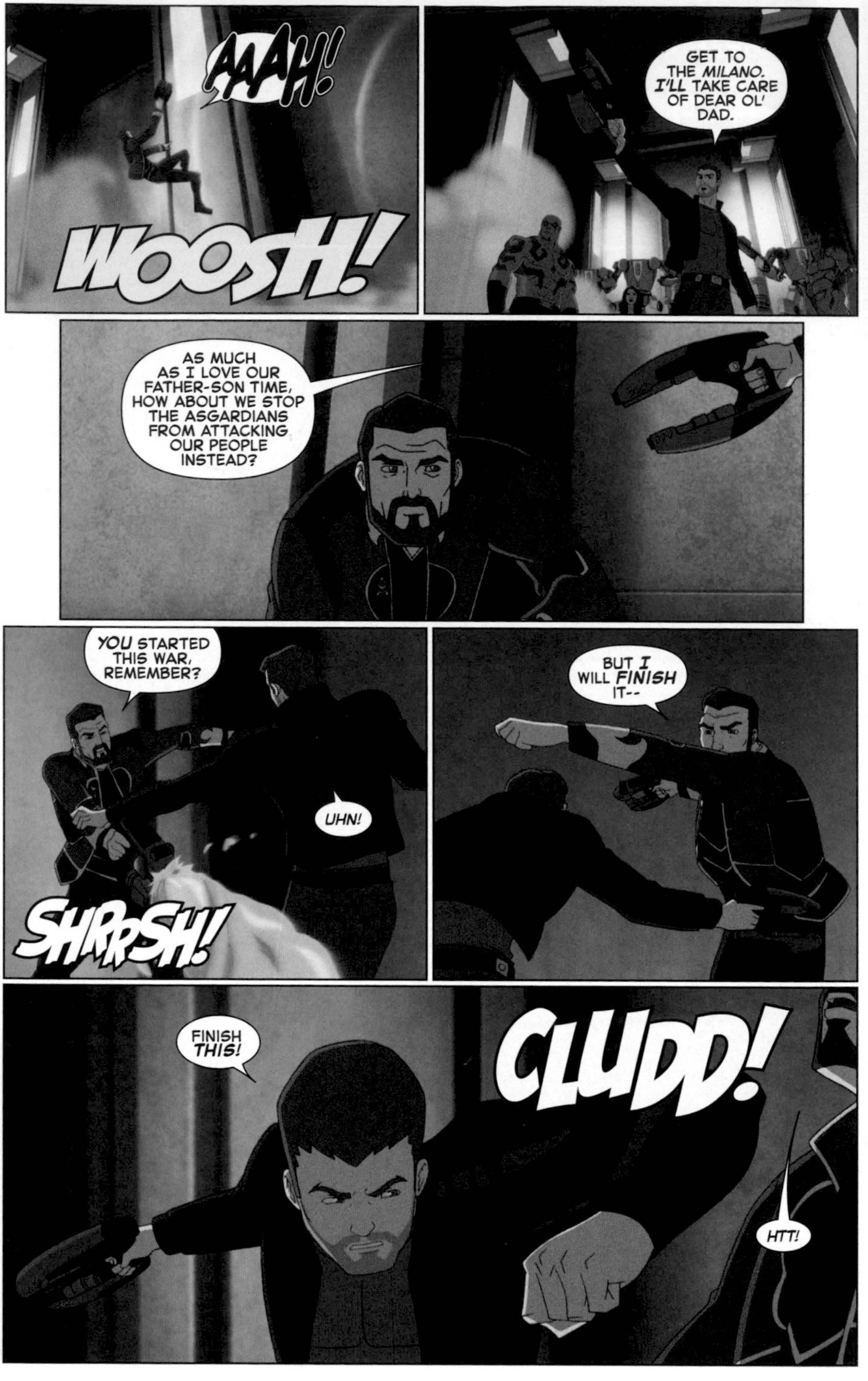
AAAH!
WOOSH!
GET TO THE MILANO. I'LL TAKE CARE OF DEAR OL' DAD.
AS MUCH AS I LOVE OUR FATHER-SON TIME, HOW ABOUT WE STOP THE ASGARDIANS FROM ATTACKING OUR PEOPLE INSTEAD?
YOU STARTED THIS WAR, REMEMBER?
UHN!
SHRRSH!
BUT I WILL FINISH IT--
FINISH THIS!
CLUDD!
HTT!

MEANWHILE...

--SSSSSSSS!

FRSSSSS--

GIVE THIS UP, DAD! YOUR KINGDOM IS SUFFERING FOR *NO GOOD REASON!*

I HAVE THE VIDEO PROOF THAT *LOKI* ACTUALLY TOOK THE COSMIC SEED!

ARE YOU *SURE* ABOUT THAT?

WHAT?! YOU *ERASED* IT?

I CONFISCATED YOUR *HELMET*--YOU DIDN'T SEE THAT COMING?

OF *COURSE* I WANT THIS WAR--

SO YOU ACTUALLY *WANT* THIS WAR?

FROOOSH!

FROOOSH!

--BECAUSE *THIS* TIME I KNOW I CAN *WIN!*

KR-SH!

AAAH!

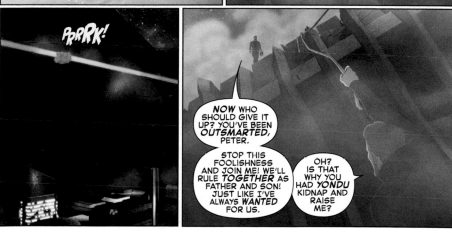

PRRRK!

NOW WHO SHOULD GIVE IT UP? YOU'VE BEEN *OUTSMARTED,* PETER.

STOP THIS FOOLISHNESS AND JOIN ME! WE'LL RULE *TOGETHER* AS FATHER AND SON! JUST LIKE I'VE ALWAYS *WANTED* FOR US.

OH? IS THAT WHY YOU HAD *YONDU* KIDNAP AND RAISE ME?

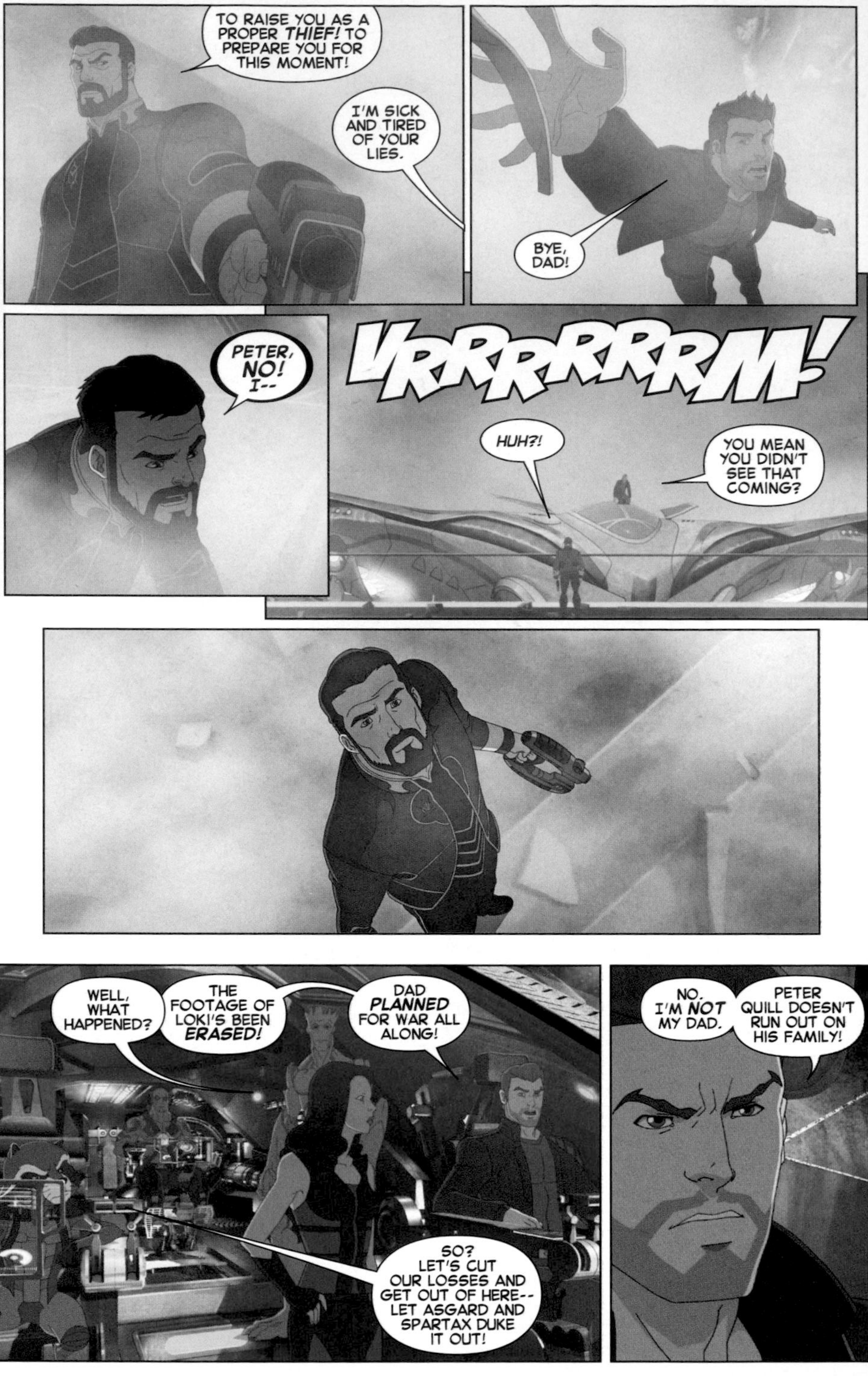
TO RAISE YOU AS A PROPER THIEF! TO PREPARE YOU FOR THIS MOMENT!
I'M SICK AND TIRED OF YOUR LIES.
BYE, DAD!
PETER, NO! I--
VRRRRRRRM!
HUH?!
YOU MEAN YOU DIDN'T SEE THAT COMING?
WELL, WHAT HAPPENED?
THE FOOTAGE OF LOKI'S BEEN ERASED!
DAD PLANNED FOR WAR ALL ALONG!
SO? LET'S CUT OUR LOSSES AND GET OUT OF HERE-- LET ASGARD AND SPARTAX DUKE IT OUT!
NO. I'M NOT MY DAD.
PETER QUILL DOESN'T RUN OUT ON HIS FAMILY!

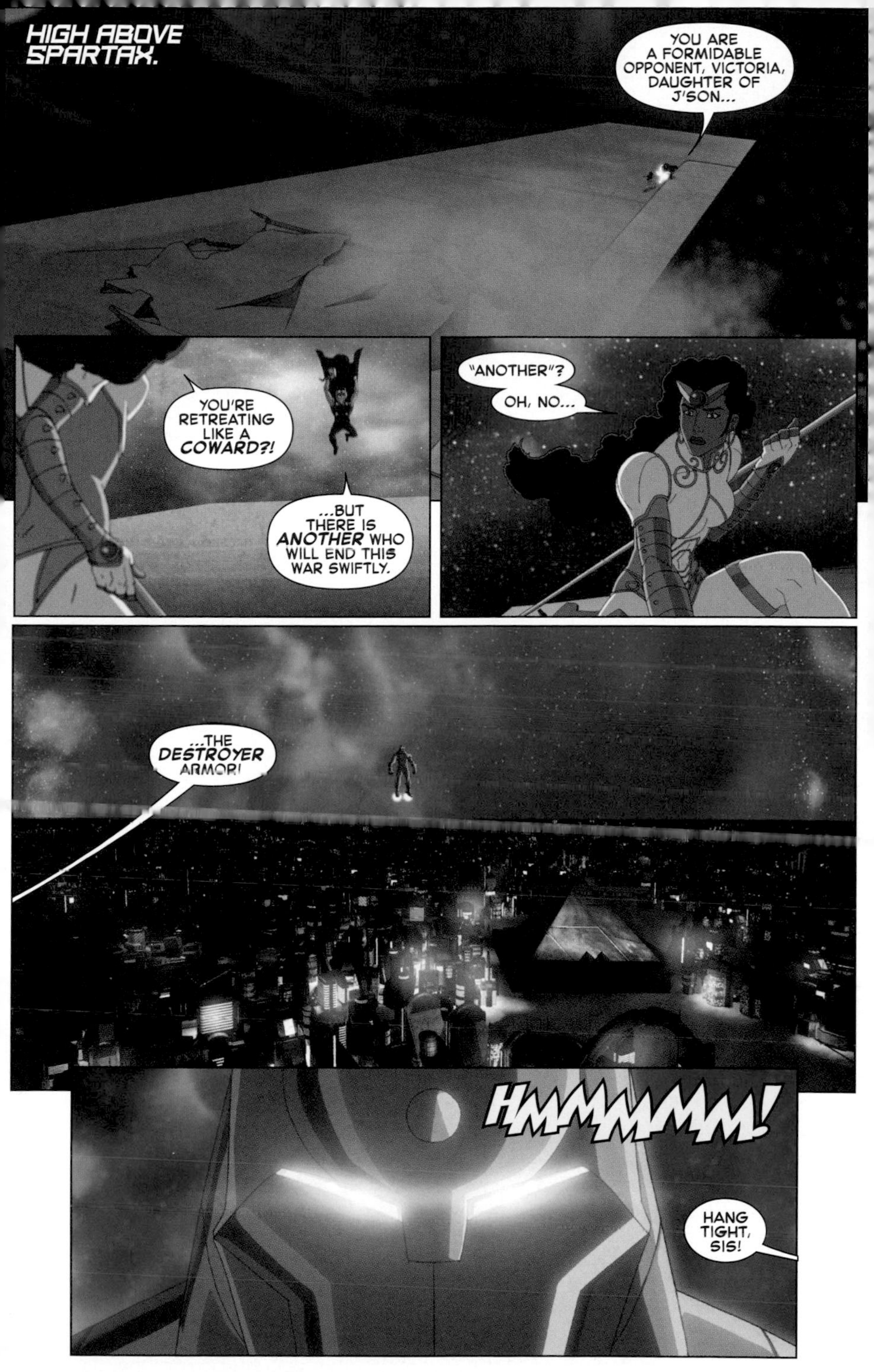
HIGH ABOVE SPARTAX.
YOU ARE A FORMIDABLE OPPONENT, VICTORIA, DAUGHTER OF J'SON...
YOU'RE RETREATING LIKE A COWARD?!
...BUT THERE IS ANOTHER WHO WILL END THIS WAR SWIFTLY.
"ANOTHER"?
OH, NO...
...THE DESTROYER ARMOR!
HMMMMM!
HANG TIGHT, SIS!

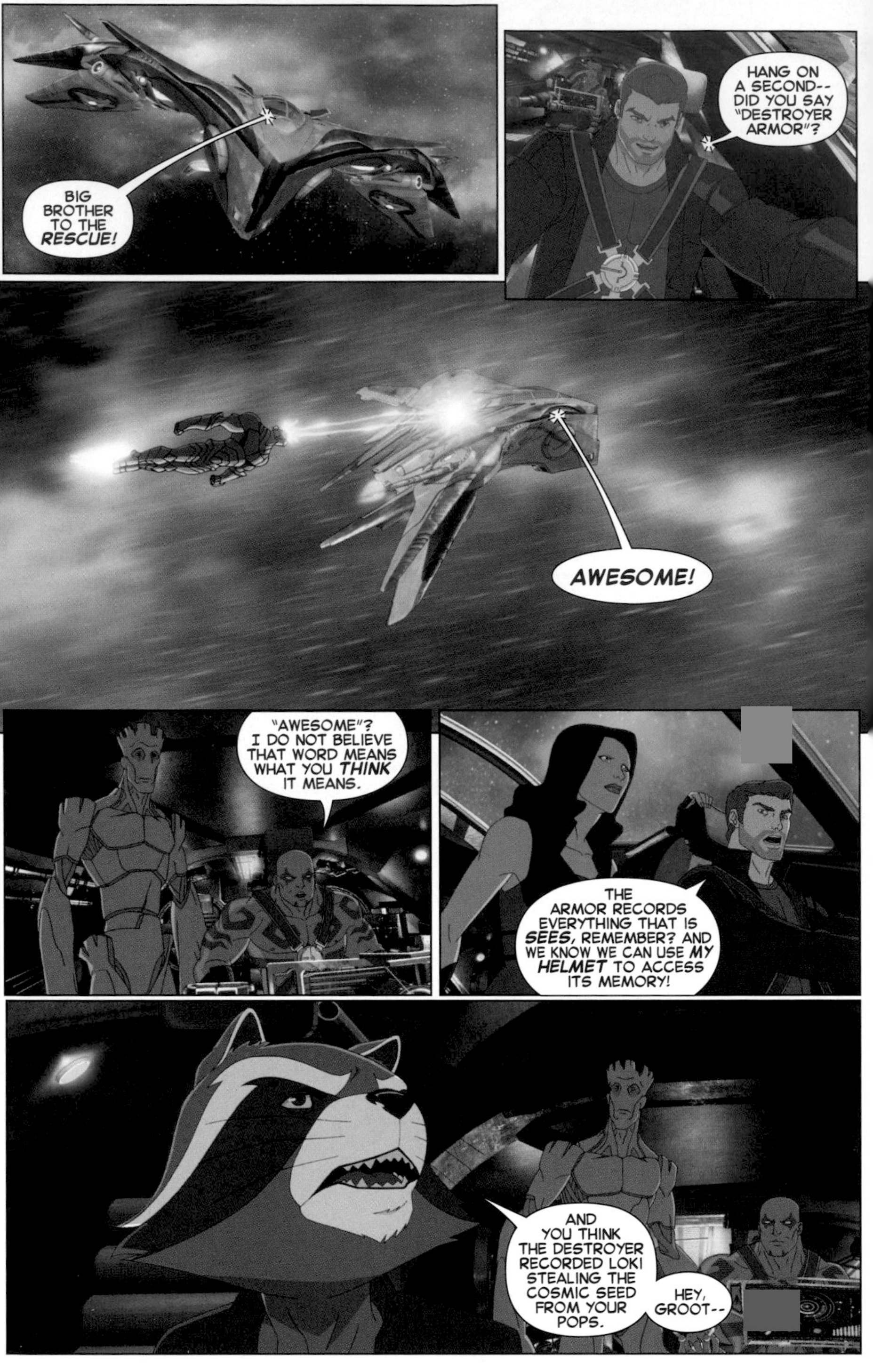
BIG BROTHER TO THE RESCUE!
HANG ON A SECOND-- DID YOU SAY "DESTROYER ARMOR"?
AWESOME!
"AWESOME"? I DO NOT BELIEVE THAT WORD MEANS WHAT YOU THINK IT MEANS.
THE ARMOR RECORDS EVERYTHING THAT IS SEES, REMEMBER? AND WE KNOW WE CAN USE MY HELMET TO ACCESS ITS MEMORY!
AND YOU THINK THE DESTROYER RECORDED LOKI STEALING THE COSMIC SEED FROM YOUR POPS.
HEY, GROOT--

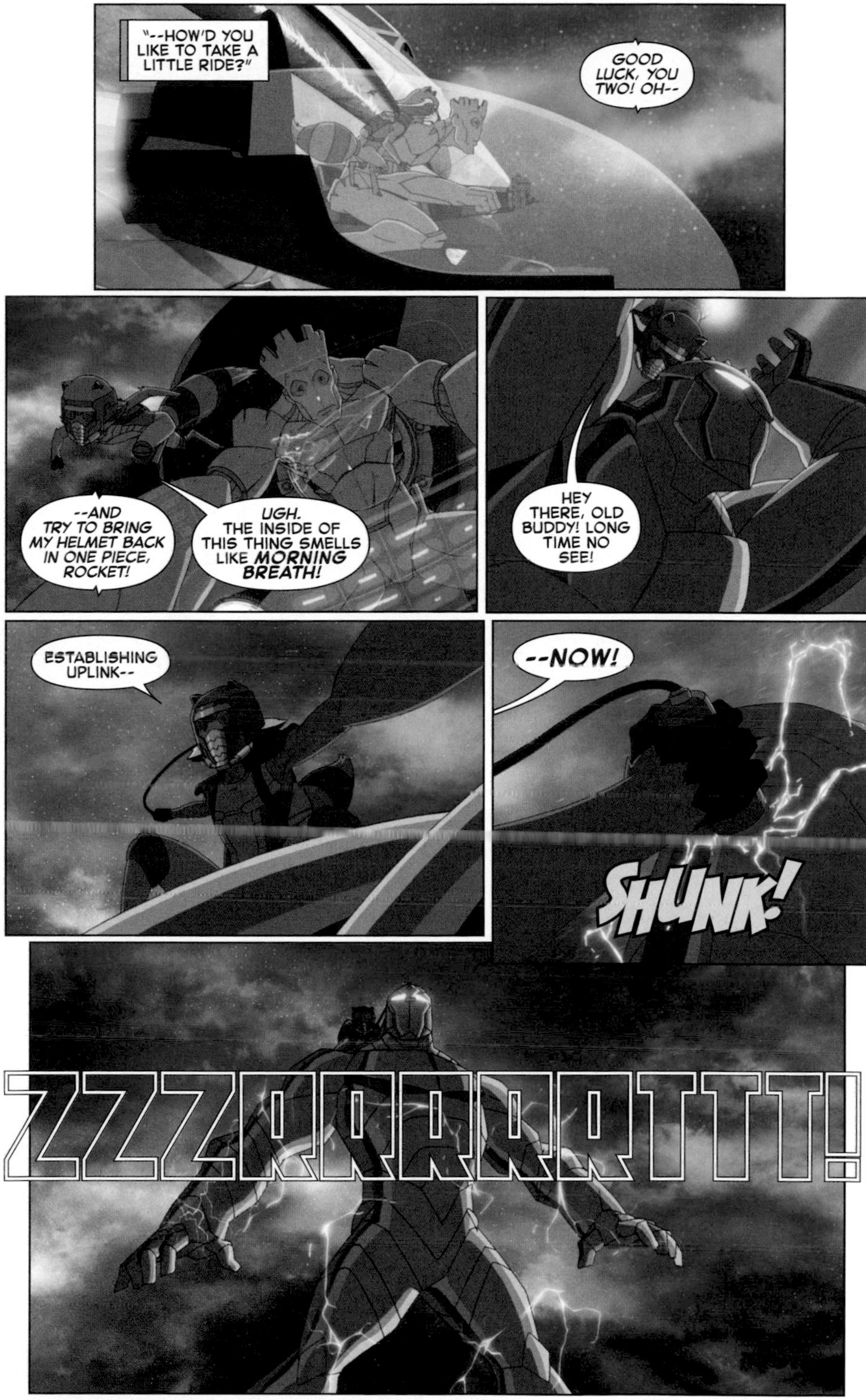
"--HOW'D YOU LIKE TO TAKE A LITTLE RIDE?"
GOOD LUCK, YOU TWO! OH--
--AND TRY TO BRING MY HELMET BACK IN ONE PIECE, ROCKET!
UGH. THE INSIDE OF THIS THING SMELLS LIKE MORNING BREATH!
HEY THERE, OLD BUDDY! LONG TIME NO SEE!
ESTABLISHING UPLINK--
--NOW!
SHUNK!
ZZZRRRRTTT!

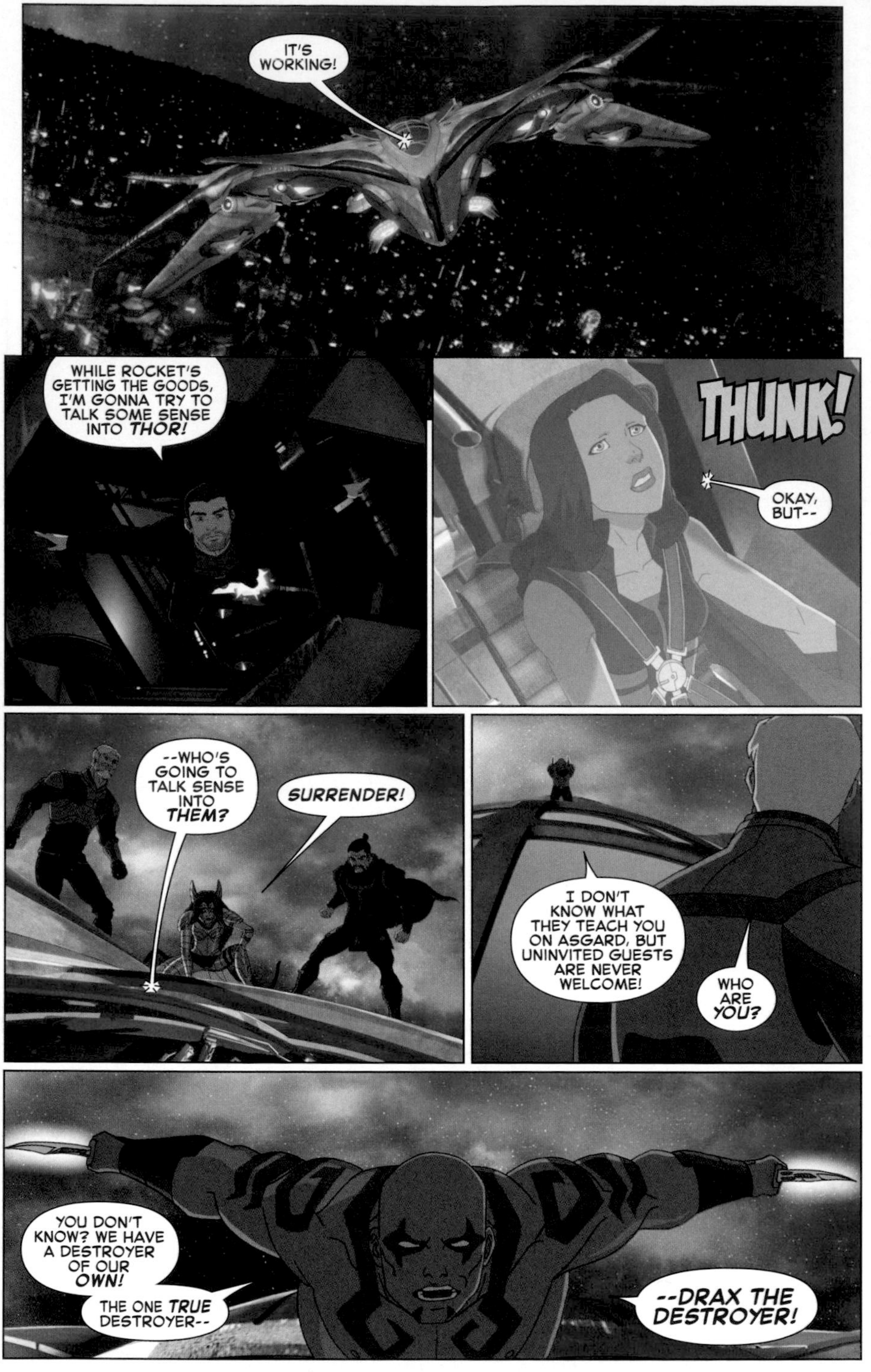
IT'S WORKING!
WHILE ROCKET'S GETTING THE GOODS, I'M GONNA TRY TO TALK SOME SENSE INTO THOR!
THUNK!
OKAY, BUT--
--WHO'S GOING TO TALK SENSE INTO THEM?
SURRENDER!
I DON'T KNOW WHAT THEY TEACH YOU ON ASGARD, BUT UNINVITED GUESTS ARE NEVER WELCOME!
WHO ARE YOU?
YOU DON'T KNOW? WE HAVE A DESTROYER OF OUR OWN!
THE ONE TRUE DESTROYER--
--DRAX THE DESTROYER!

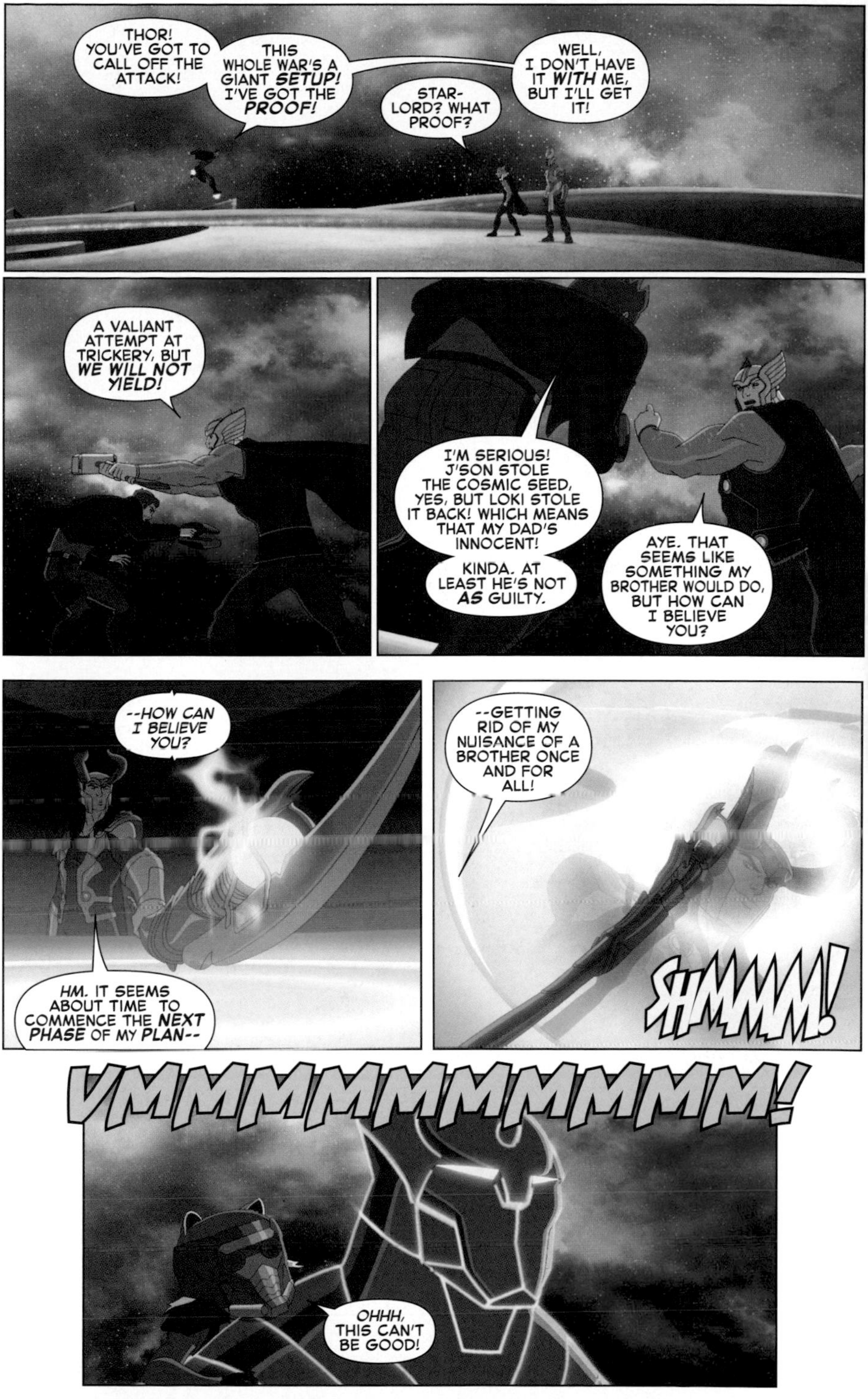
THOR! YOU'VE GOT TO CALL OFF THE ATTACK!
THIS WHOLE WAR'S A GIANT SETUP! I'VE GOT THE PROOF!
STAR-LORD? WHAT PROOF?
WELL, I DON'T HAVE IT WITH ME, BUT I'LL GET IT!
A VALIANT ATTEMPT AT TRICKERY, BUT WE WILL NOT YIELD!
I'M SERIOUS! J'SON STOLE THE COSMIC SEED, YES, BUT LOKI STOLE IT BACK! WHICH MEANS THAT MY DAD'S INNOCENT!
KINDA. AT LEAST HE'S NOT AS GUILTY.
AYE. THAT SEEMS LIKE SOMETHING MY BROTHER WOULD DO, BUT HOW CAN I BELIEVE YOU?
--HOW CAN I BELIEVE YOU?
HM. IT SEEMS ABOUT TIME TO COMMENCE THE NEXT PHASE OF MY PLAN--
--GETTING RID OF MY NUISANCE OF A BROTHER ONCE AND FOR ALL!
SHMMM!
VMMMMMMMMMMMM!
OHHH, THIS CAN'T BE GOOD!

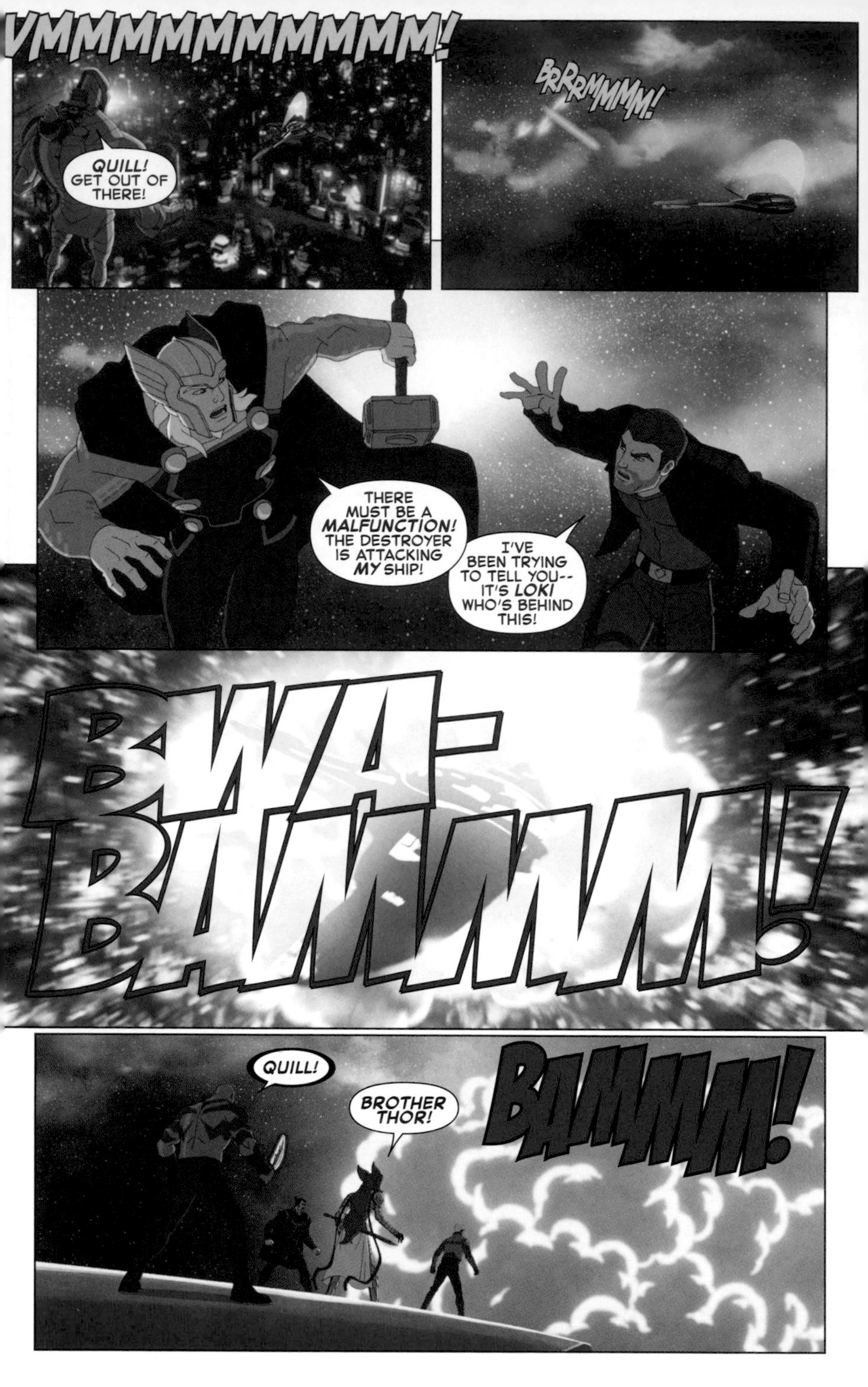
VMMMMMMMMMMM!
QUILL! GET OUT OF THERE!
BRRRMMMM!
THERE MUST BE A MALFUNCTION! THE DESTROYER IS ATTACKING MY SHIP!
I'VE BEEN TRYING TO TELL YOU-- IT'S LOKI WHO'S BEHIND THIS!
BWA-BAMMMM!
QUILL!
BROTHER THOR!
BAMMMM!

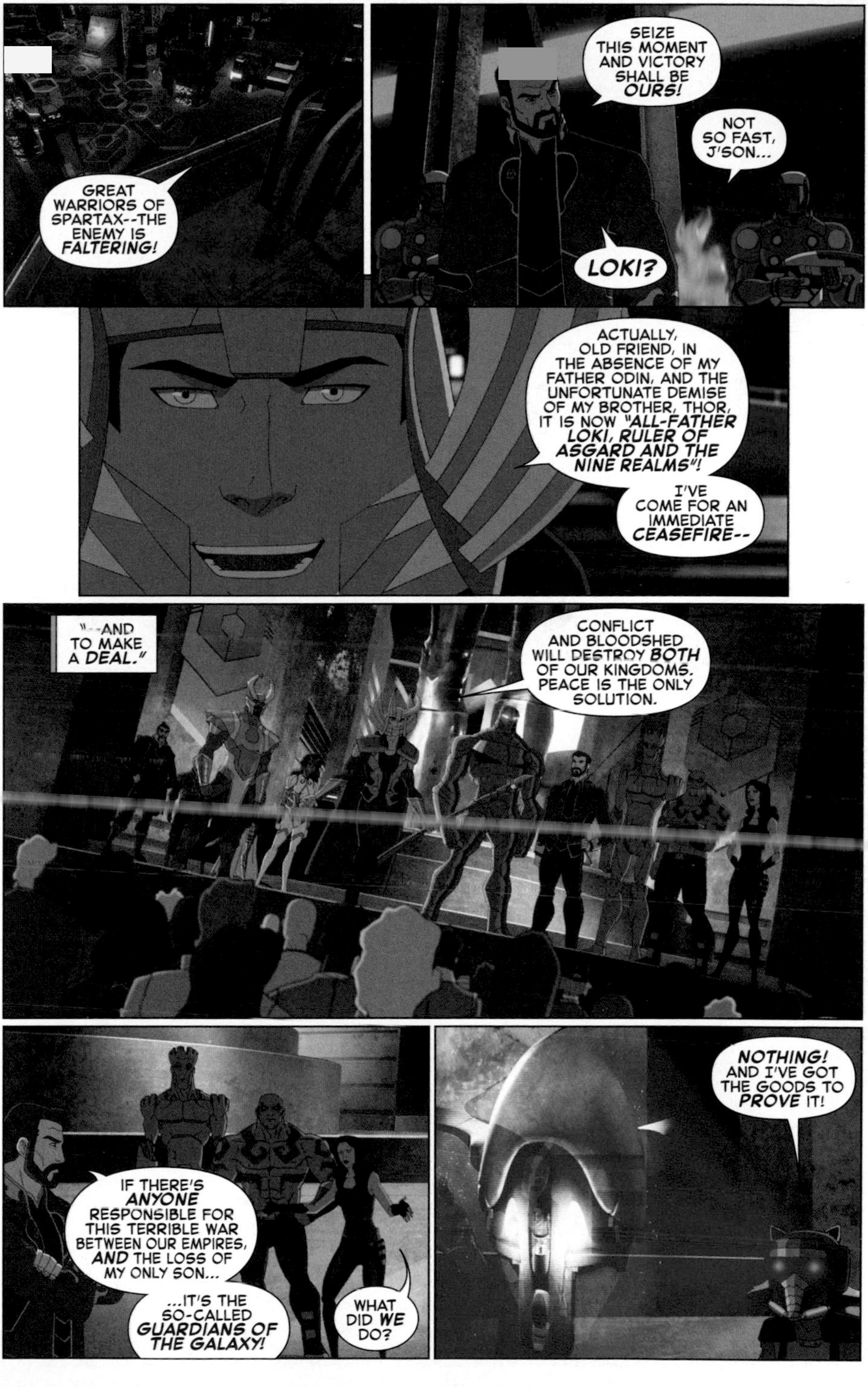
GREAT WARRIORS OF SPARTAX--THE ENEMY IS FALTERING!
SEIZE THIS MOMENT AND VICTORY SHALL BE OURS!
NOT SO FAST, J'SON...
LOKI?
ACTUALLY, OLD FRIEND, IN THE ABSENCE OF MY FATHER ODIN, AND THE UNFORTUNATE DEMISE OF MY BROTHER, THOR, IT IS NOW "ALL-FATHER LOKI, RULER OF ASGARD AND THE NINE REALMS"!
I'VE COME FOR AN IMMEDIATE CEASEFIRE--
"--AND TO MAKE A DEAL."
CONFLICT AND BLOODSHED WILL DESTROY BOTH OF OUR KINGDOMS. PEACE IS THE ONLY SOLUTION.
IF THERE'S ANYONE RESPONSIBLE FOR THIS TERRIBLE WAR BETWEEN OUR EMPIRES, AND THE LOSS OF MY ONLY SON...
...IT'S THE SO-CALLED GUARDIANS OF THE GALAXY!
WHAT DID WE DO?
NOTHING! AND I'VE GOT THE GOODS TO PROVE IT!

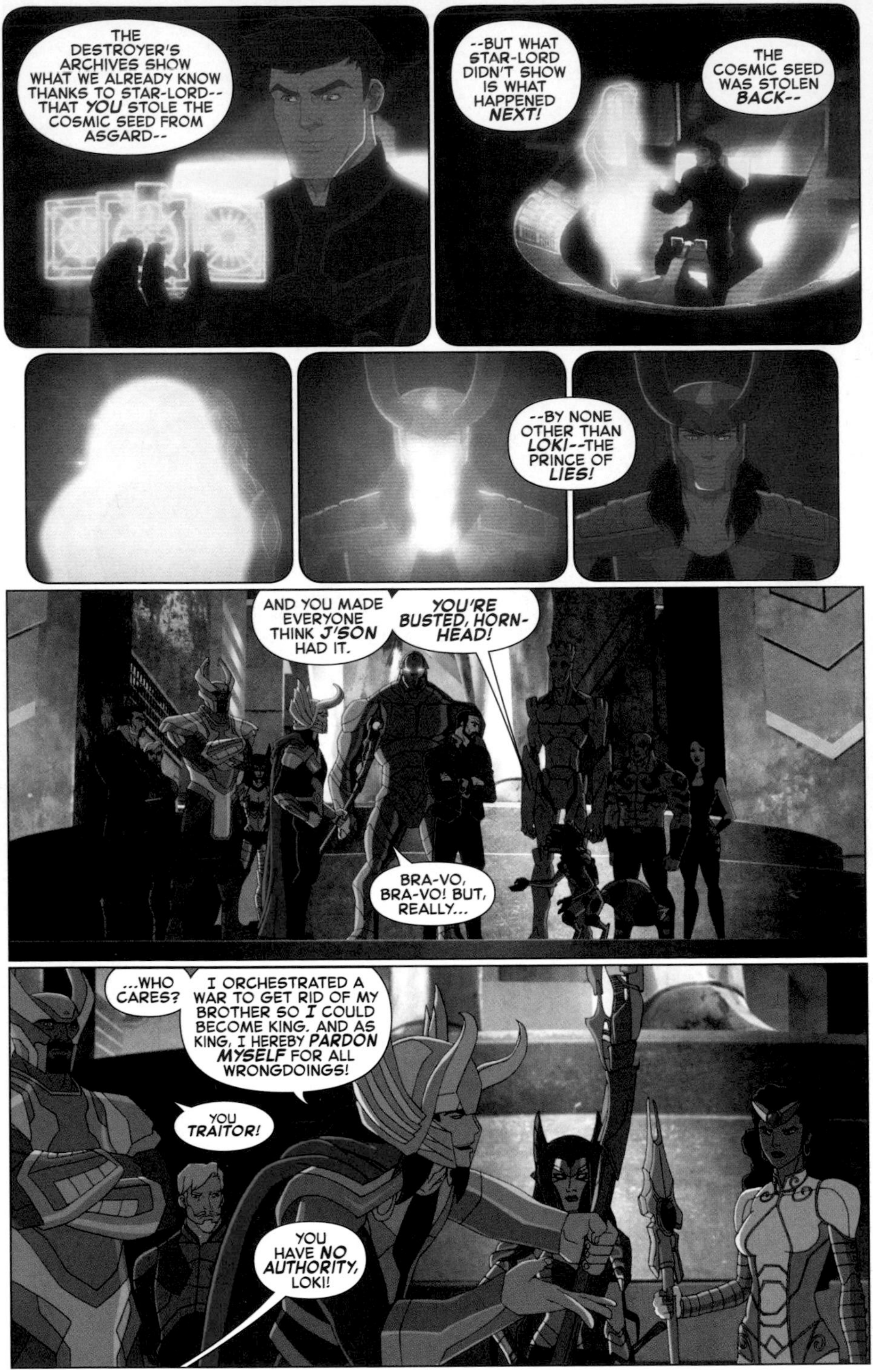
THE DESTROYER'S ARCHIVES SHOW WHAT WE ALREADY KNOW THANKS TO STAR-LORD-- THAT YOU STOLE THE COSMIC SEED FROM ASGARD--
--BUT WHAT STAR-LORD DIDN'T SHOW IS WHAT HAPPENED NEXT!
THE COSMIC SEED WAS STOLEN BACK--
--BY NONE OTHER THAN LOKI--THE PRINCE OF LIES!
AND YOU MADE EVERYONE THINK J'SON HAD IT.
YOU'RE BUSTED, HORN-HEAD!
BRA-VO, BRA-VO! BUT, REALLY...
...WHO CARES?
I ORCHESTRATED A WAR TO GET RID OF MY BROTHER SO I COULD BECOME KING. AND AS KING, I HEREBY PARDON MYSELF FOR ALL WRONGDOINGS!
YOU TRAITOR!
YOU HAVE NO AUTHORITY, LOKI!

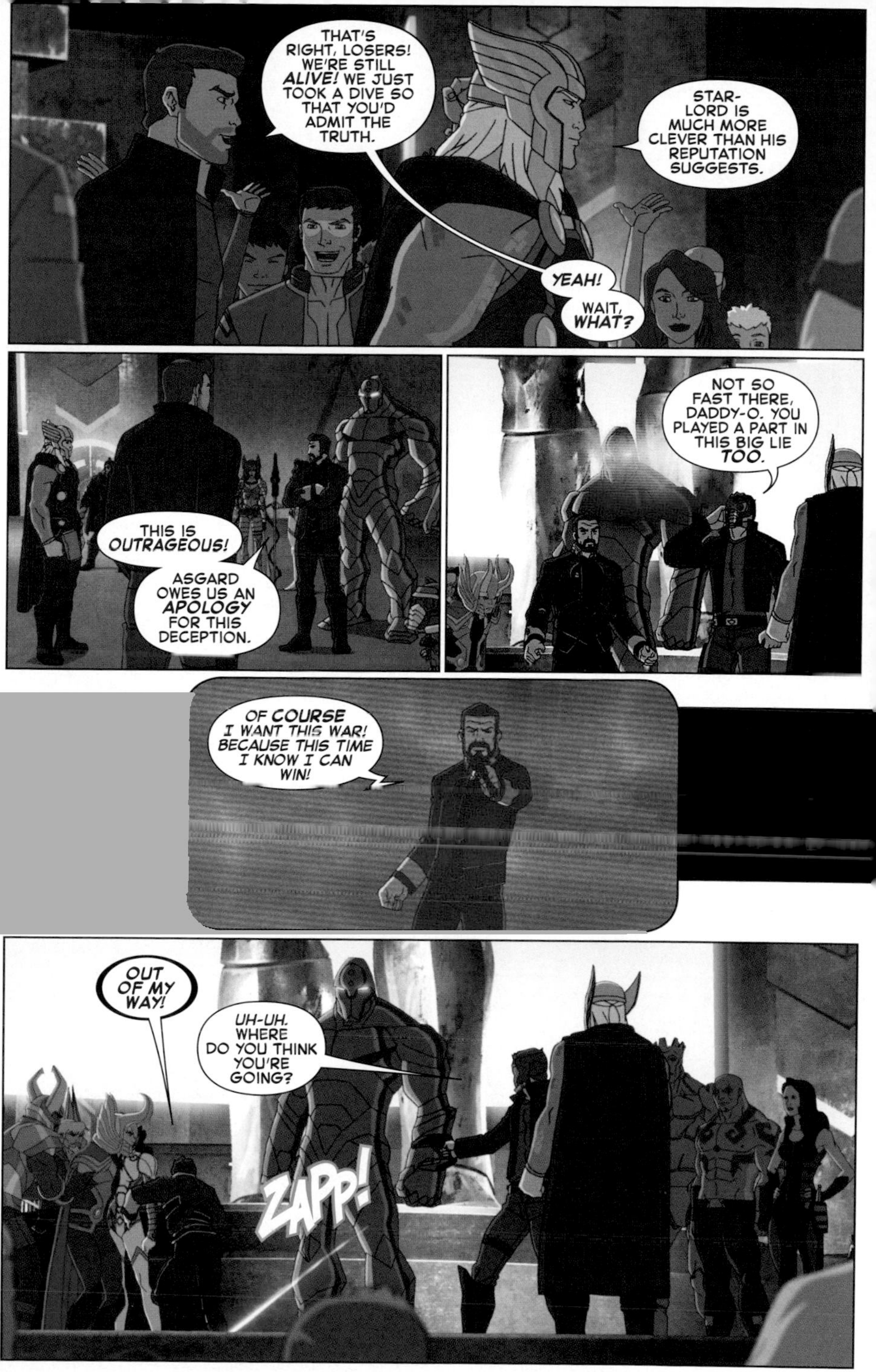
THAT'S RIGHT, LOSERS! WE'RE STILL ALIVE! WE JUST TOOK A DIVE SO THAT YOU'D ADMIT THE TRUTH.
STAR-LORD IS MUCH MORE CLEVER THAN HIS REPUTATION SUGGESTS.
YEAH!
WAIT, WHAT?
THIS IS OUTRAGEOUS!
ASGARD OWES US AN APOLOGY FOR THIS DECEPTION.
NOT SO FAST THERE, DADDY-O. YOU PLAYED A PART IN THIS BIG LIE TOO.
OF COURSE I WANT THIS WAR! BECAUSE THIS TIME I KNOW I CAN WIN!
OUT OF MY WAY!
UH-UH. WHERE DO YOU THINK YOU'RE GOING?
ZAPP!

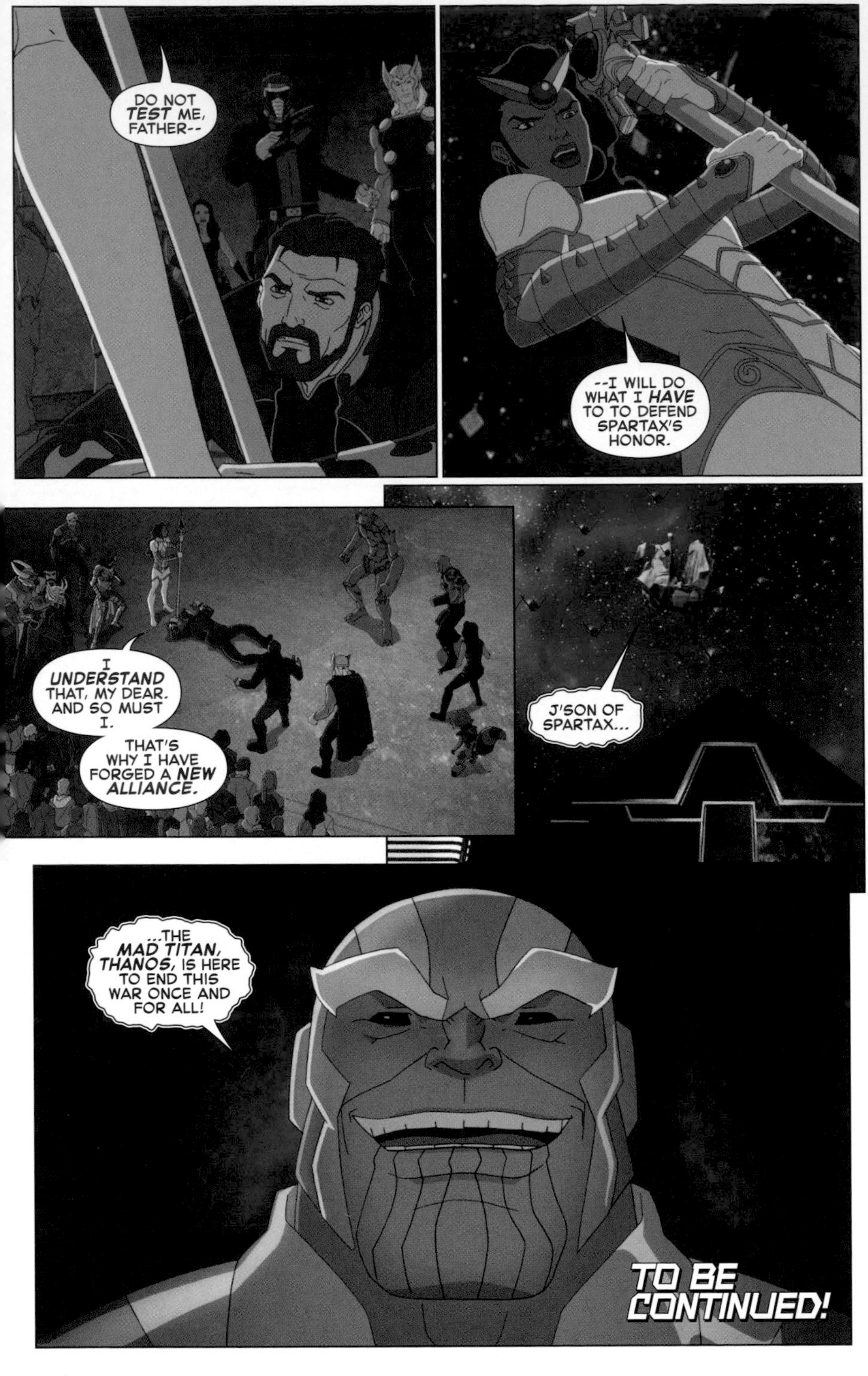
DO NOT TEST ME, FATHER--
--I WILL DO WHAT I HAVE TO TO DEFEND SPARTAX'S HONOR.
I UNDERSTAND THAT, MY DEAR. AND SO MUST I.
THAT'S WHY I HAVE FORGED A NEW ALLIANCE.
J'SON OF SPARTAX...
...THE MAD TITAN, THANOS, IS HERE TO END THIS WAR ONCE AND FOR ALL!
TO BE CONTINUED!

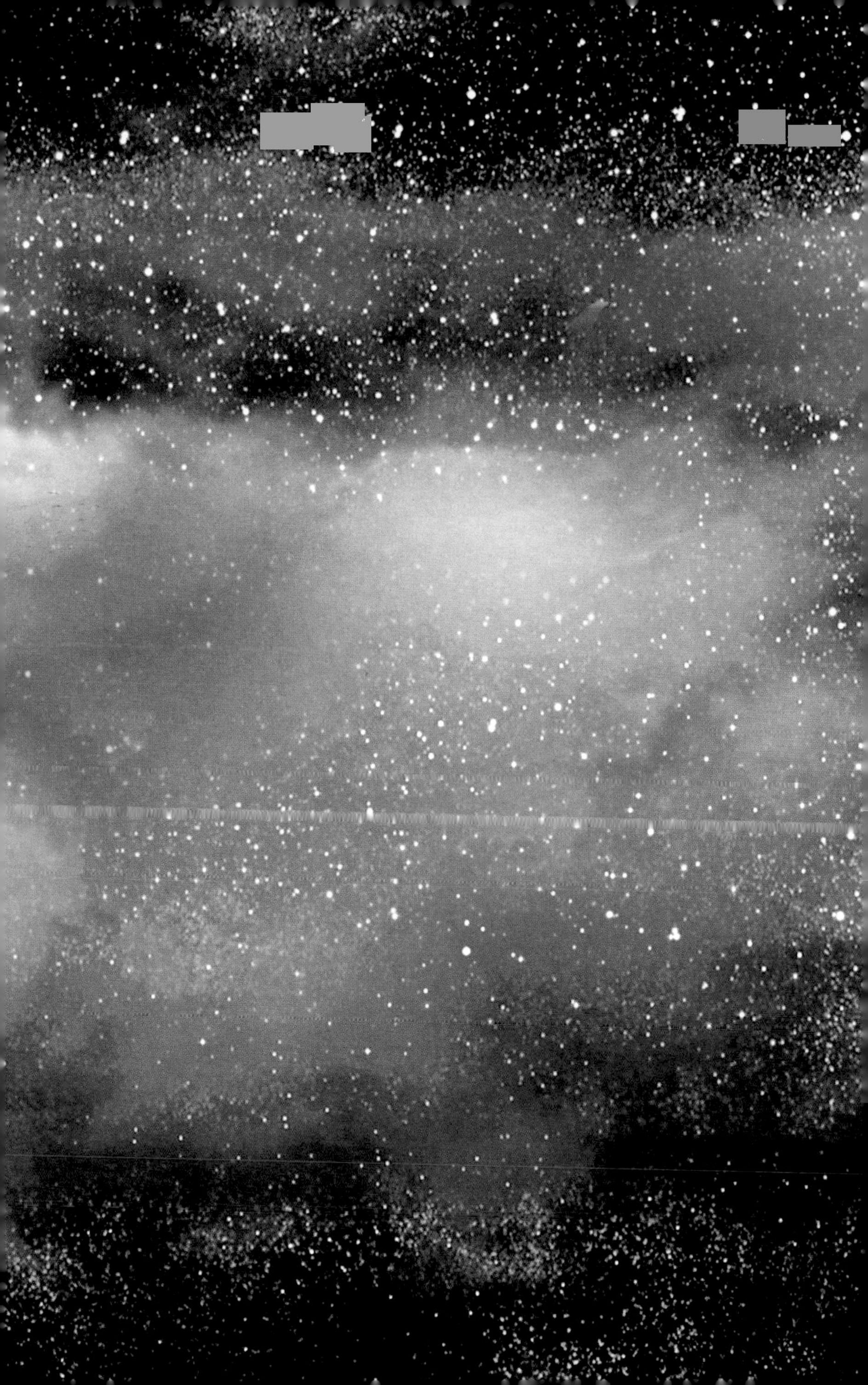

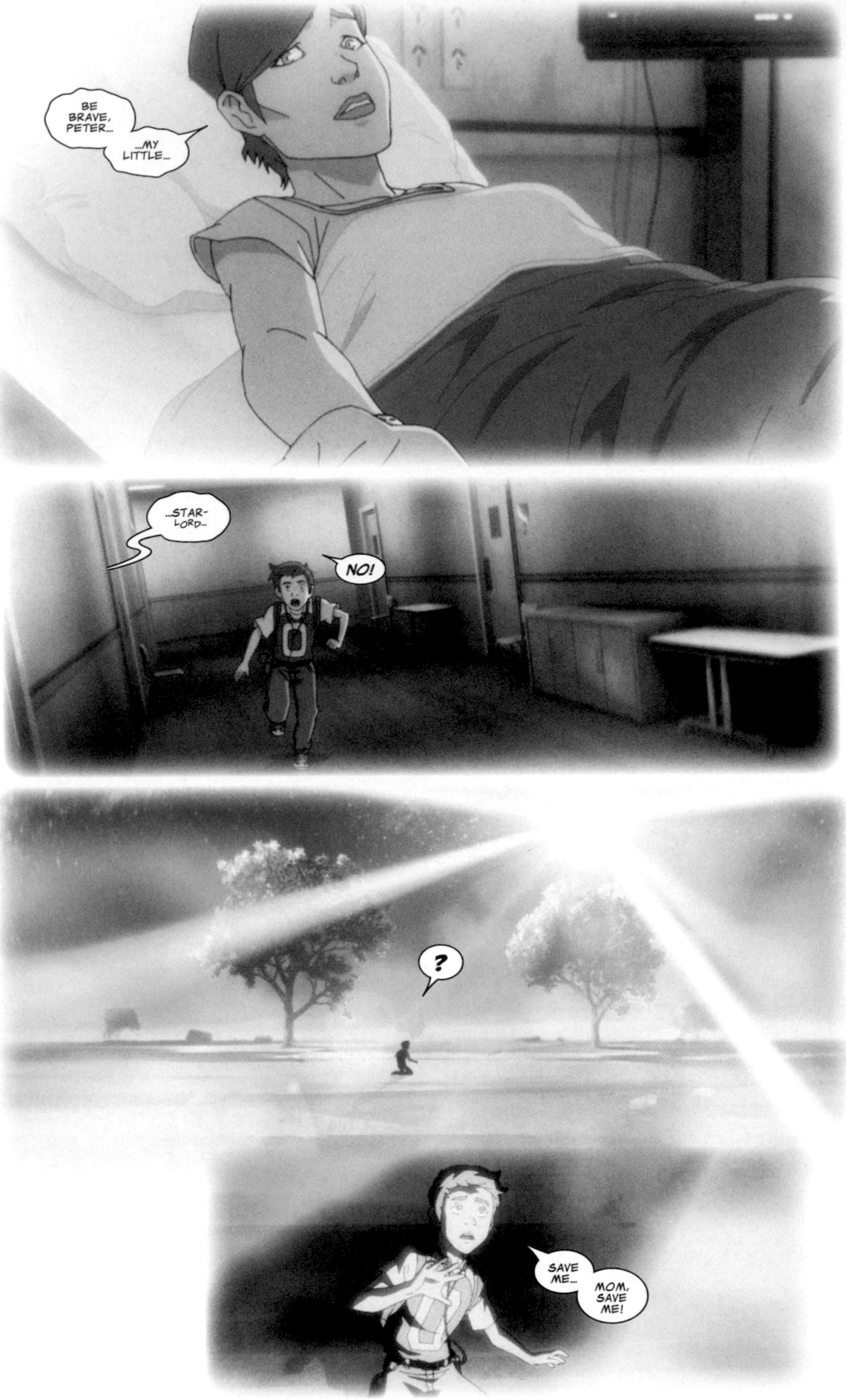
BE BRAVE, PETER...
...MY LITTLE...
...STAR-LORD...
NO!
?
SAVE ME...
MOM, SAVE ME!

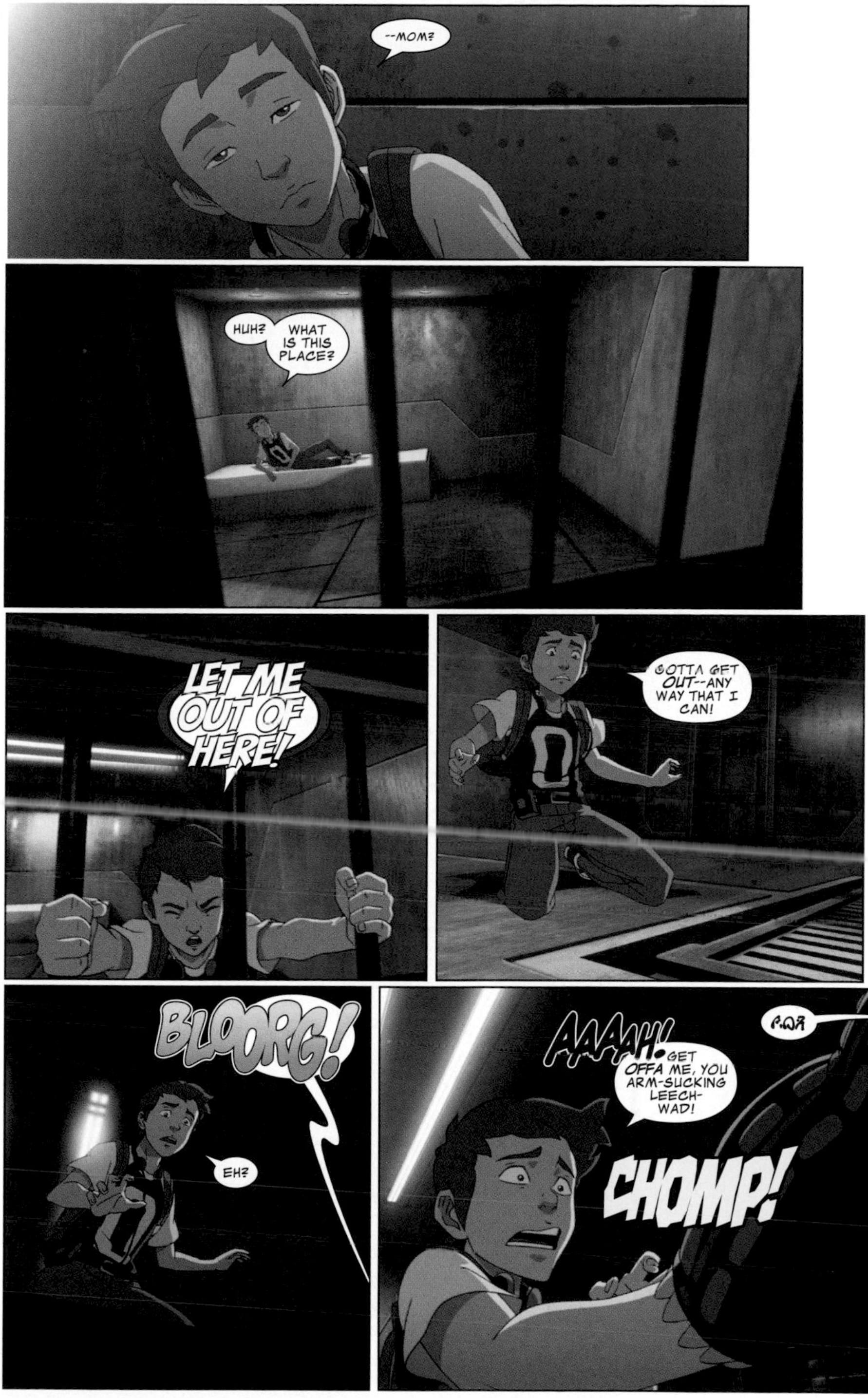
--MOM?
HUH?
WHAT IS THIS PLACE?
LET ME OUT OF HERE!
GOTTA GET OUT--ANY WAY THAT I CAN!
BLOORG!
EH?
AAAAH!
GET OFFA ME, YOU ARM-SUCKING LEECH-WAD!
CHOMP!

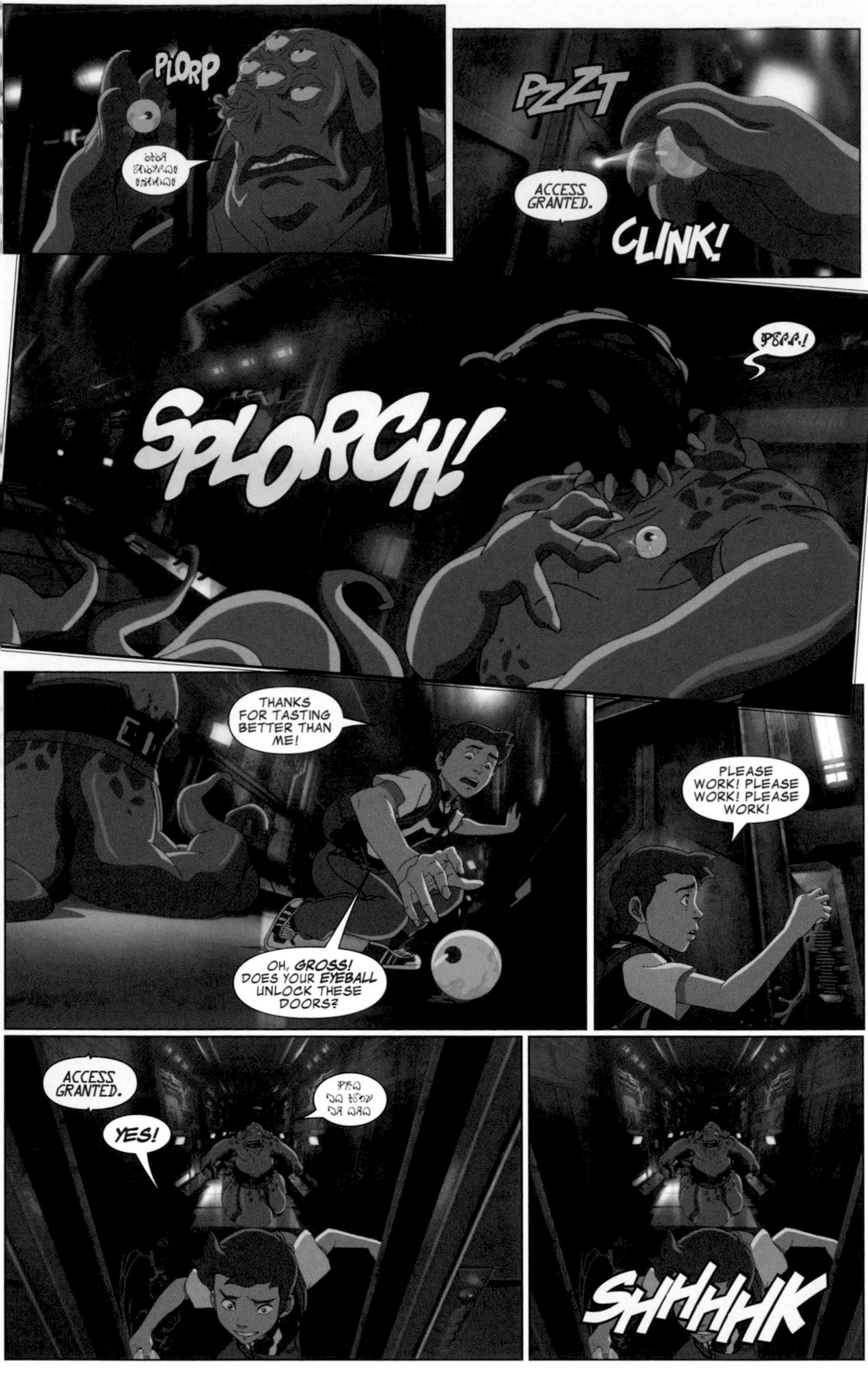
PLORP
PZZT
ACCESS GRANTED.
CLINK!
SPLORCH!
THANKS FOR TASTING BETTER THAN ME!
OH, GROSS! DOES YOUR EYEBALL UNLOCK THESE DOORS?
PLEASE WORK! PLEASE WORK! PLEASE WORK!
ACCESS GRANTED.
YES!
SHHHHK

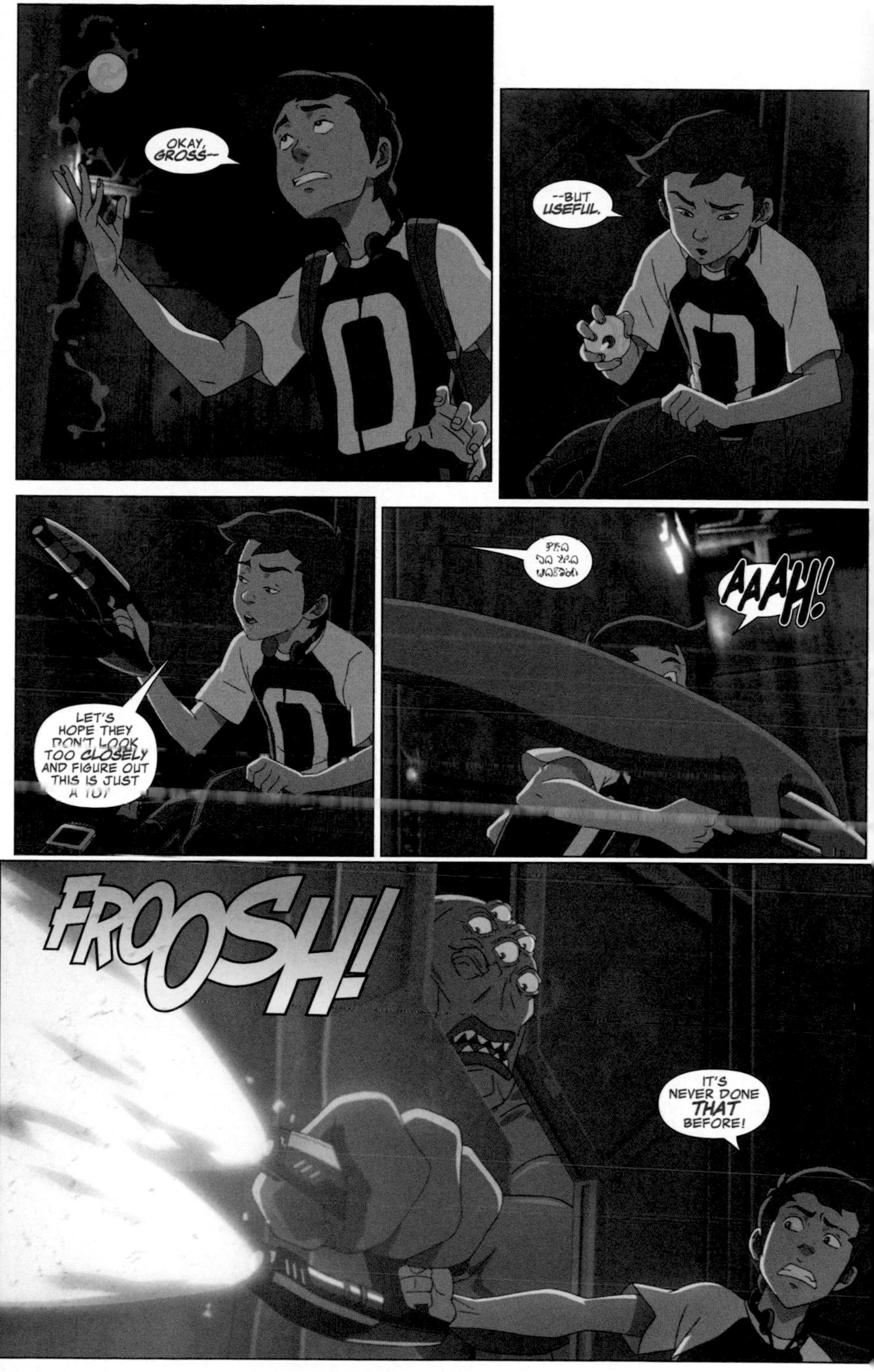
OKAY, GROSS--
--BUT USEFUL.
LET'S HOPE THEY DON'T LOOK TOO CLOSELY AND FIGURE OUT THIS IS JUST
FROOSH!
IT'S NEVER DONE THAT BEFORE!

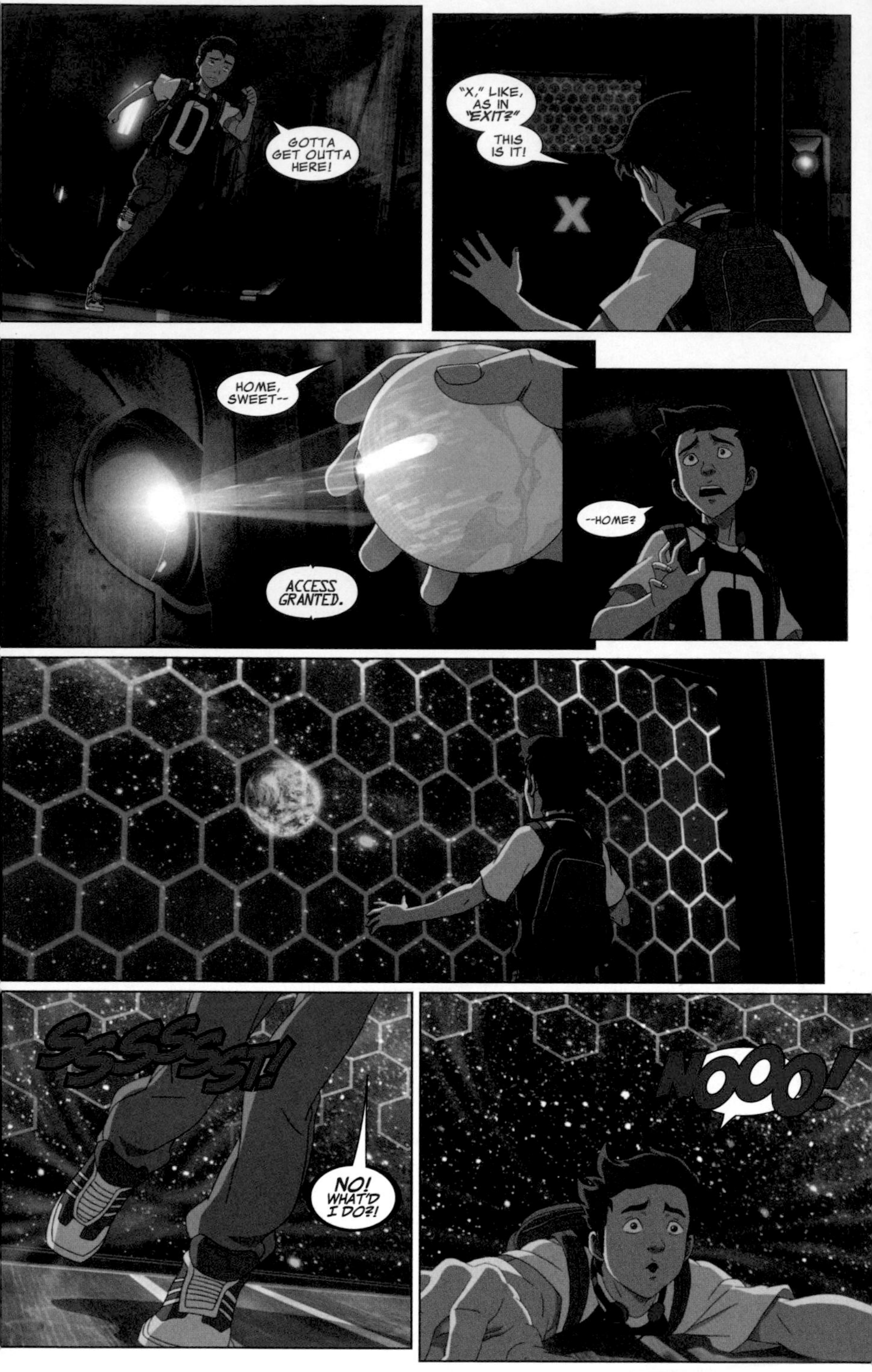
GOTTA GET OUTTA HERE!
"X," LIKE, AS IN EXIT?"
THIS IS IT!
HOME, SWEET--
--HOME?
ACCESS GRANTED.
SSSSSST!
NO! WHAT'D I DO?!
NOOO!

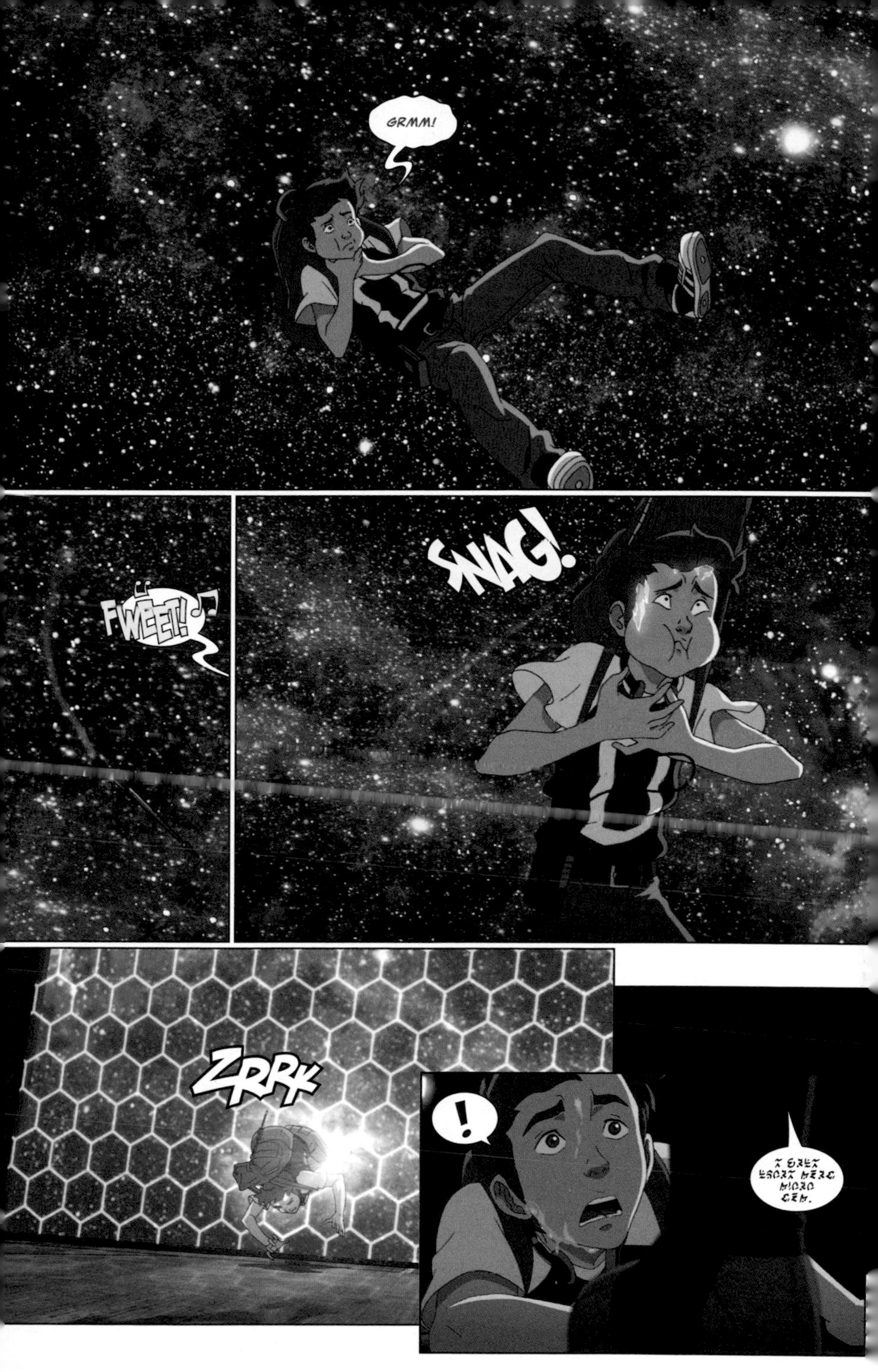
GRMM!
FWEET!
SNAG!
ZRRK
!

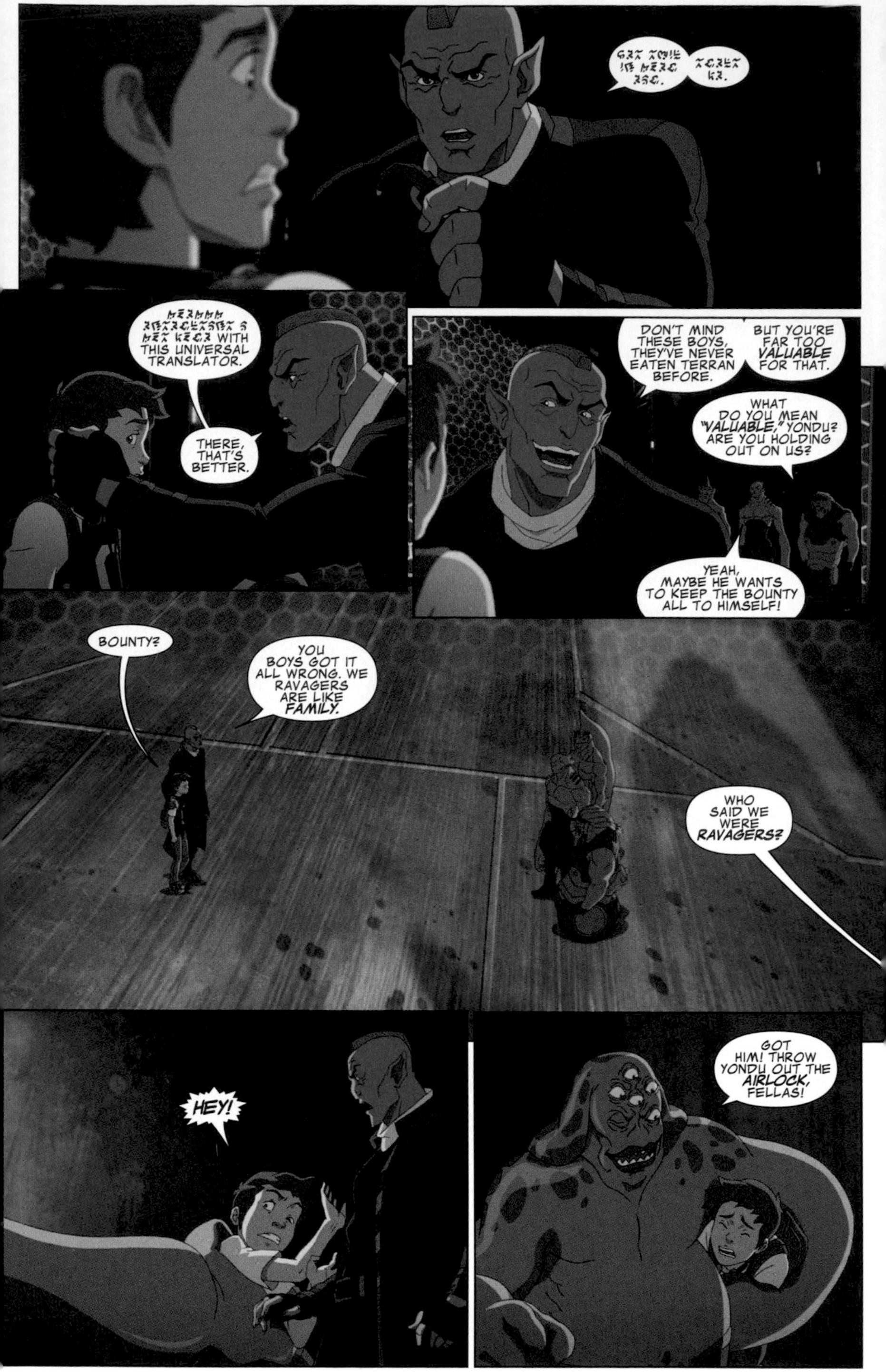

WITH THIS UNIVERSAL TRANSLATOR.
THERE, THAT'S BETTER.
DON'T MIND THESE BOYS, THEY'VE NEVER EATEN TERRAN BEFORE.
BUT YOU'RE FAR TOO VALUABLE FOR THAT.
WHAT DO YOU MEAN "VALUABLE," YONDU? ARE YOU HOLDING OUT ON US?
YEAH, MAYBE HE WANTS TO KEEP THE BOUNTY ALL TO HIMSELF!
BOUNTY?
YOU BOYS GOT IT ALL WRONG. WE RAVAGERS ARE LIKE FAMILY.
WHO SAID WE WERE RAVAGERS?
HEY!
GOT HIM! THROW YONDU OUT THE AIRLOCK, FELLAS!

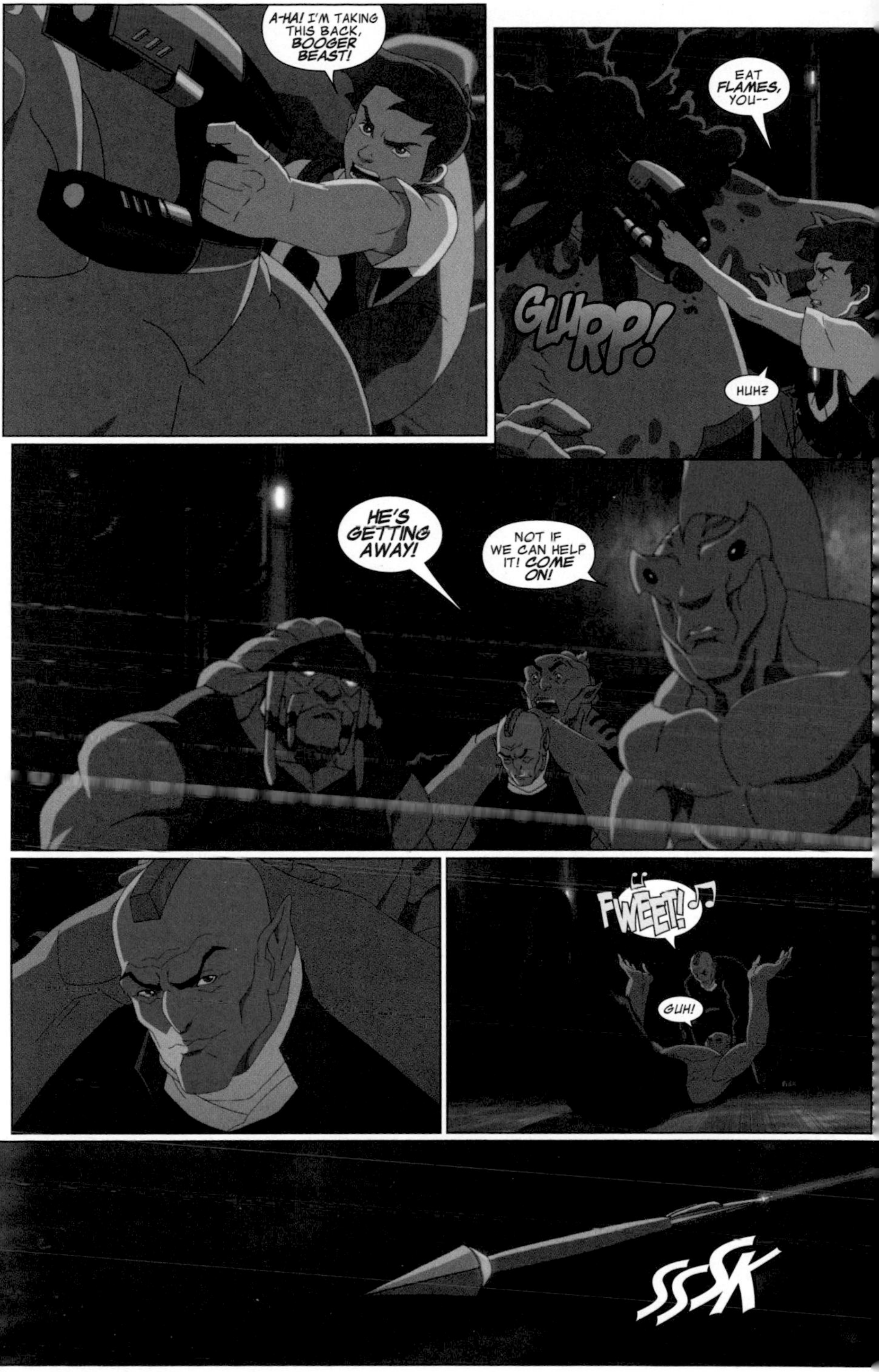
A-HA! I'M TAKING THIS BACK, BOOGER BEAST!
EAT FLAMES, YOU--
GLURP!
HUH?
HE'S GETTING AWAY!
NOT IF WE CAN HELP IT! COME ON!
FWEET!
GUH!
SSSK

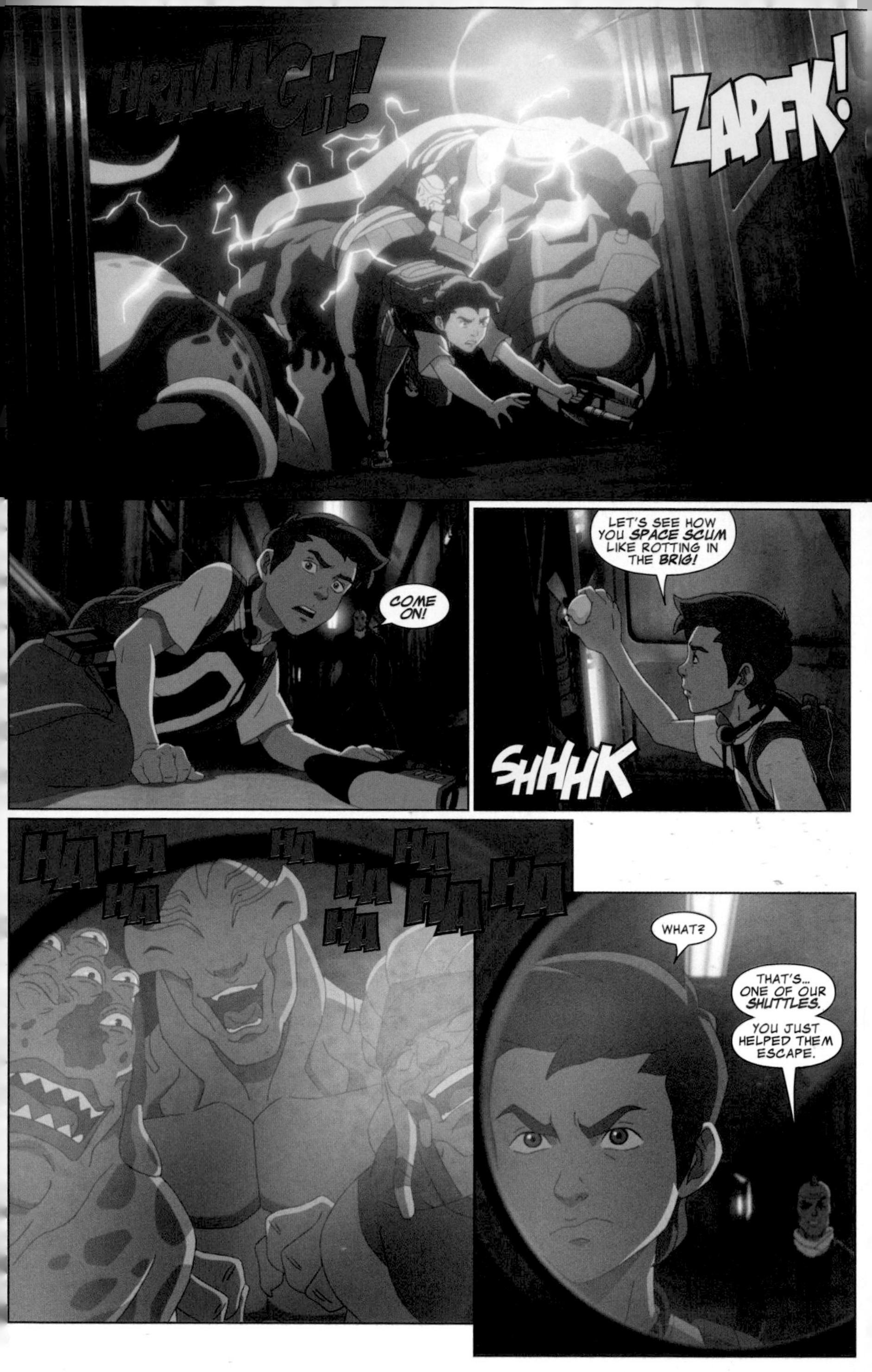

HRUAAAGH!
ZAPFK!
COME ON!
LET'S SEE HOW YOU SPACE SCUM LIKE ROTTING IN THE BRIG!
SHHHK
HA HA HA HA HA HA HA HA HA HA
WHAT?
THAT'S... ONE OF OUR SHUTTLES.
YOU JUST HELPED THEM ESCAPE.

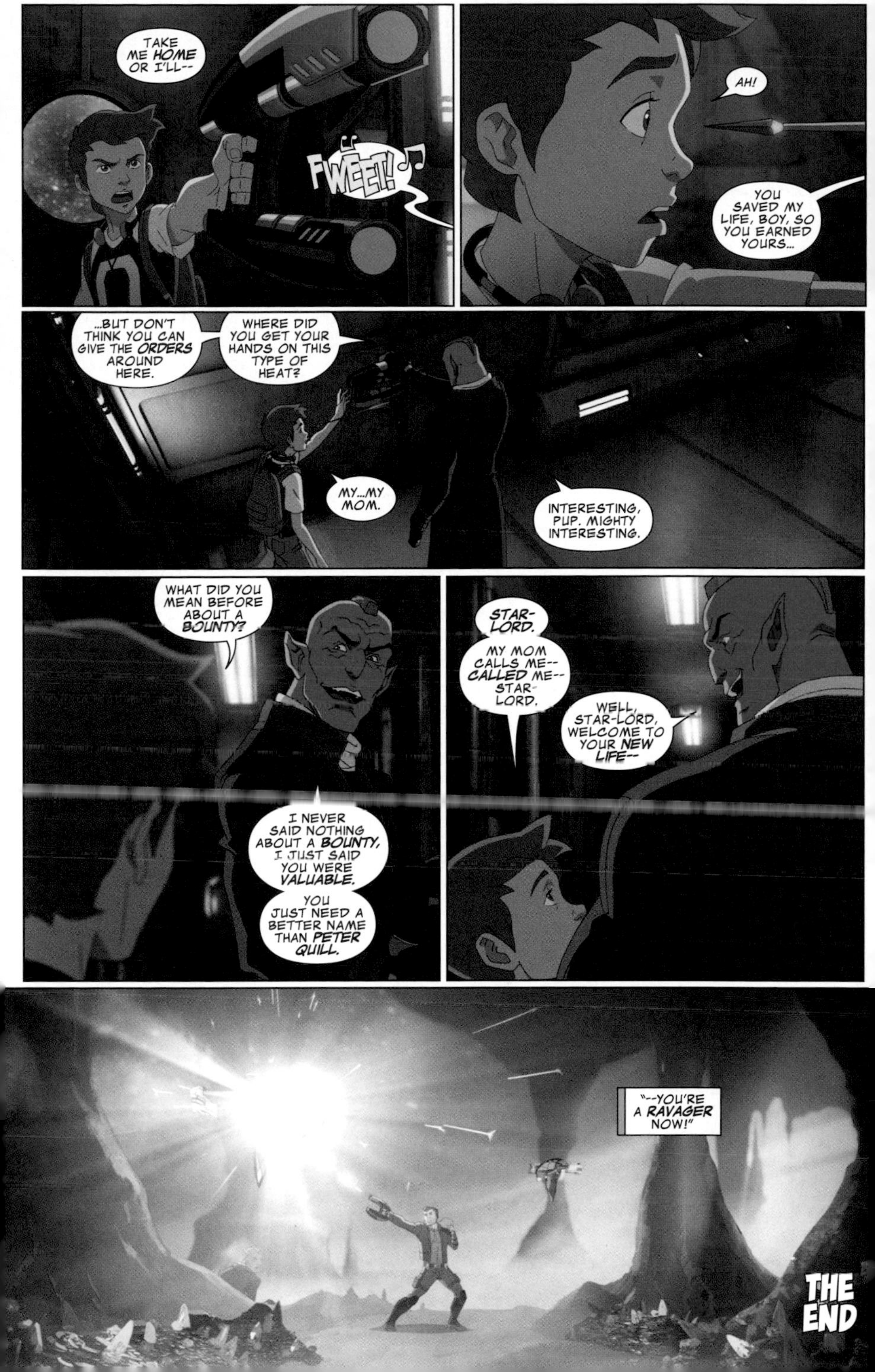
TAKE ME HOME OR I'LL--
FWEET!
AH!
YOU SAVED MY LIFE, BOY, SO YOU EARNED YOURS...
...BUT DON'T THINK YOU CAN GIVE THE ORDERS AROUND HERE.
WHERE DID YOU GET YOUR HANDS ON THIS TYPE OF HEAT?
MY...MY MOM.
INTERESTING, PUP. MIGHTY INTERESTING.
WHAT DID YOU MEAN BEFORE ABOUT A BOUNTY?
I NEVER SAID NOTHING ABOUT A BOUNTY, I JUST SAID YOU WERE VALUABLE.
YOU JUST NEED A BETTER NAME THAN PETER QUILL.
STAR-LORD.
MY MOM CALLS ME--CALLED ME--STAR-LORD.
WELL, STAR-LORD, WELCOME TO YOUR NEW LIFE--
"--YOU'RE A RAVAGER NOW!"
THE END

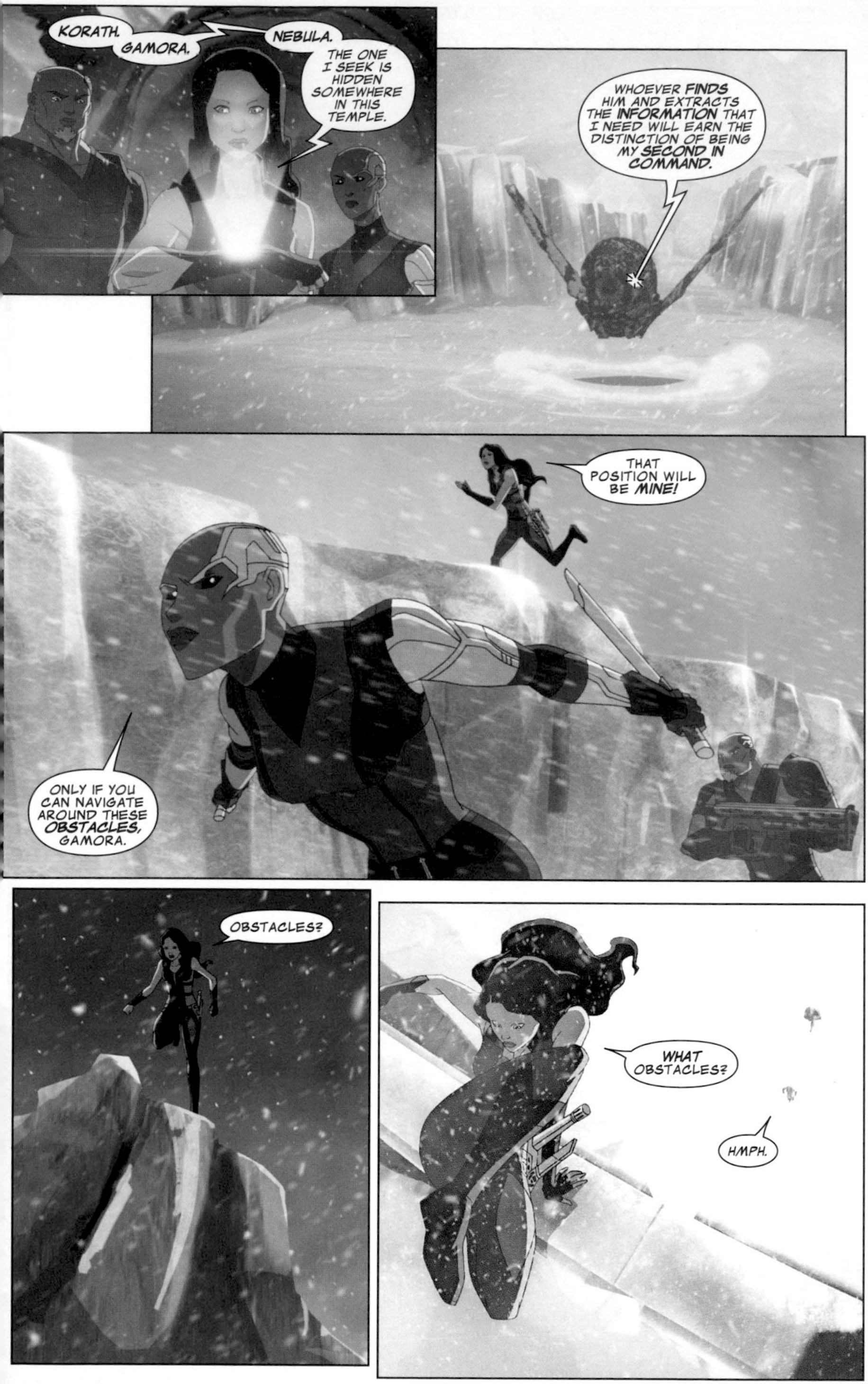
KORATH.
GAMORA.
NEBULA.
THE ONE I SEEK IS HIDDEN SOMEWHERE IN THIS TEMPLE.
WHOEVER FINDS HIM AND EXTRACTS THE INFORMATION THAT I NEED WILL EARN THE DISTINCTION OF BEING MY SECOND IN COMMAND.
THAT POSITION WILL BE MINE!
ONLY IF YOU CAN NAVIGATE AROUND THESE OBSTACLES, GAMORA.
OBSTACLES?
WHAT OBSTACLES?
HMPH.

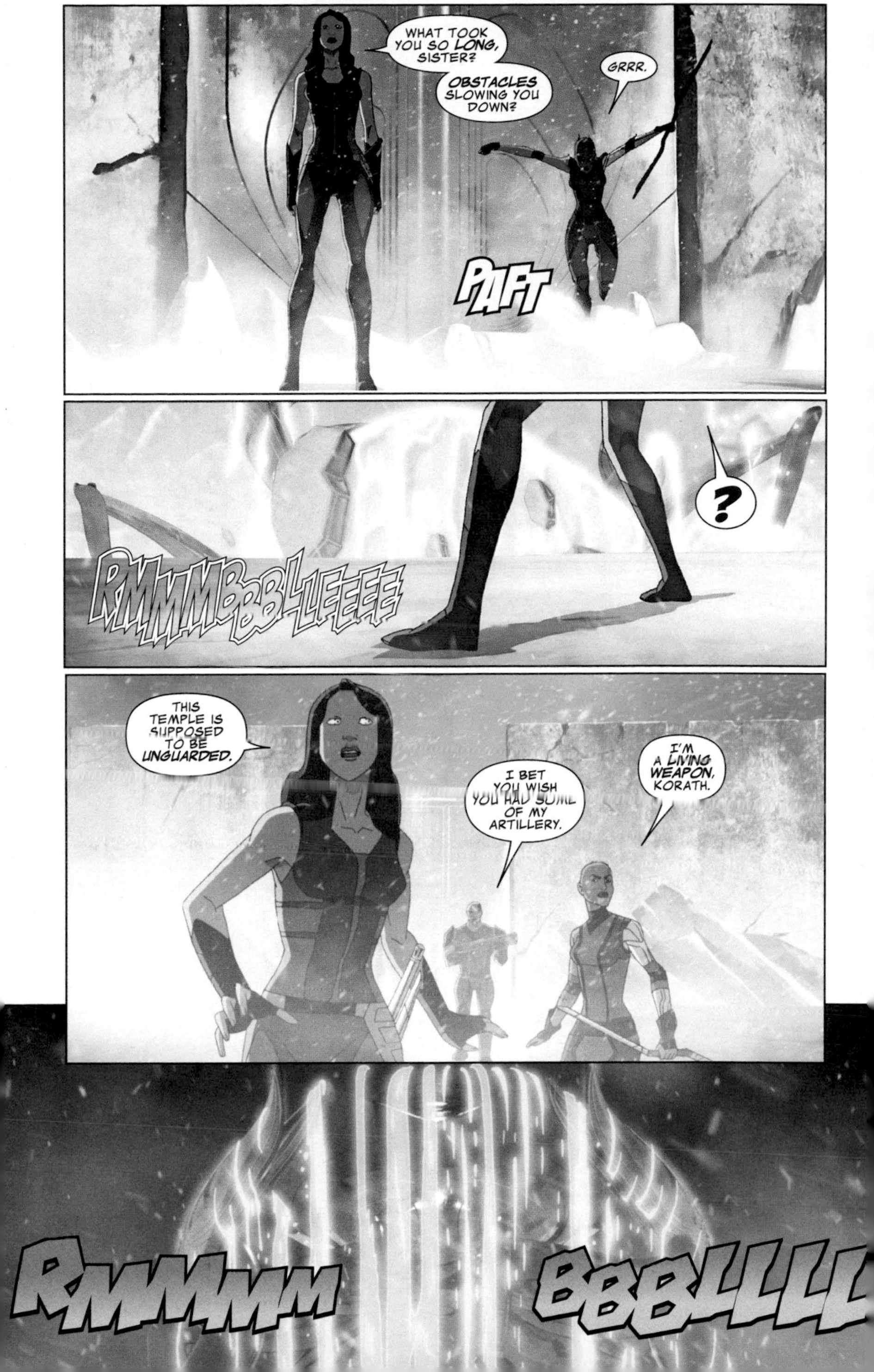
WHAT TOOK YOU SO LONG, SISTER?
OBSTACLES SLOWING YOU DOWN?
GRRR.
PAFT
?
RMMMBBBLLEEEE
THIS TEMPLE IS SUPPOSED TO BE UNGUARDED.
I BET YOU WISH YOU HAD SOME OF MY ARTILLERY.
I'M A LIVING WEAPON, KORATH.
RMMMMM
BBBLLLL

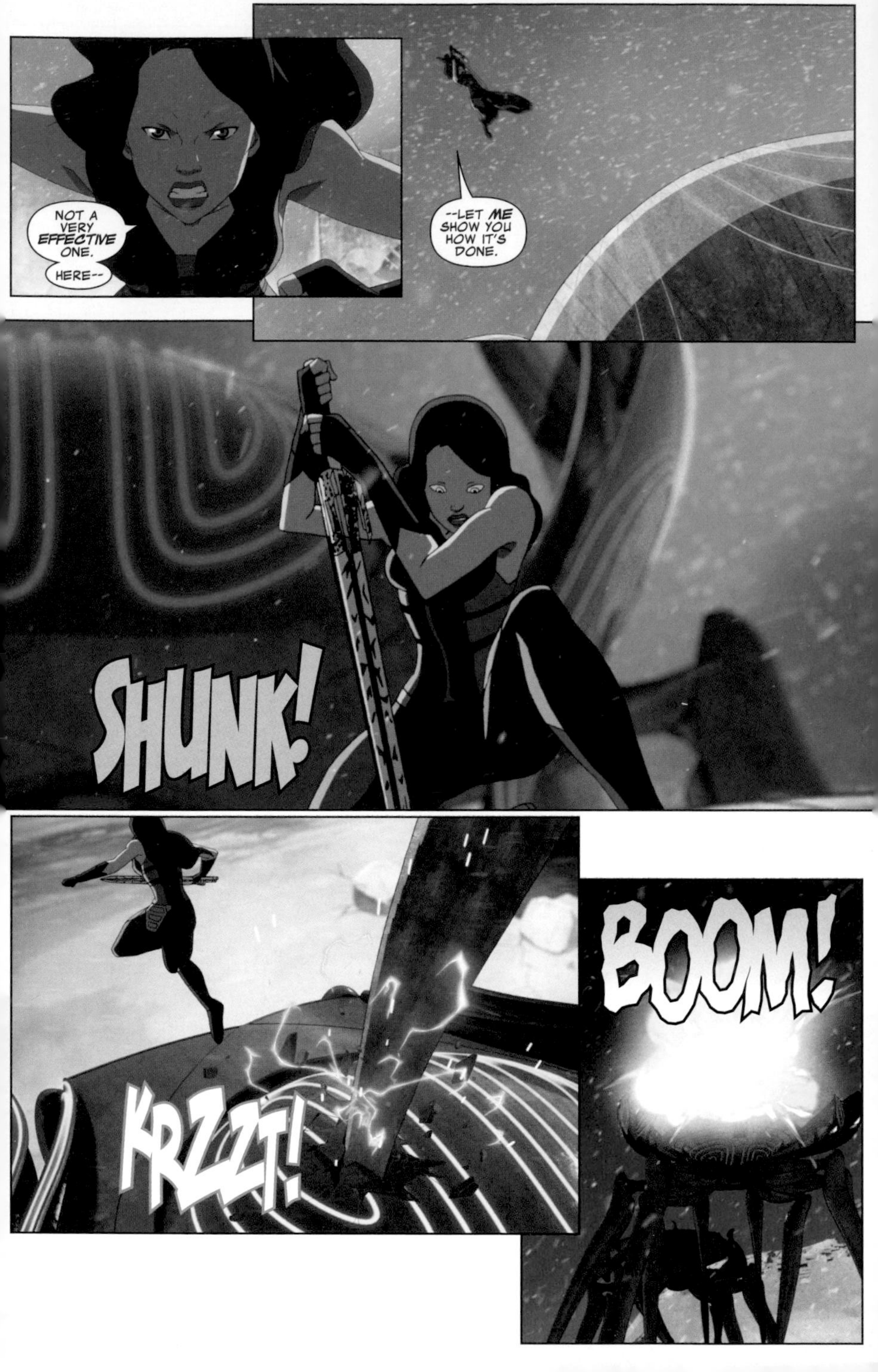
NOT A VERY EFFECTIVE ONE.
HERE--
--LET ME SHOW YOU HOW IT'S DONE.
SHUNK!
KRZZT!
BOOM!

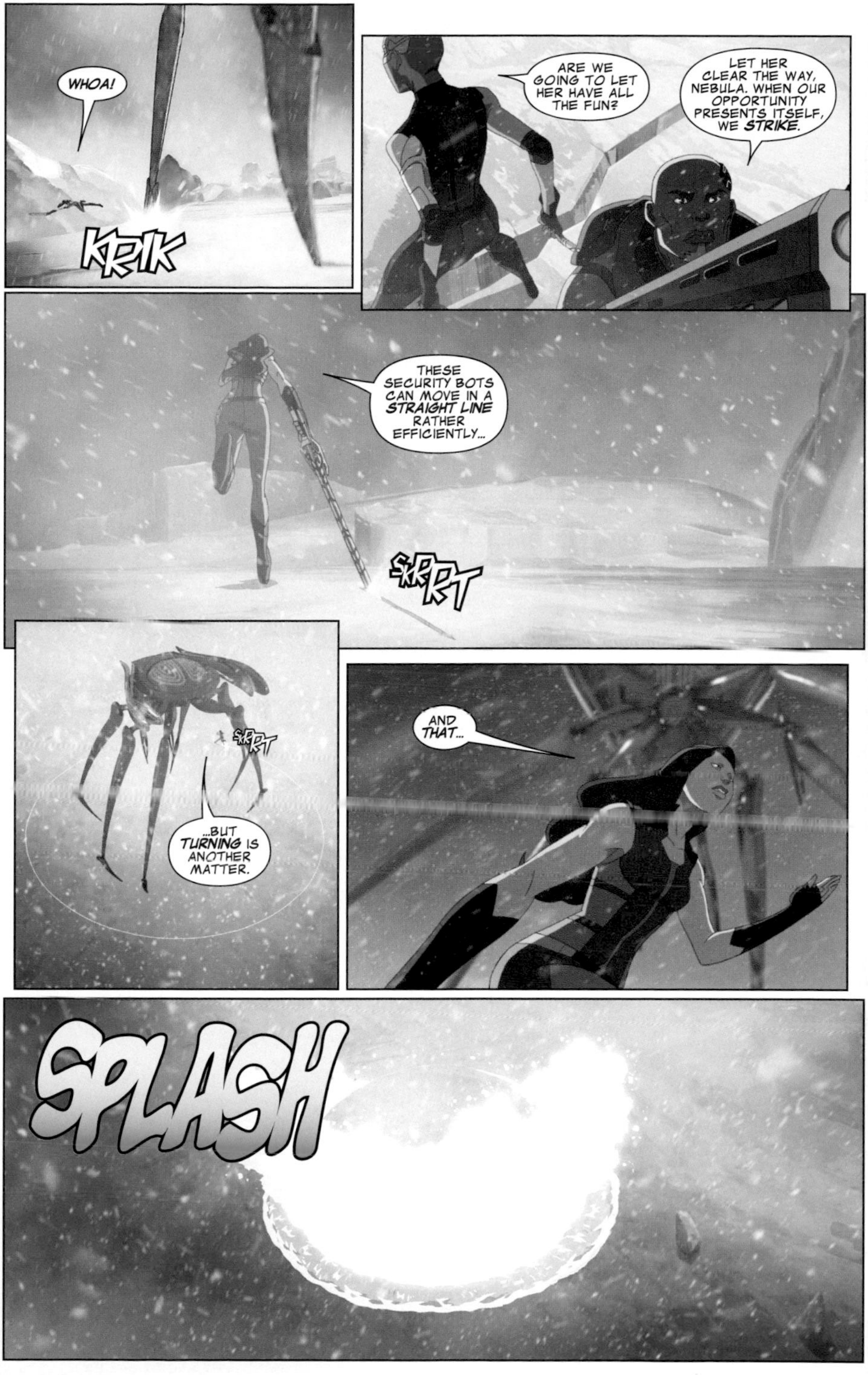
WHOA!
KRIK
ARE WE GOING TO LET HER HAVE ALL THE FUN?
LET HER CLEAR THE WAY, NEBULA. WHEN OUR OPPORTUNITY PRESENTS ITSELF, WE STRIKE.
THESE SECURITY BOTS CAN MOVE IN A STRAIGHT LINE RATHER EFFICIENTLY...
SKRRRT
SKRRT
...BUT TURNING IS ANOTHER MATTER.
AND THAT...
SPLASH

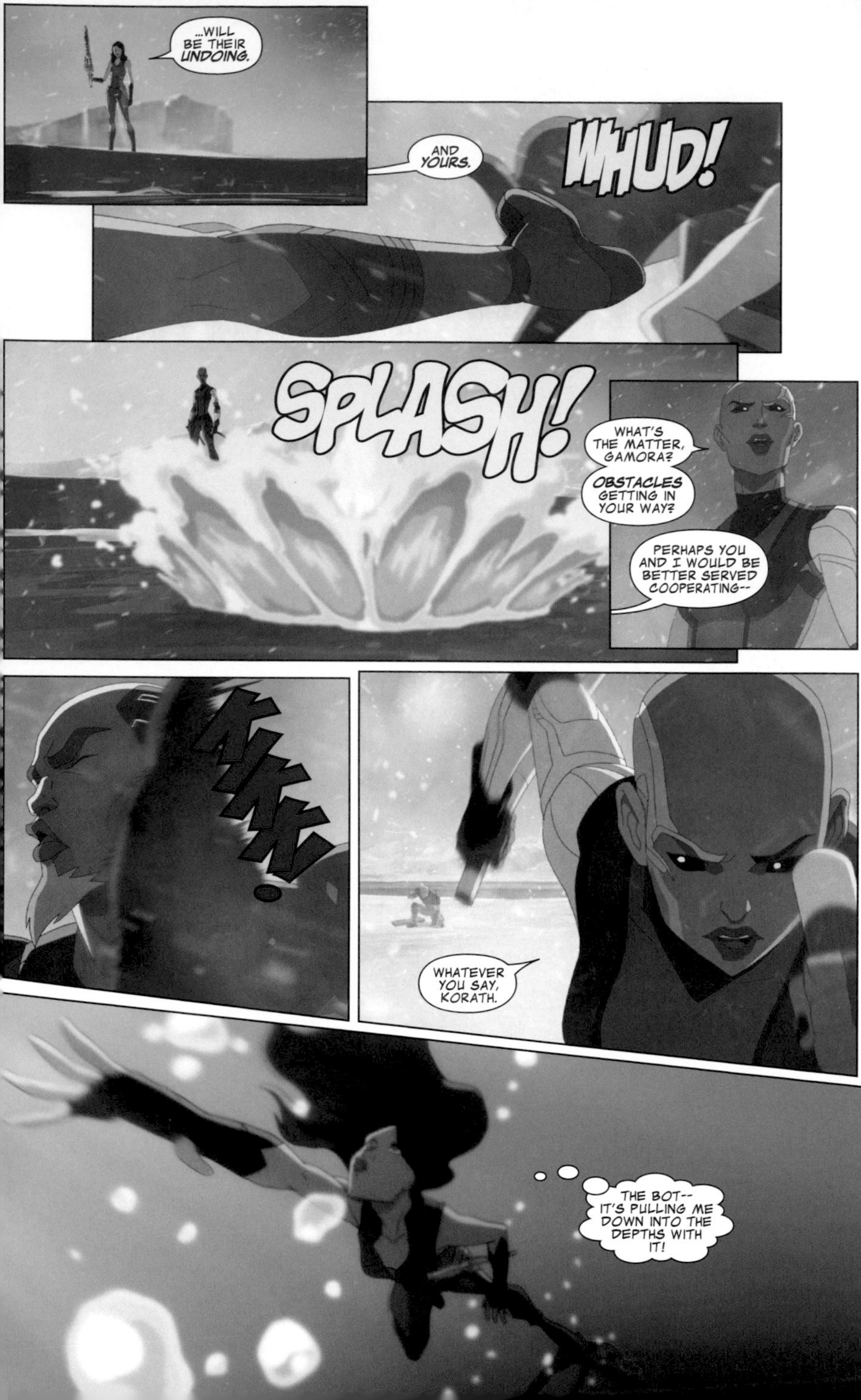
...WILL BE THEIR UNDOING.
AND YOURS.
WHUD!
SPLASH!
WHAT'S THE MATTER, GAMORA?
OBSTACLES GETTING IN YOUR WAY?
PERHAPS YOU AND I WOULD BE BETTER SERVED COOPERATING--
KIKK!
WHATEVER YOU SAY, KORATH.
THE BOT-- IT'S PULLING ME DOWN INTO THE DEPTHS WITH IT!

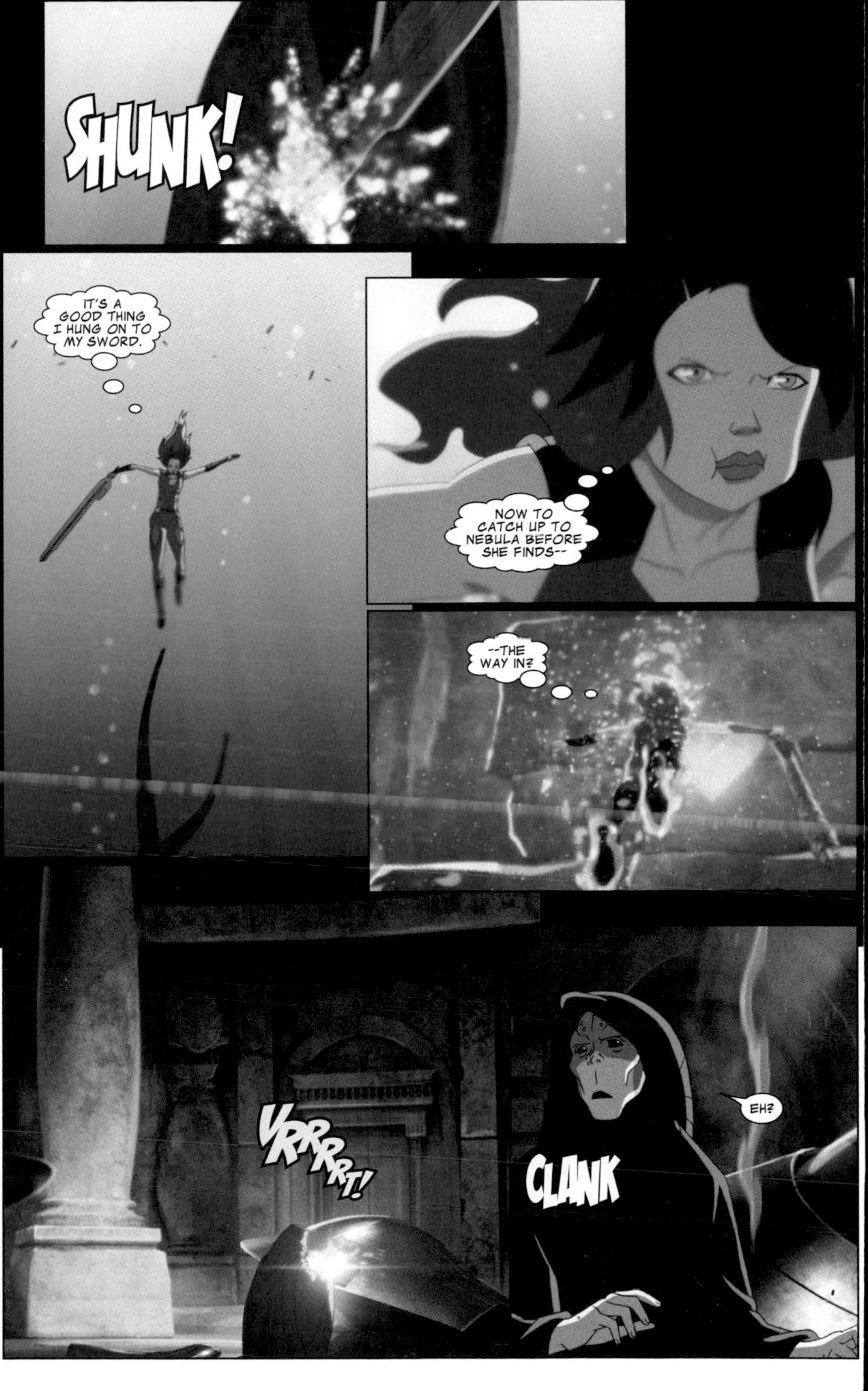
SHUNK!
IT'S A GOOD THING I HUNG ON TO MY SWORD.
NOW TO CATCH UP TO NEBULA BEFORE SHE FINDS--
--THE WAY IN?
VRRRRT!
CLANK
EH?

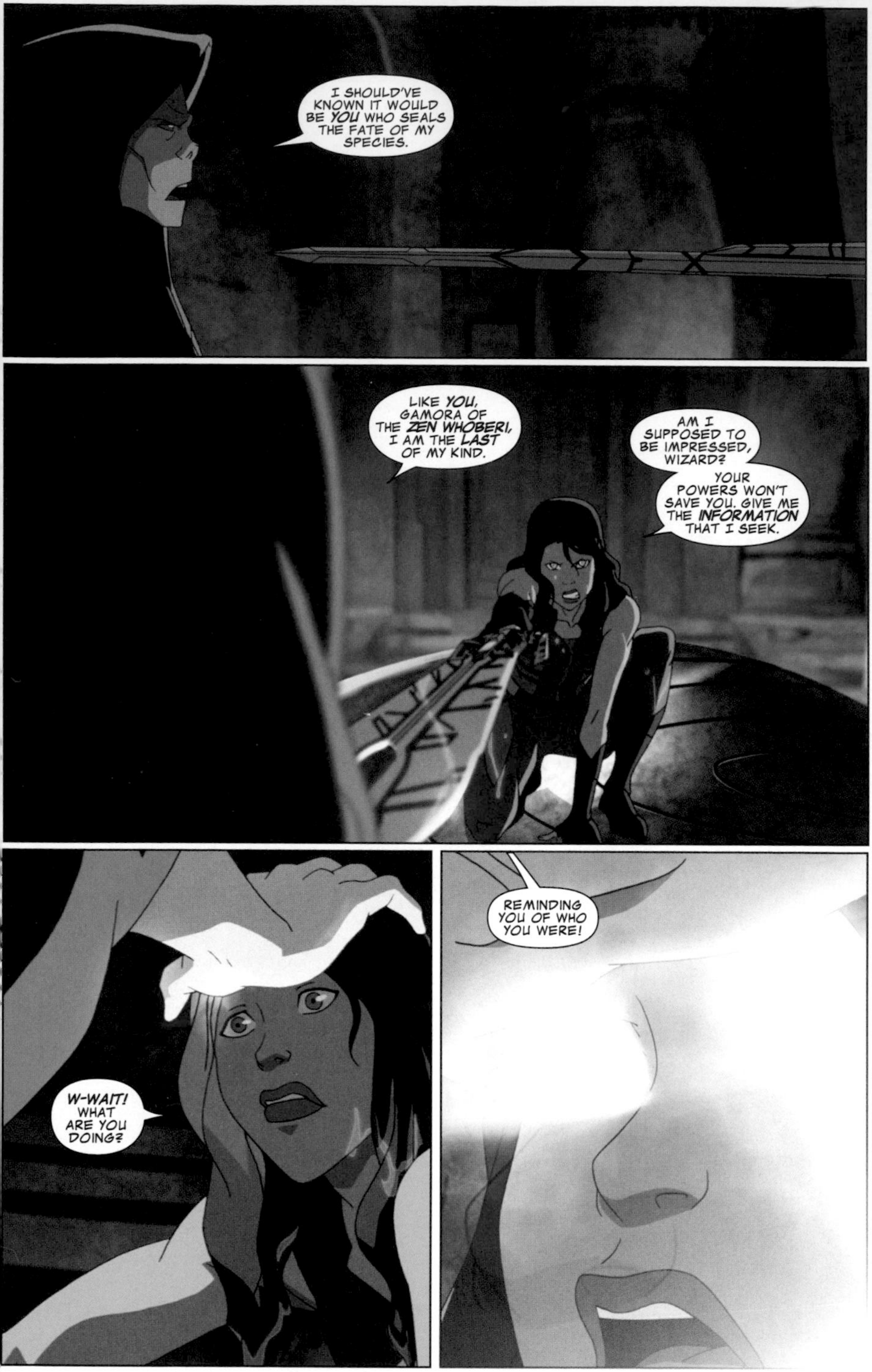
I SHOULD'VE KNOWN IT WOULD BE YOU WHO SEALS THE FATE OF MY SPECIES.
LIKE YOU, GAMORA OF THE ZEN WHOBERI, I AM THE LAST OF MY KIND.
AM I SUPPOSED TO BE IMPRESSED, WIZARD?
YOUR POWERS WON'T SAVE YOU. GIVE ME THE INFORMATION THAT I SEEK.
W-WAIT! WHAT ARE YOU DOING?
REMINDING YOU OF WHO YOU WERE!

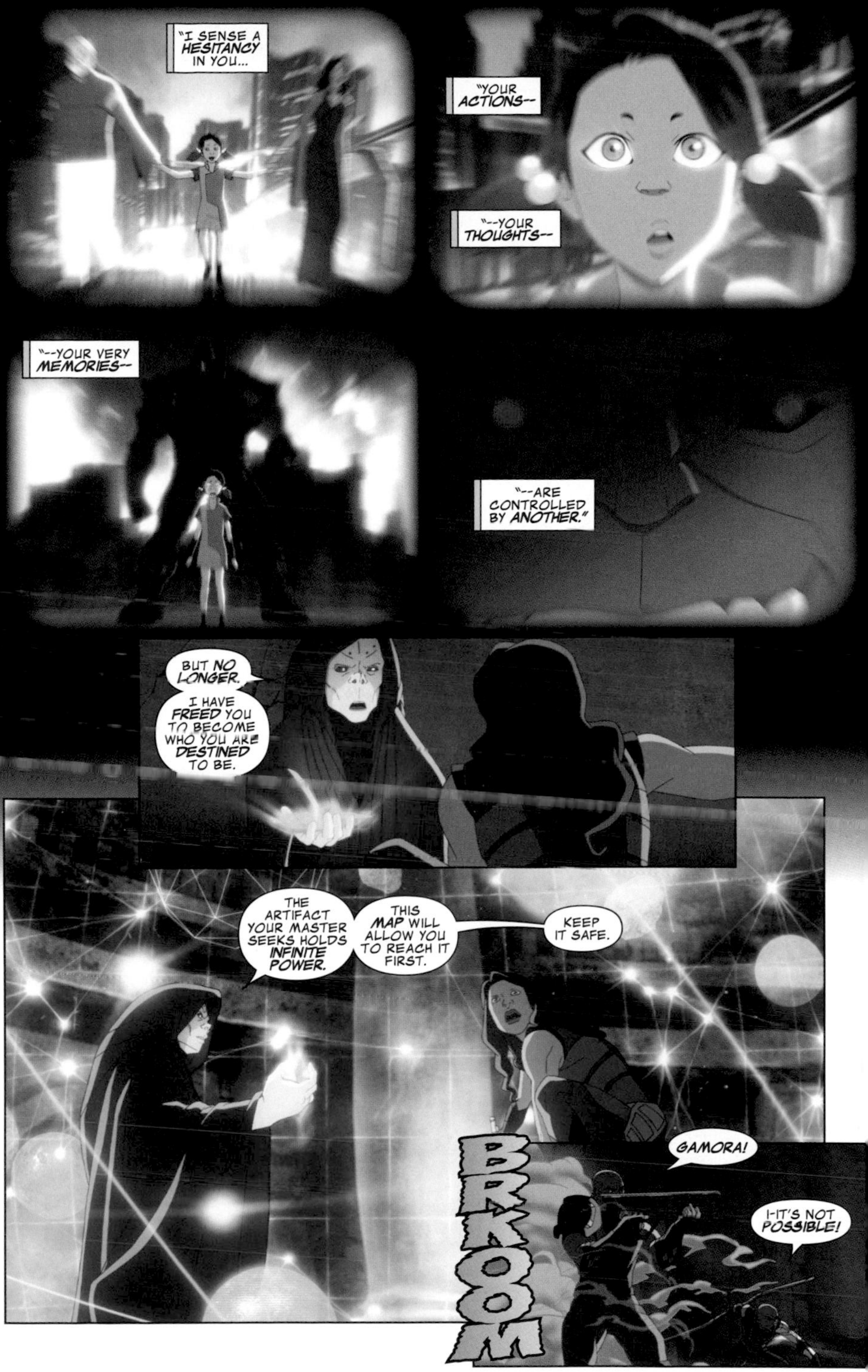
"I SENSE A HESITANCY IN YOU...
"YOUR ACTIONS--
"--YOUR THOUGHTS--
"--YOUR VERY MEMORIES--
"--ARE CONTROLLED BY ANOTHER."
BUT NO LONGER.
I HAVE FREED YOU TO BECOME WHO YOU ARE DESTINED TO BE.
THE ARTIFACT YOUR MASTER SEEKS HOLDS INFINITE POWER.
THIS MAP WILL ALLOW YOU TO REACH IT FIRST.
KEEP IT SAFE.
BRKOOM
GAMORA!
I-IT'S NOT POSSIBLE!

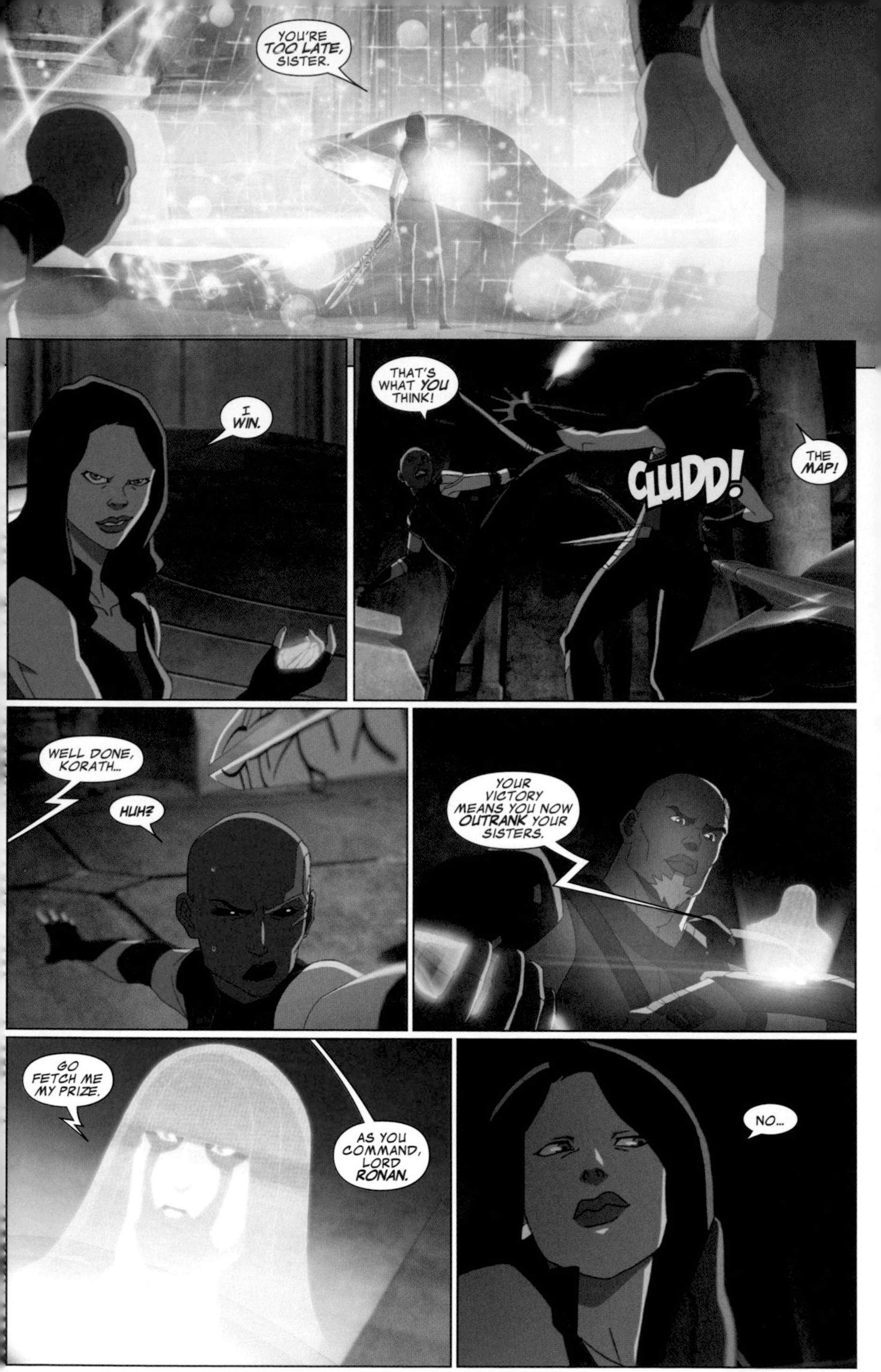

YOU'RE TOO LATE, SISTER.
I WIN.
THAT'S WHAT YOU THINK!
CLUDD!
THE MAP!
WELL DONE, KORATH...
HUH?
YOUR VICTORY MEANS YOU NOW OUTRANK YOUR SISTERS.
GO FETCH ME MY PRIZE.
AS YOU COMMAND, LORD RONAN.
NO...

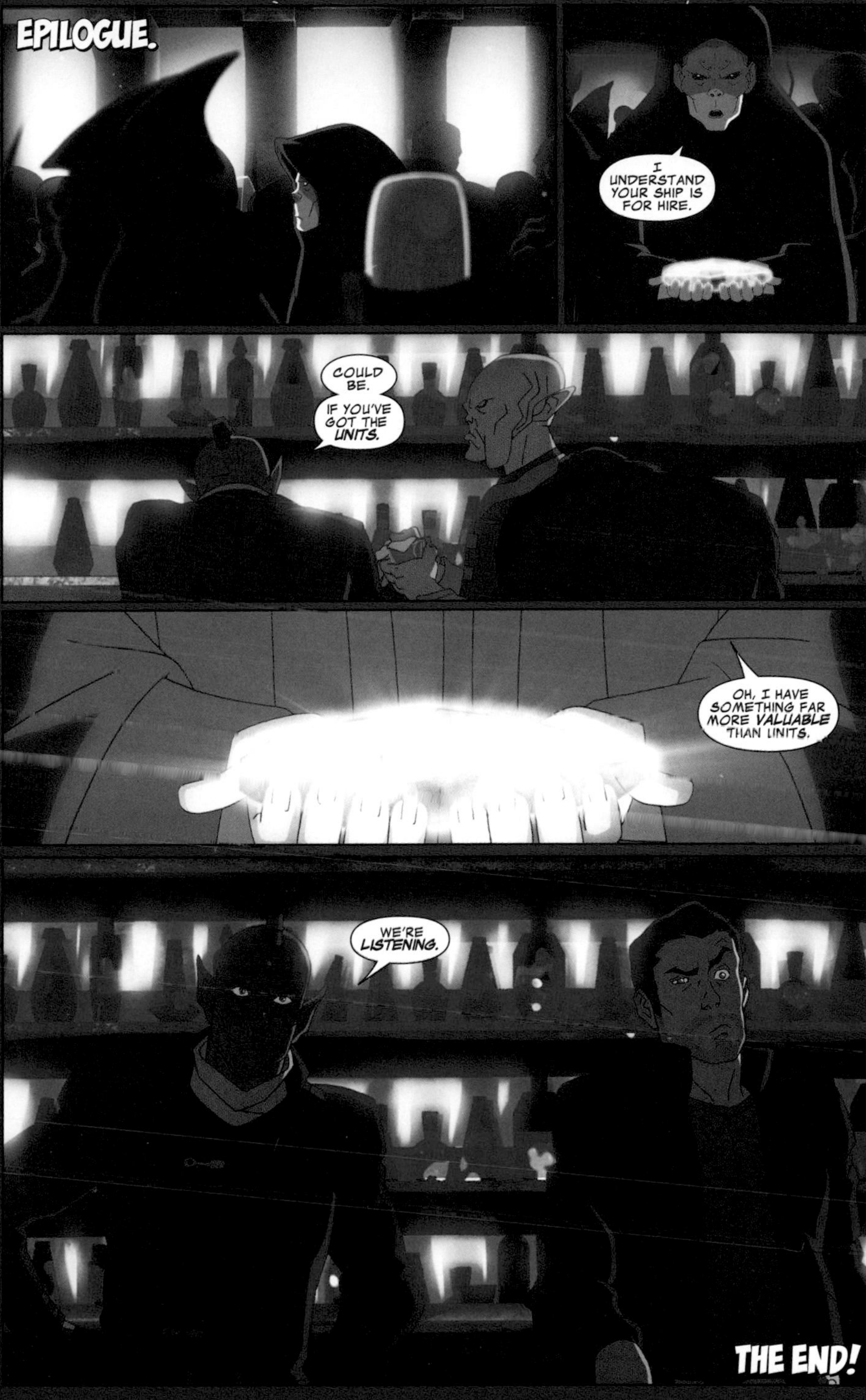

EPILOGUE.
I UNDERSTAND YOUR SHIP IS FOR HIRE.
COULD BE.
IF YOU'VE GOT THE UNITS.
OH, I HAVE SOMETHING FAR MORE VALUABLE THAN UNITS.
WE'RE LISTENING.
THE END!

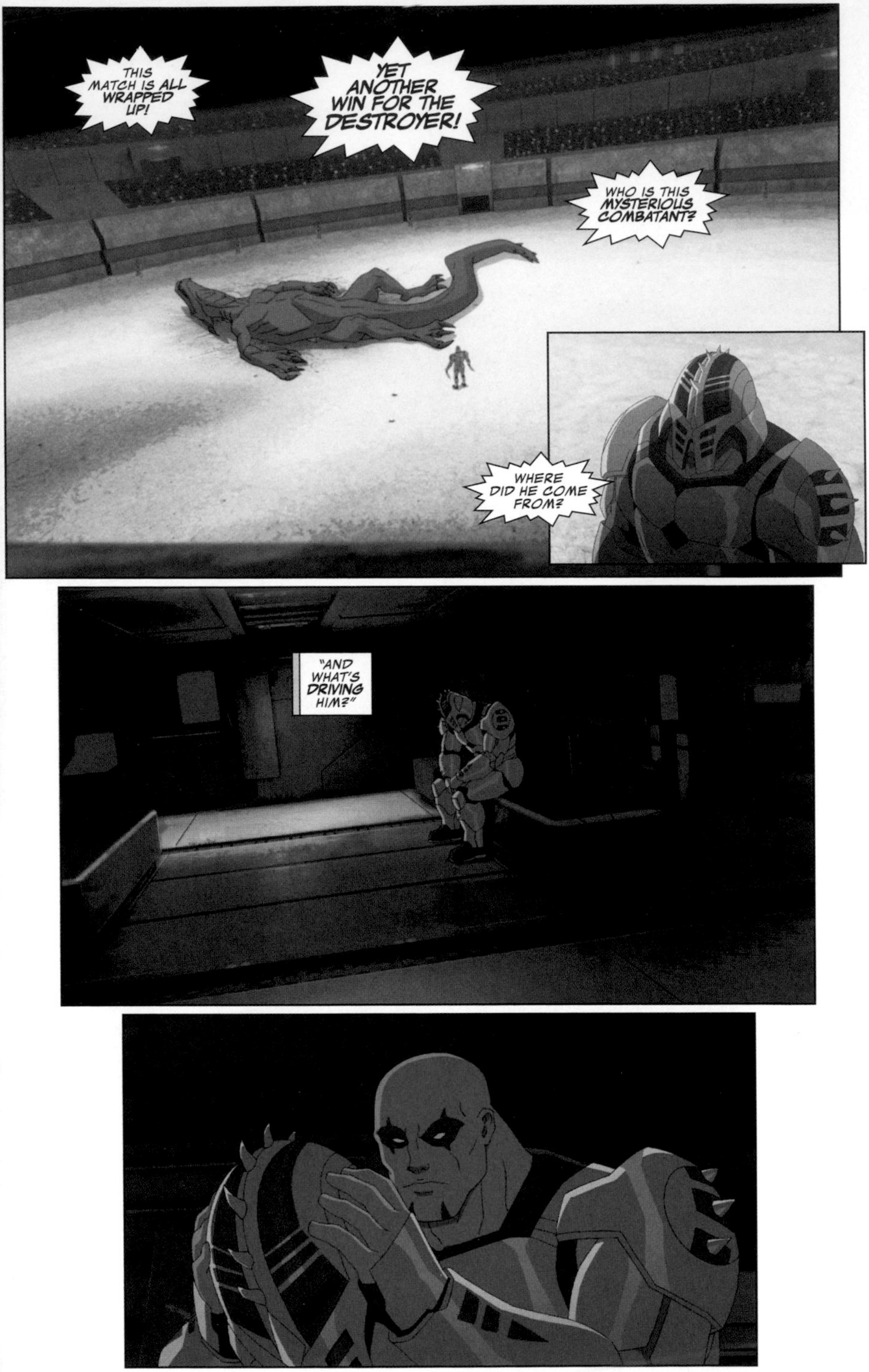
THIS MATCH IS ALL WRAPPED UP!
YET ANOTHER WIN FOR THE DESTROYER!
WHO IS THIS MYSTERIOUS COMBATANT?
WHERE DID HE COME FROM?
"AND WHAT'S DRIVING HIM?"

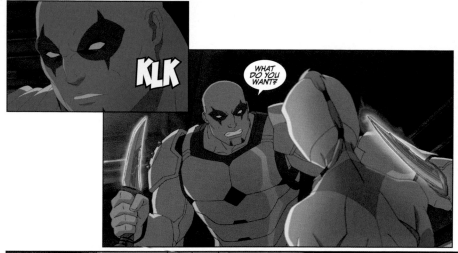

KLK

WHAT DO YOU WANT?

YOU FIGHT *MY FATHER* NEXT.

I'M WONDERING...

...COULD YOU LET *HIM* WIN?

YOU REMIND ME OF SOMEONE I CARED FOR LONG AGO.

BUT SHE WAS TAKEN AWAY FROM ME BY SOMEONE VERY *EVIL*.

I *MUST* DEFEAT YOUR FATHER. BUT I PROMISE...

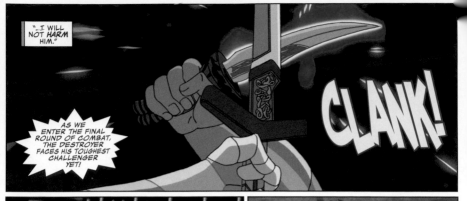

"...I WILL NOT HARM HIM."

AS WE ENTER THE FINAL ROUND OF COMBAT, THE DESTROYER FACES HIS TOUGHEST CHALLENGER YET!

CLANK!

WHOOSH!

WHOOSH!

NO SURPRISE SINCE THERE'S A LOT AT STAKE!

THE CHAMPION WILL EARN THE RIGHT TO SERVE AS ENFORCER AND STAND AT THE RIGHT HAND OF RONAN THE ACCUSER!

CLANK!

CLINK!

HNN!

WHUDD!

IT'S ALL OVER BUT THE SLAYING--

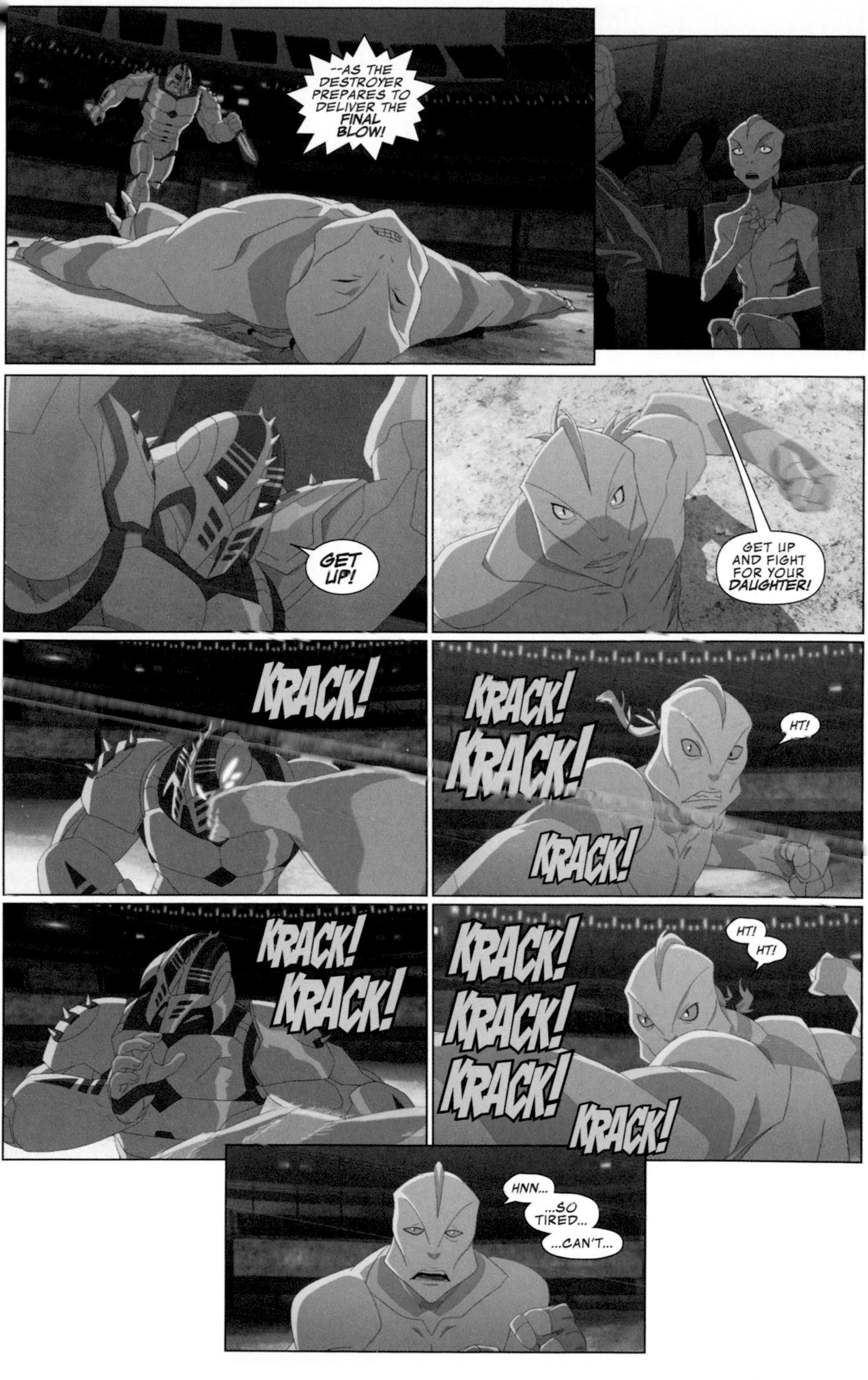
--AS THE DESTROYER PREPARES TO DELIVER THE FINAL BLOW!
GET UP!
GET UP AND FIGHT FOR YOUR DAUGHTER!
KRACK!
KRACK!
KRACK!
HT!
KRACK!
KRACK!
KRACK!
KRACK!
KRACK!
KRACK!
HT!
HT!
KRACK!
HNN...
...SO TIRED...
...CAN'T...

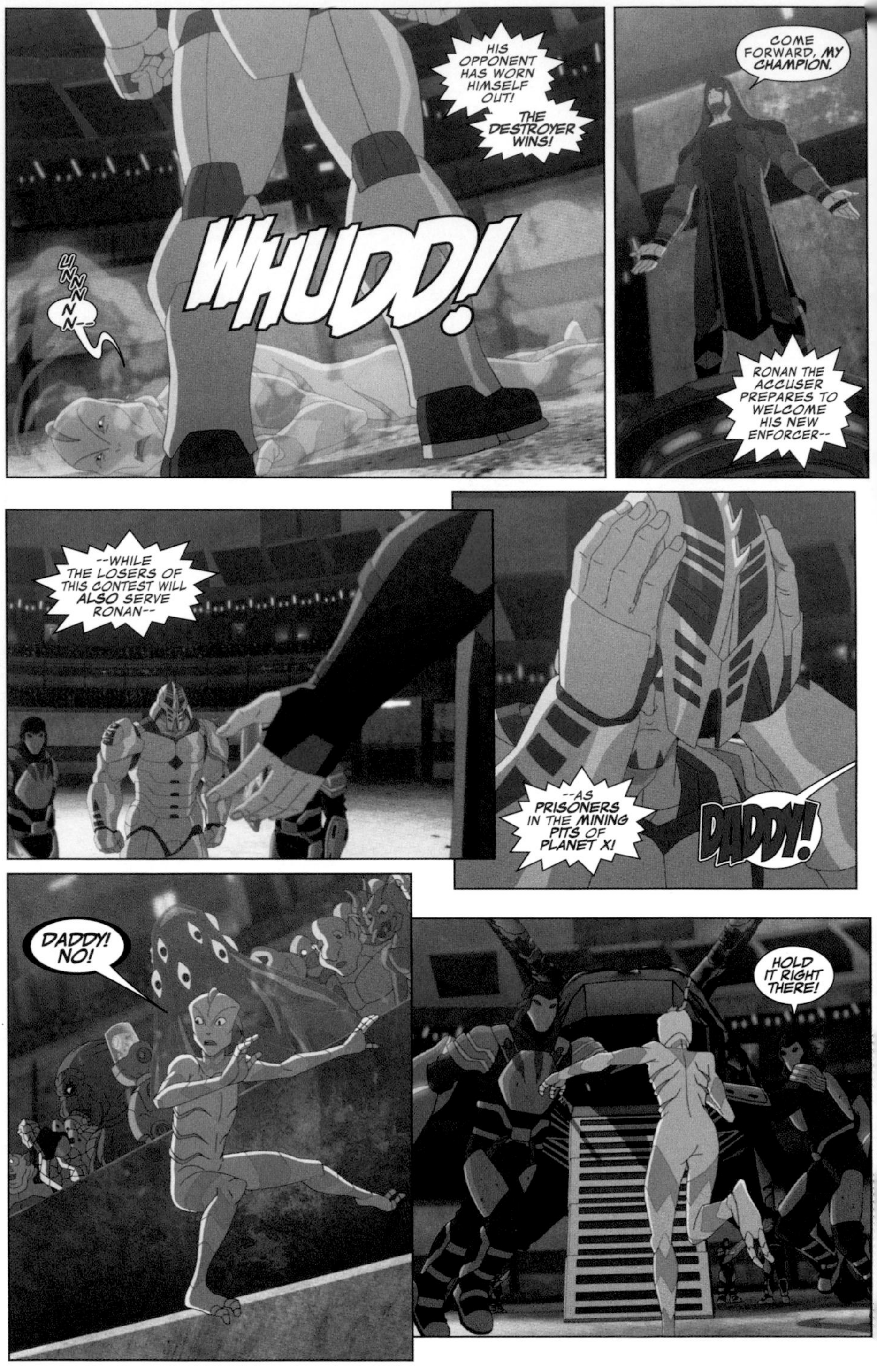

HIS OPPONENT HAS WORN HIMSELF OUT!
THE DESTROYER WINS!
WHUDD!
UNNNNN--
COME FORWARD, MY CHAMPION.
RONAN THE ACCUSER PREPARES TO WELCOME HIS NEW ENFORCER--
--WHILE THE LOSERS OF THIS CONTEST WILL ALSO SERVE RONAN--
--AS PRISONERS IN THE MINING PITS OF PLANET X!
DADDY!
DADDY! NO!
HOLD IT RIGHT THERE!

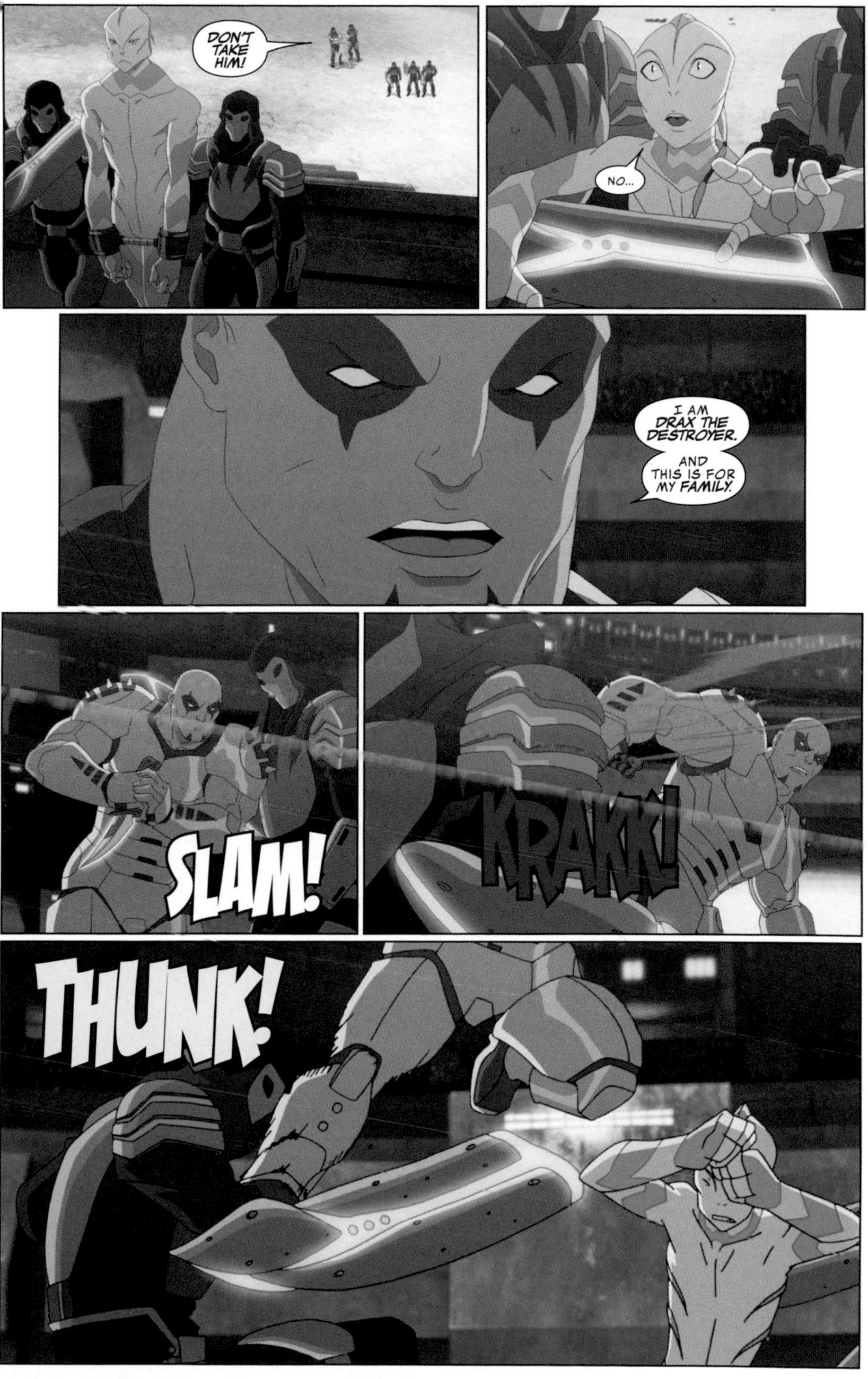
DON'T TAKE HIM!
NO...
I AM DRAX THE DESTROYER.
AND THIS IS FOR MY FAMILY.
SLAM!
KRAKK!
THUNK!

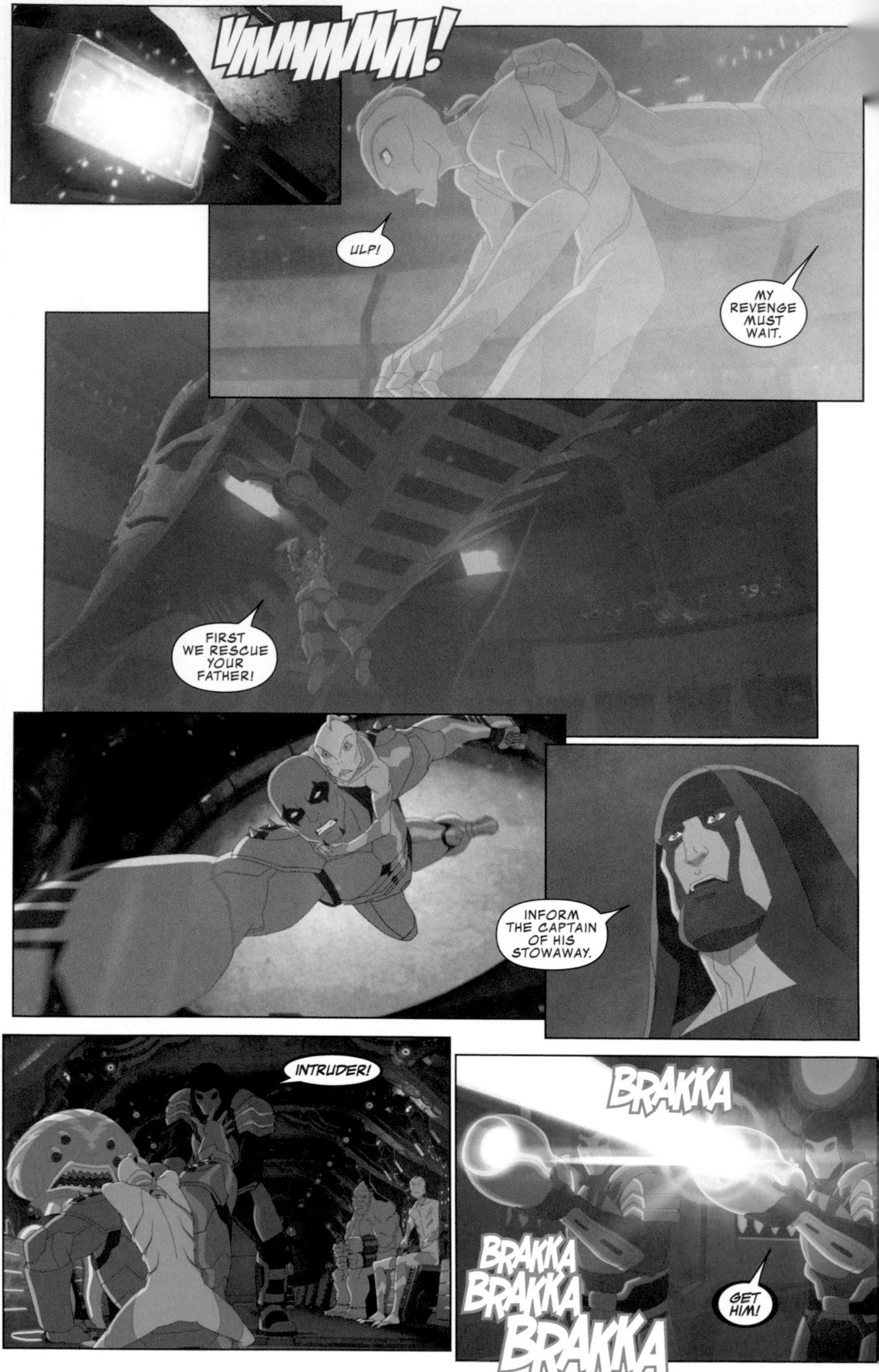
VMMMMMM!
ULP!
MY REVENGE MUST WAIT.
FIRST WE RESCUE YOUR FATHER!
INFORM THE CAPTAIN OF HIS STOWAWAY.
INTRUDER!
BRAKKA
BRAKKA BRAKKA BRAKKA
GET HIM!

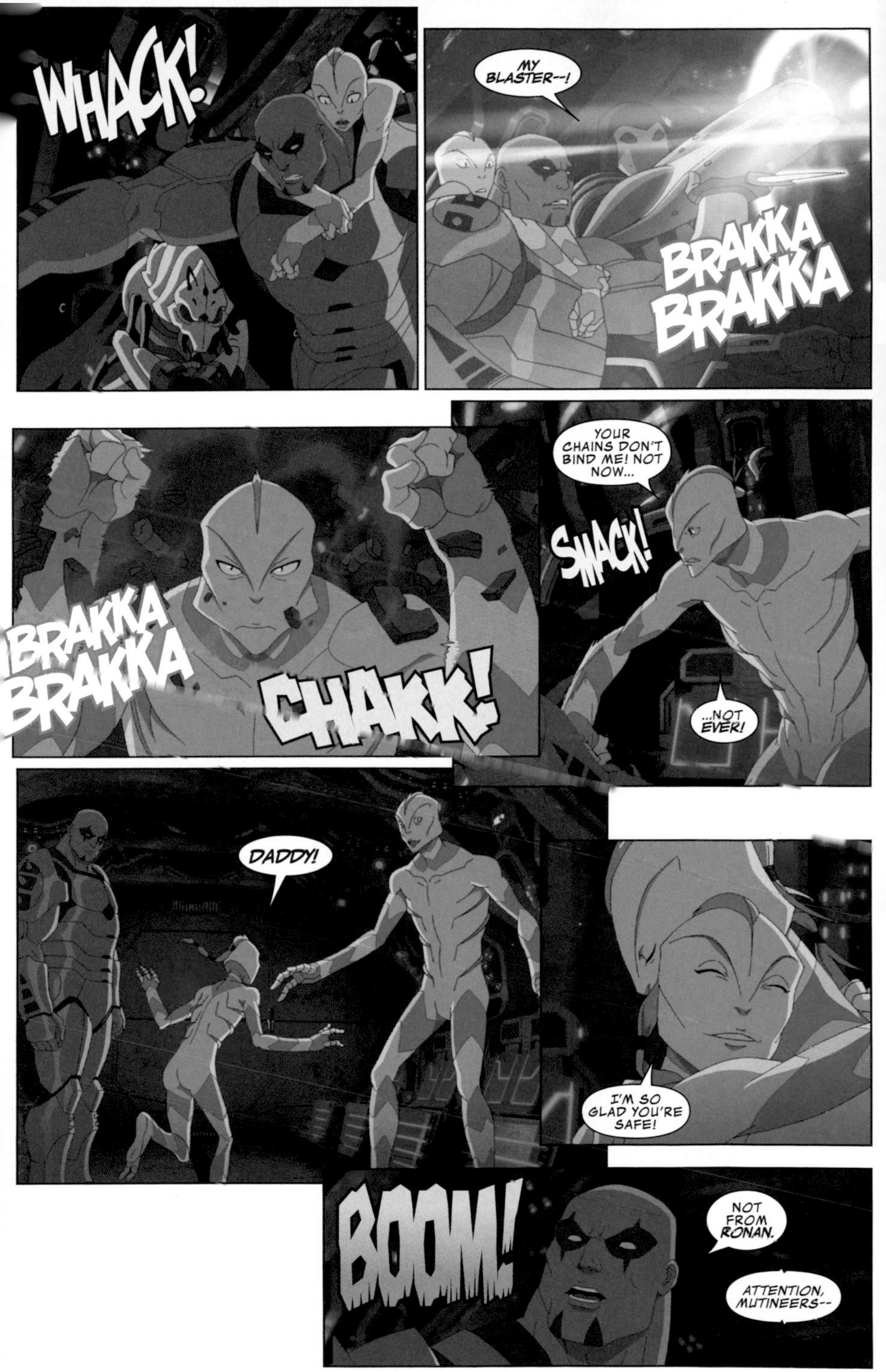
WHACK!
MY BLASTER--!
BRAKKA BRAKKA
BRAKKA BRAKKA
CHAKK!
YOUR CHAINS DON'T BIND ME! NOT NOW...
SMACK!
...NOT EVER!
DADDY!
I'M SO GLAD YOU'RE SAFE!
BOOM!
NOT FROM RONAN.
ATTENTION, MUTINEERS--

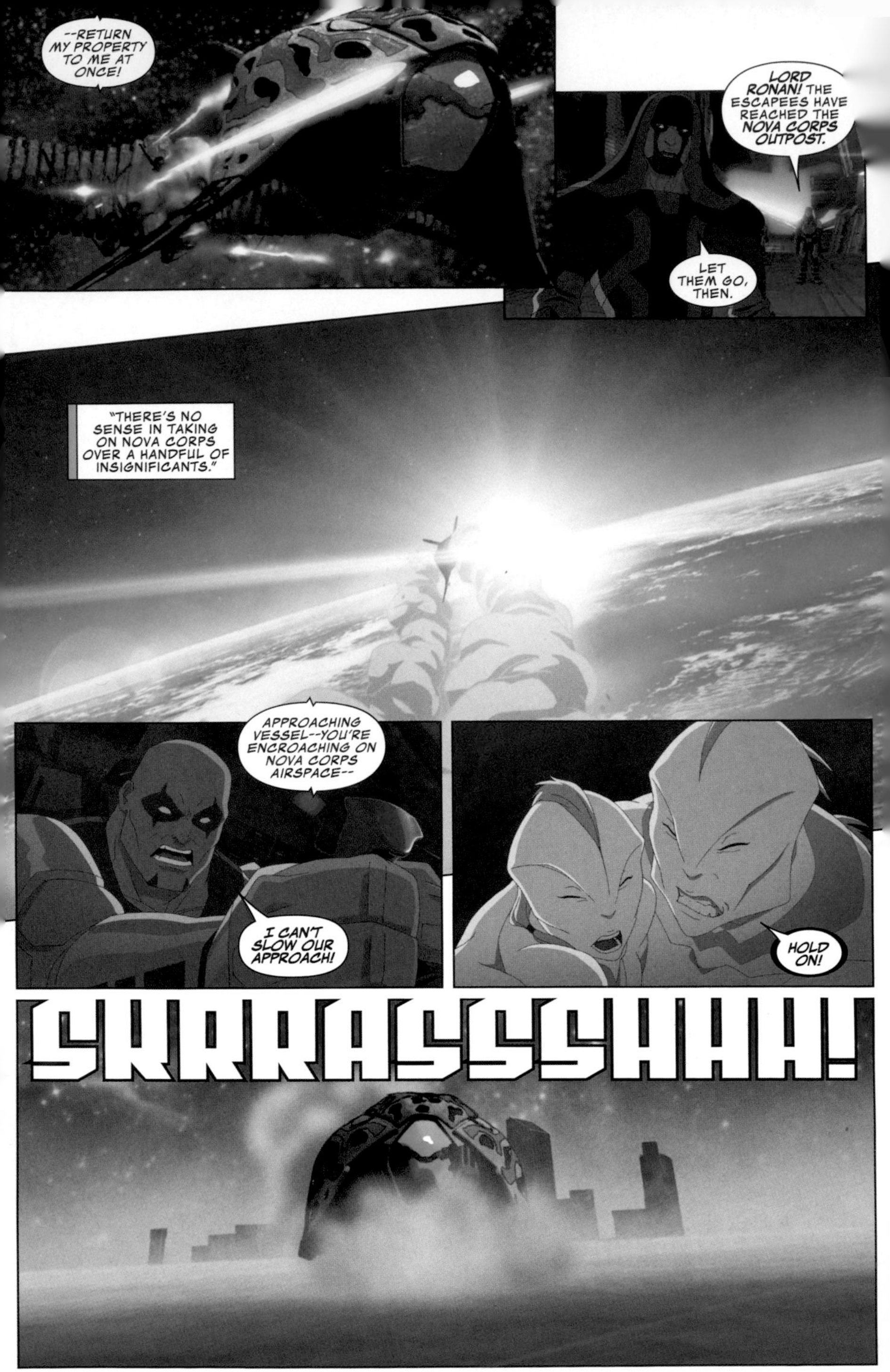
--RETURN MY PROPERTY TO ME AT ONCE!
LORD RONAN! THE ESCAPEES HAVE REACHED THE NOVA CORPS OUTPOST.
LET THEM GO, THEN.
"THERE'S NO SENSE IN TAKING ON NOVA CORPS OVER A HANDFUL OF INSIGNIFICANTS."
APPROACHING VESSEL--YOU'RE ENCROACHING ON NOVA CORPS AIRSPACE--
I CAN'T SLOW OUR APPROACH!
HOLD ON!
SKRRASSSHHH!

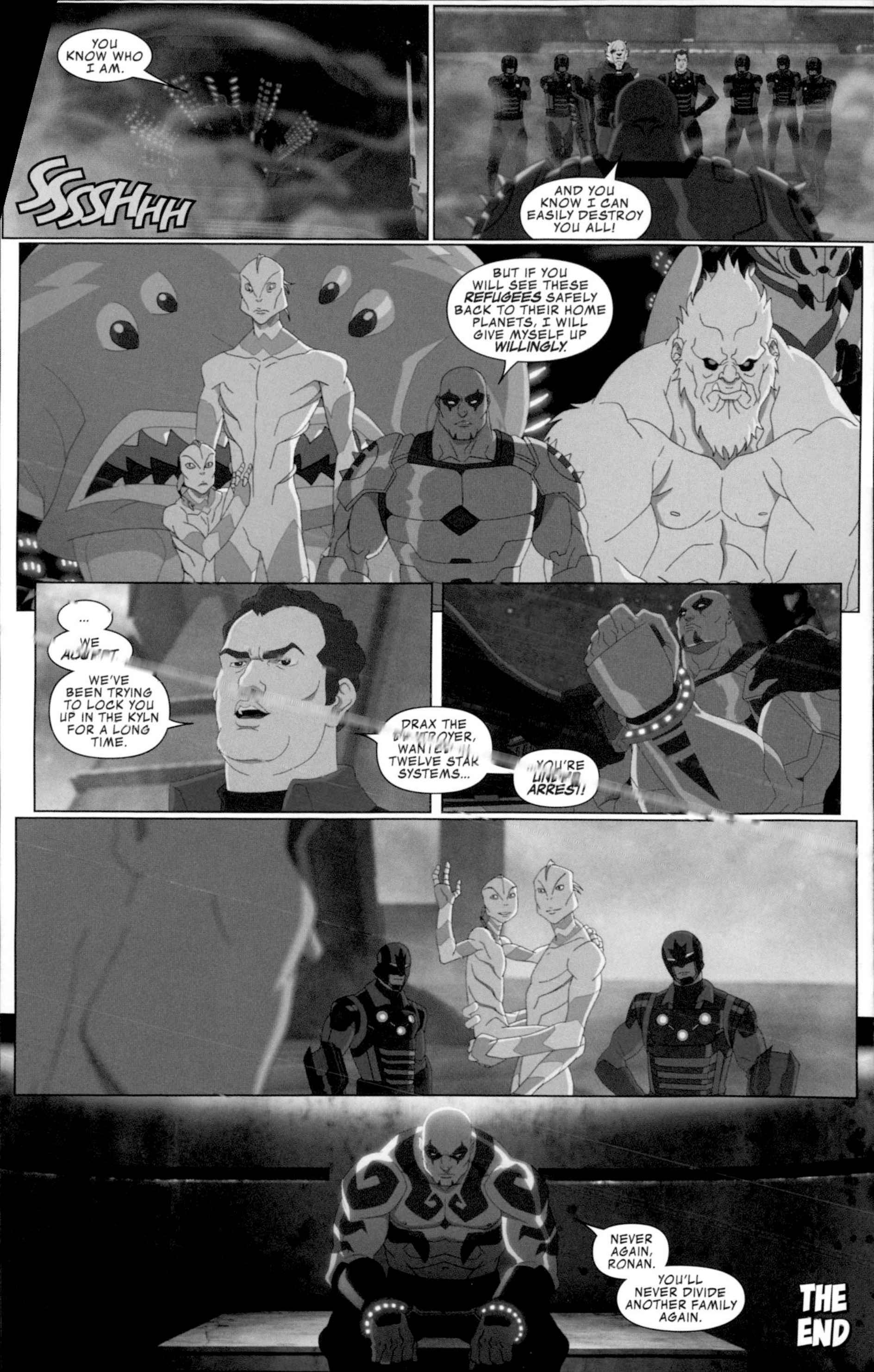
YOU KNOW WHO I AM.
SSSSHHH
AND YOU KNOW I CAN EASILY DESTROY YOU ALL!
BUT IF YOU WILL SEE THESE REFUGEES SAFELY BACK TO THEIR HOME PLANETS, I WILL GIVE MYSELF UP WILLINGLY.
... WE
WE'VE BEEN TRYING TO LOCK YOU UP IN THE KYLN FOR A LONG TIME.
DRAX THE
TWELVE STAR SYSTEMS...
YOU'RE
ARREST!
NEVER AGAIN, RONAN.
YOU'LL NEVER DIVIDE ANOTHER FAMILY AGAIN.
THE END

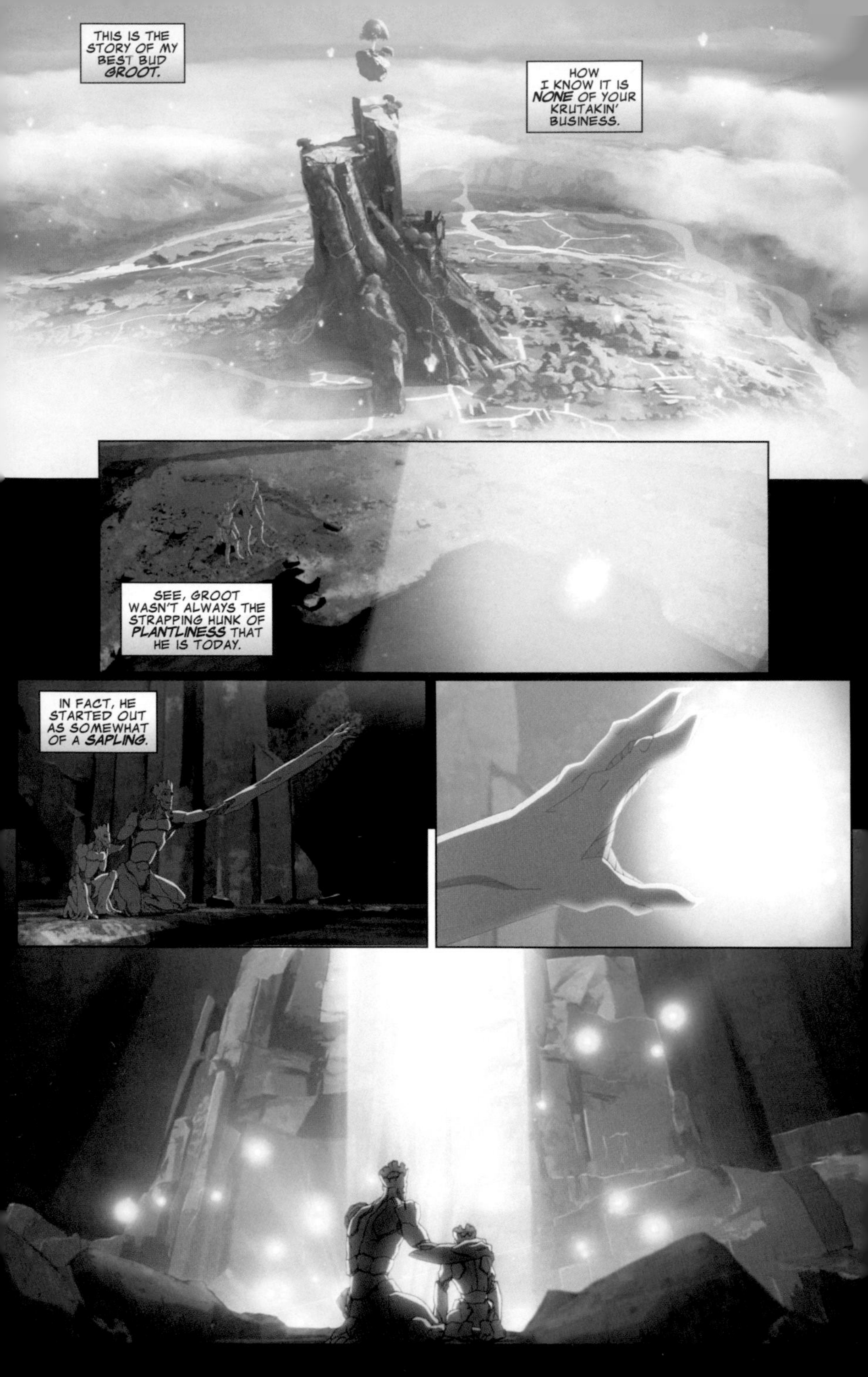
THIS IS THE STORY OF MY BEST BUD GROOT.
HOW I KNOW IT IS NONE OF YOUR KRUTAKIN' BUSINESS.
SEE, GROOT WASN'T ALWAYS THE STRAPPING HUNK OF PLANTLINESS THAT HE IS TODAY.
IN FACT, HE STARTED OUT AS SOMEWHAT OF A SAPLING.

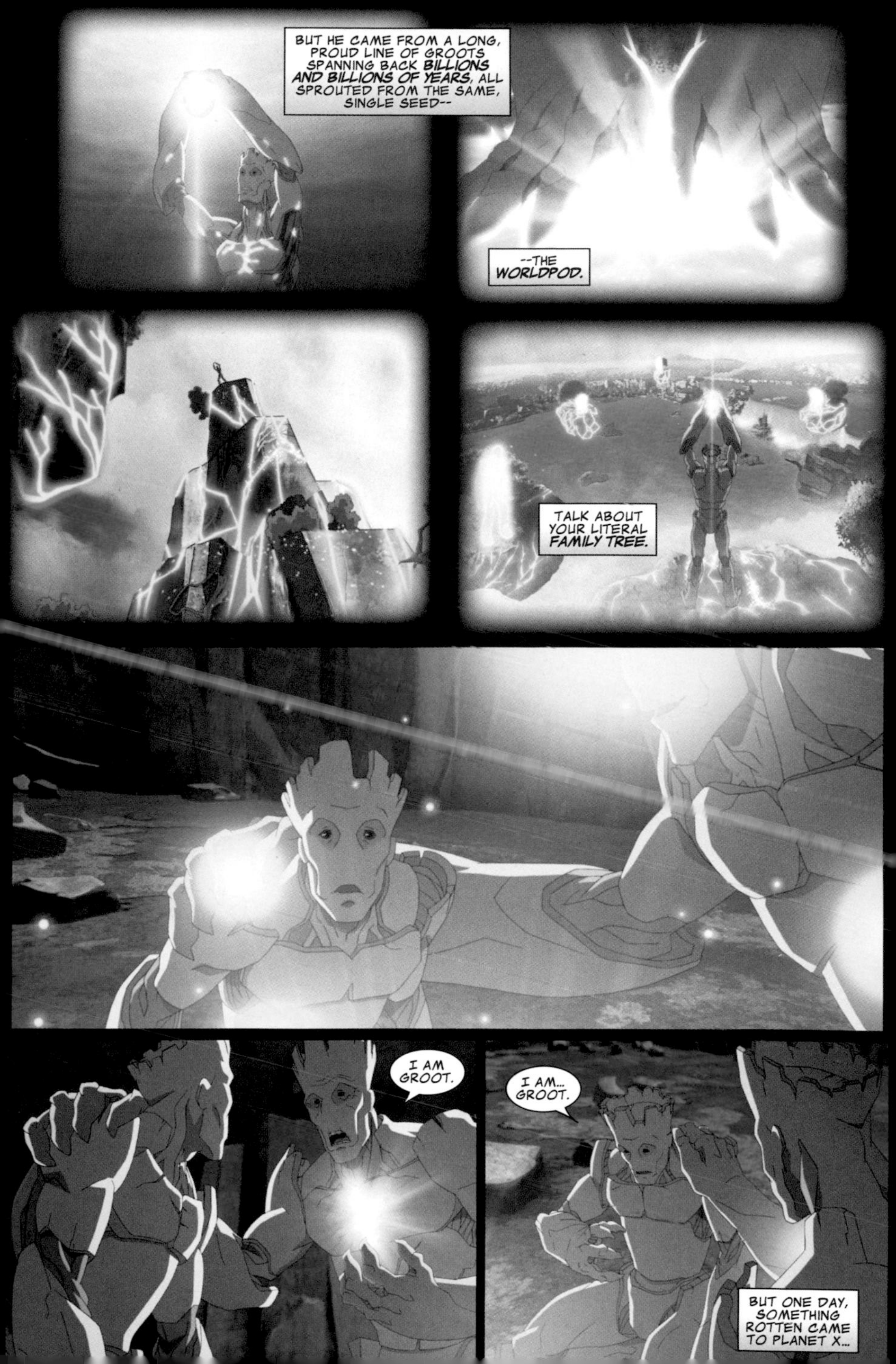
BUT HE CAME FROM A LONG, PROUD LINE OF GROOTS SPANNING BACK **BILLIONS AND BILLIONS OF YEARS**, ALL SPROUTED FROM THE SAME, SINGLE SEED--
--THE ***WORLDPOD.***
TALK ABOUT YOUR LITERAL ***FAMILY TREE.***
I AM GROOT.
I AM... GROOT.
BUT ONE DAY, SOMETHING ROTTEN CAME TO PLANET X...

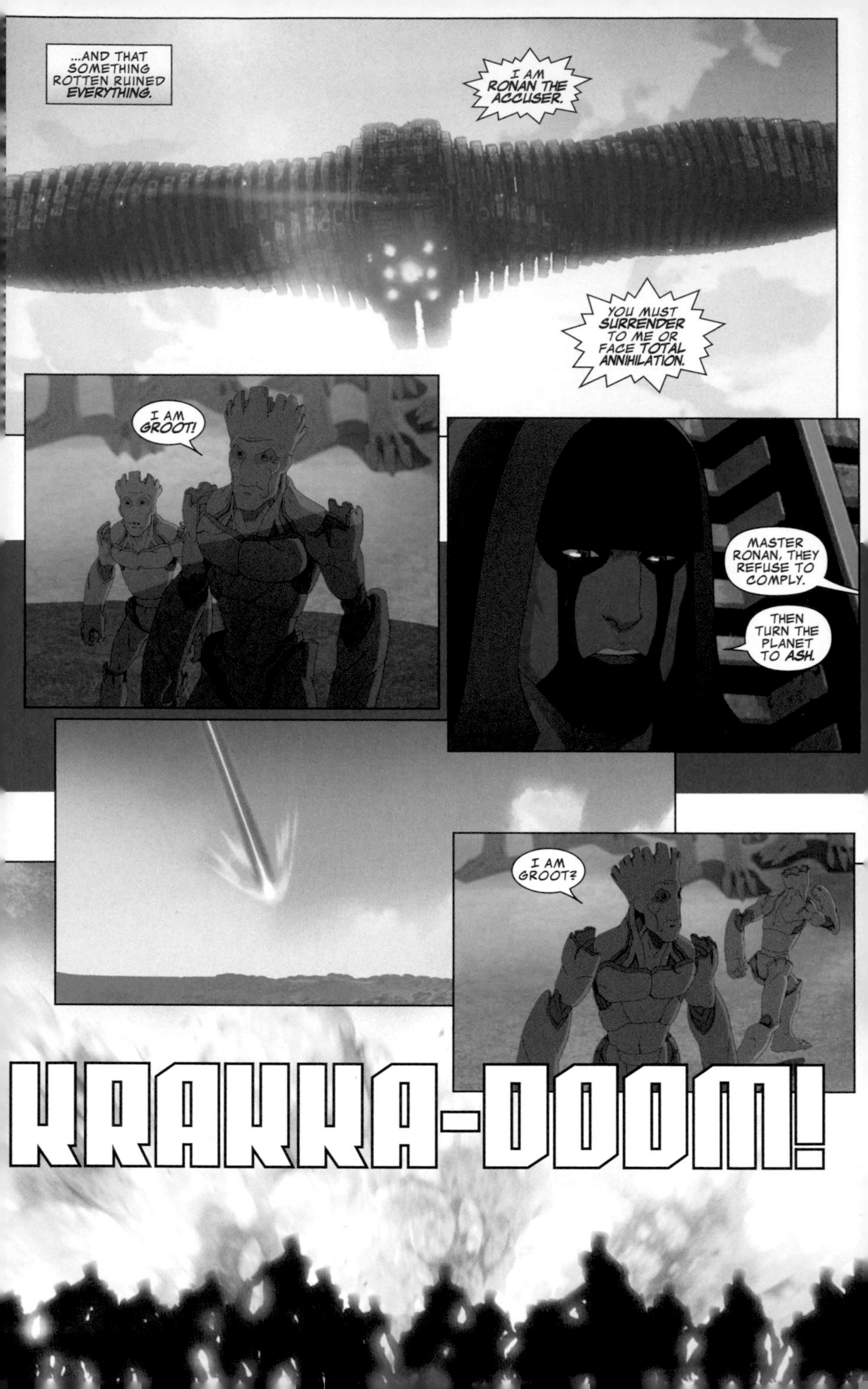
...AND THAT SOMETHING ROTTEN RUINED EVERYTHING.
I AM RONAN THE ACCUSER.
YOU MUST SURRENDER TO ME OR FACE TOTAL ANNIHILATION.
I AM GROOT!
MASTER RONAN, THEY REFUSE TO COMPLY.
THEN TURN THE PLANET TO ASH.
I AM GROOT?
KRAKKA-DOOM!

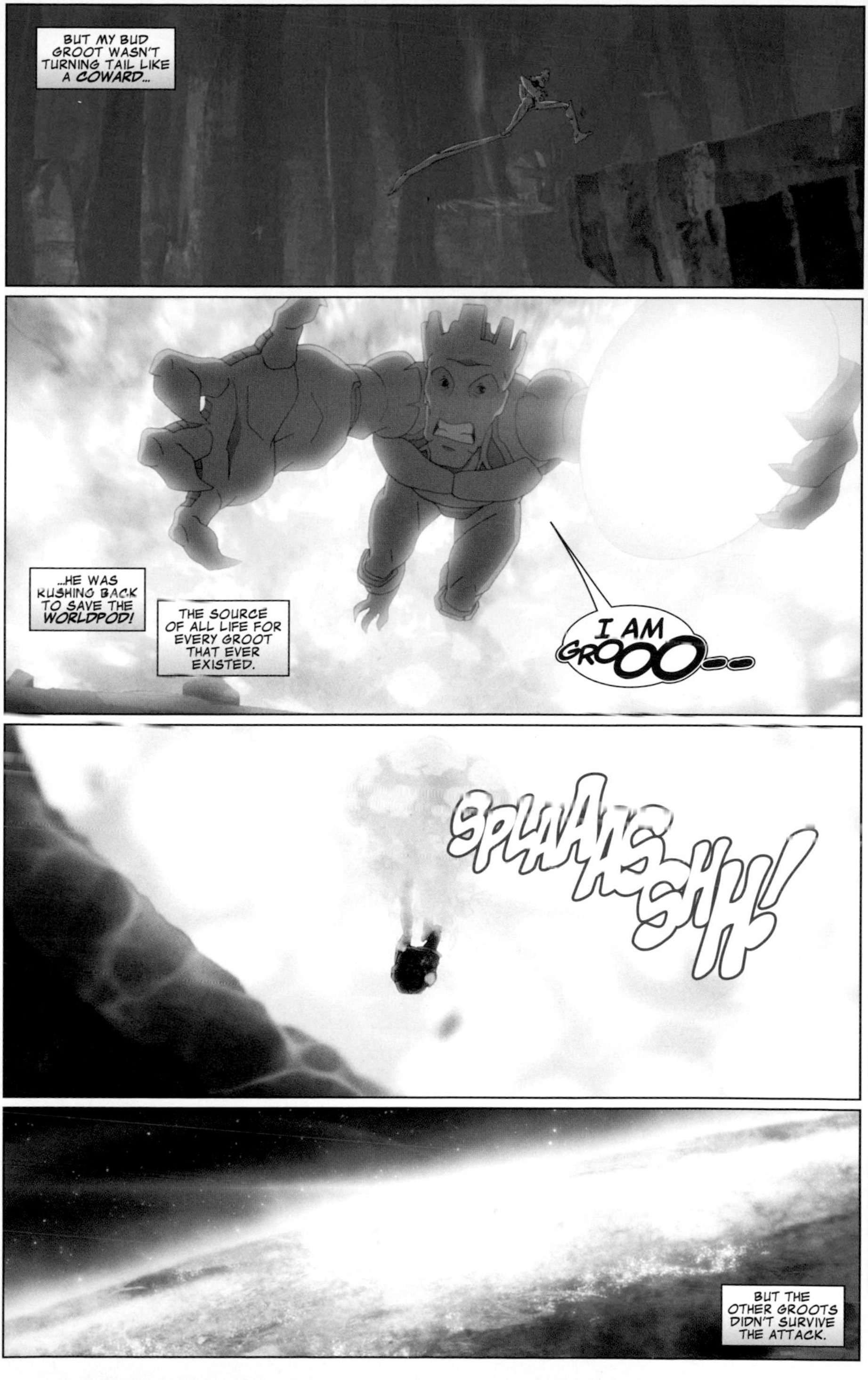
BUT MY BUD GROOT WASN'T TURNING TAIL LIKE A COWARD...
...HE WAS RUSHING BACK TO SAVE THE WORLDPOD!
THE SOURCE OF ALL LIFE FOR EVERY GROOT THAT EVER EXISTED.
I AM GROOOO--
SPLAAASSHH!
BUT THE OTHER GROOTS DIDN'T SURVIVE THE ATTACK.

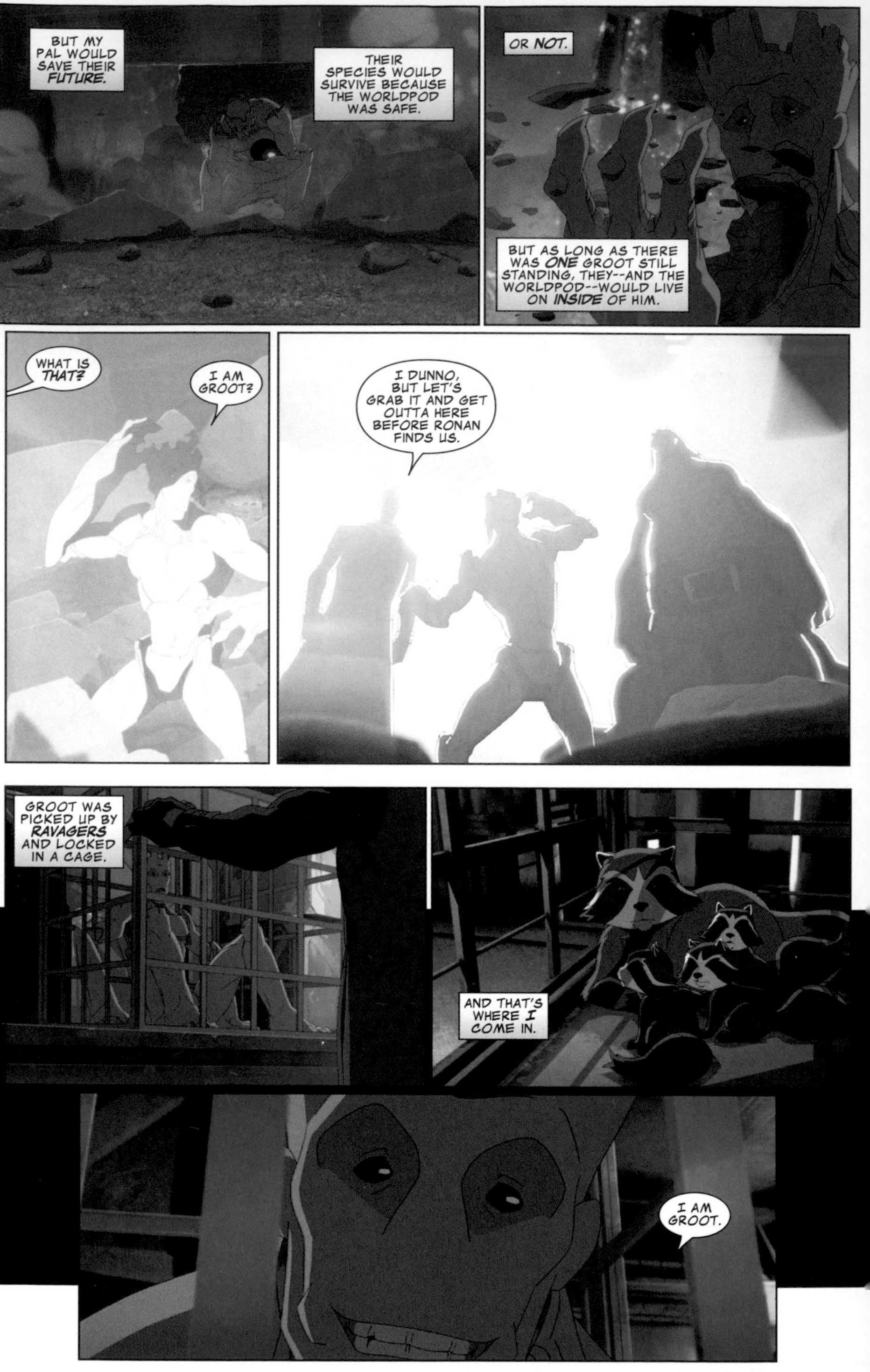
BUT MY PAL WOULD SAVE THEIR FUTURE.
THEIR SPECIES WOULD SURVIVE BECAUSE THE WORLDPOD WAS SAFE.
OR NOT.
BUT AS LONG AS THERE WAS ONE GROOT STILL STANDING, THEY--AND THE WORLDPOD--WOULD LIVE ON INSIDE OF HIM.
WHAT IS THAT?
I AM GROOT?
I DUNNO, BUT LET'S GRAB IT AND GET OUTTA HERE BEFORE RONAN FINDS US.
GROOT WAS PICKED UP BY RAVAGERS AND LOCKED IN A CAGE.
AND THAT'S WHERE I COME IN.
I AM GROOT.

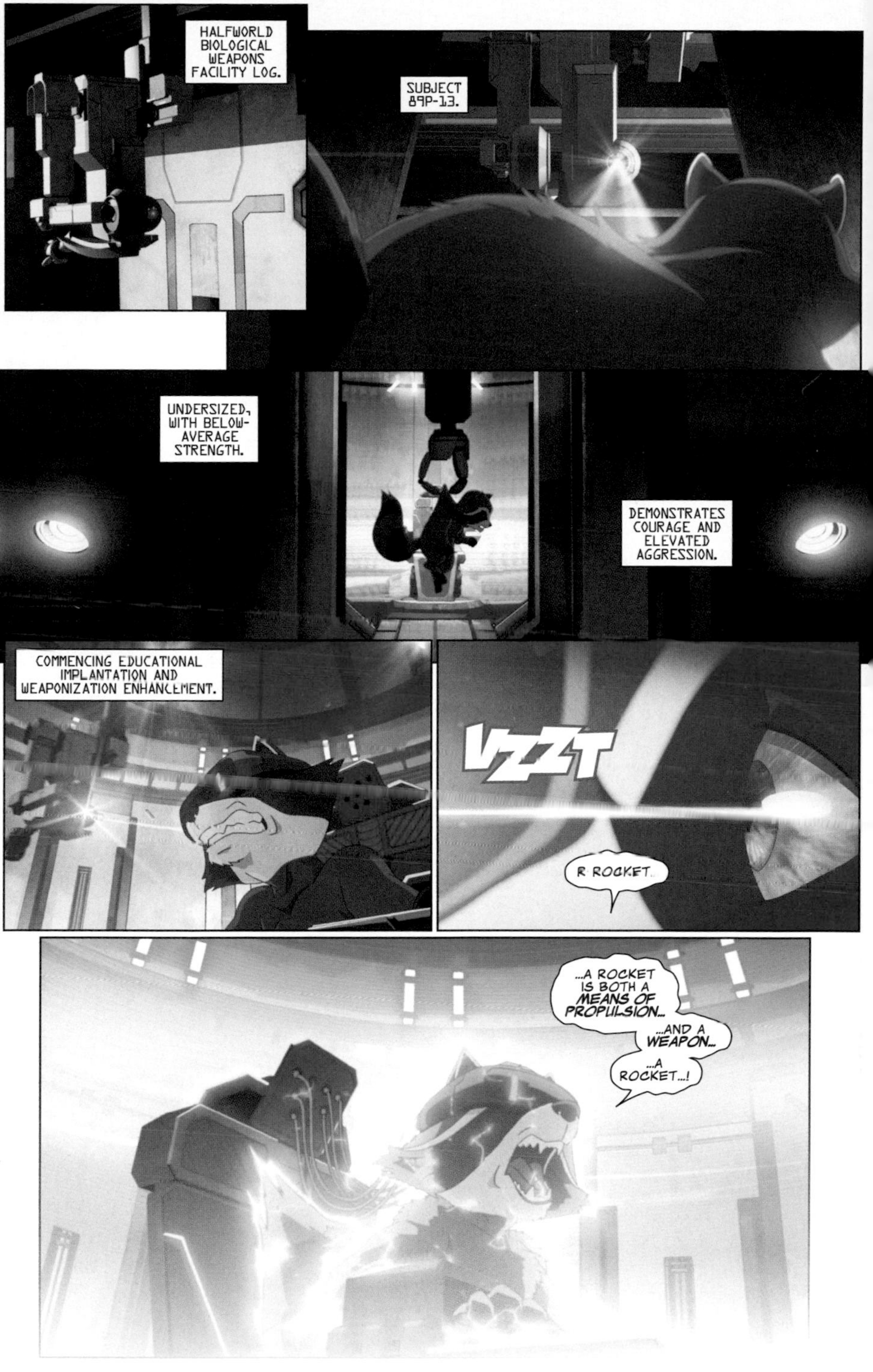
HALFWORLD BIOLOGICAL WEAPONS FACILITY LOG.
SUBJECT 89P-13.
UNDERSIZED, WITH BELOW-AVERAGE STRENGTH.
DEMONSTRATES COURAGE AND ELEVATED AGGRESSION.
COMMENCING EDUCATIONAL IMPLANTATION AND WEAPONIZATION ENHANCEMENT.
VZZT
R-ROCKET...
...A ROCKET IS BOTH A MEANS OF PROPULSION...
...AND A WEAPON...
...A ROCKET...!

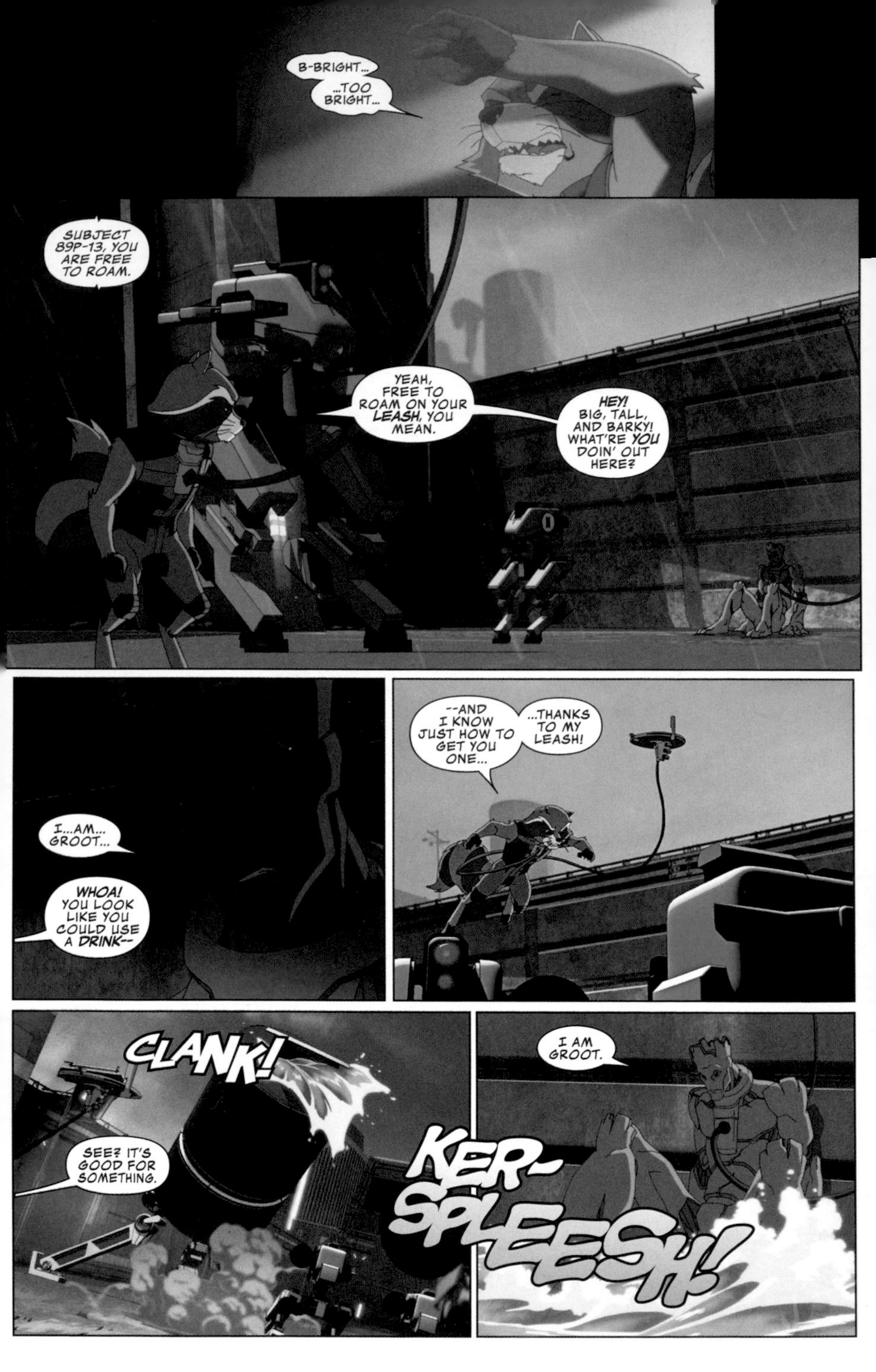
B-BRIGHT...
...TOO BRIGHT...
SUBJECT 89P-13, YOU ARE FREE TO ROAM.
YEAH, FREE TO ROAM ON YOUR LEASH, YOU MEAN.
HEY! BIG, TALL, AND BARKY! WHAT'RE YOU DOIN' OUT HERE?
I...AM... GROOT...
WHOA! YOU LOOK LIKE YOU COULD USE A DRINK--
--AND I KNOW JUST HOW TO GET YOU ONE...
...THANKS TO MY LEASH!
CLANK!
SEE? IT'S GOOD FOR SOMETHING.
KER-SPLEESH!
I AM GROOT.

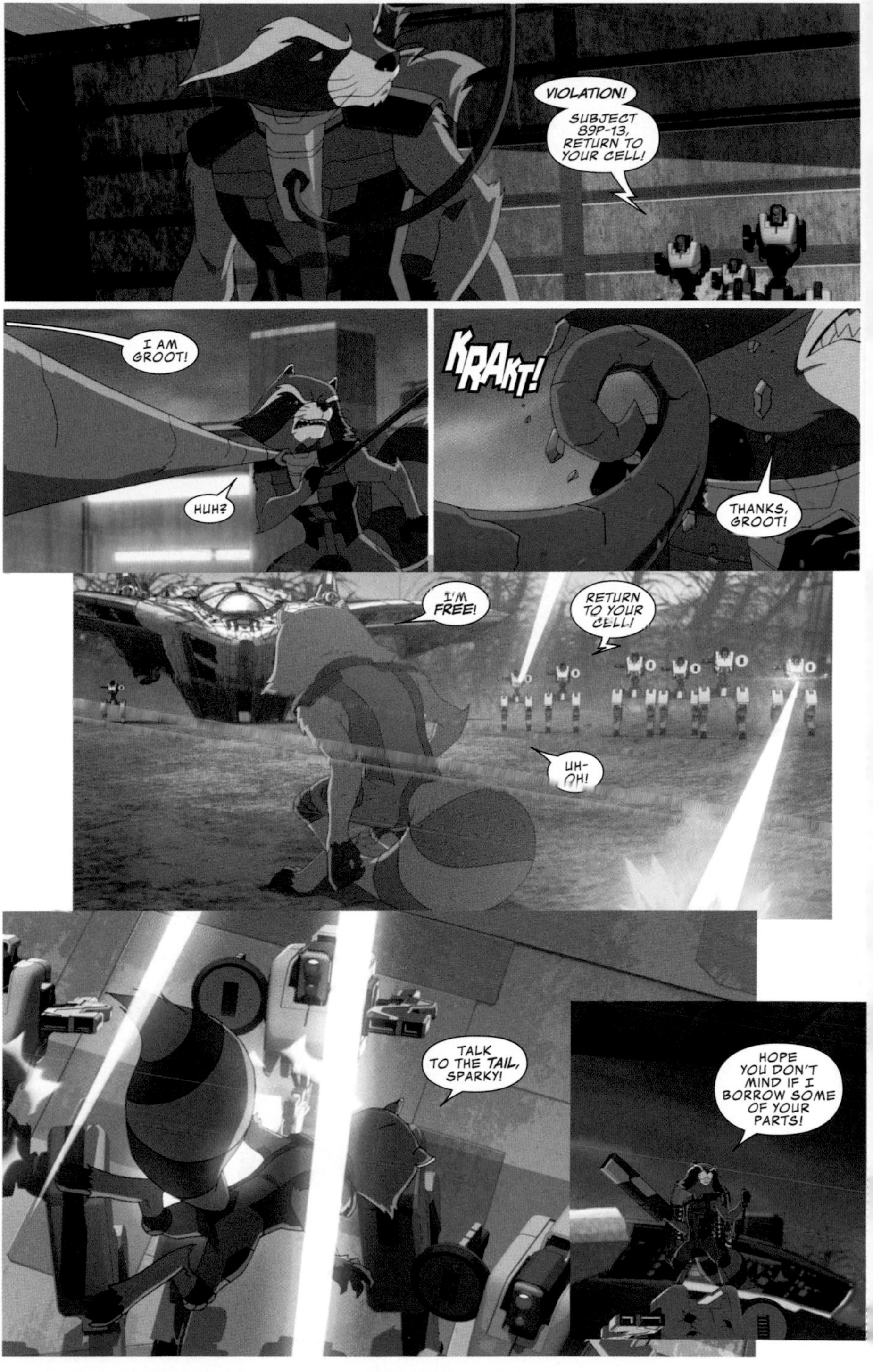
VIOLATION!
SUBJECT 89P-13, RETURN TO YOUR CELL!
I AM GROOT!
HUH?
KRAKT!
THANKS, GROOT!
I'M FREE!
RETURN TO YOUR CELL!
UH-OH!
TALK TO THE TAIL, SPARKY!
HOPE YOU DON'T MIND IF I BORROW SOME OF YOUR PARTS!

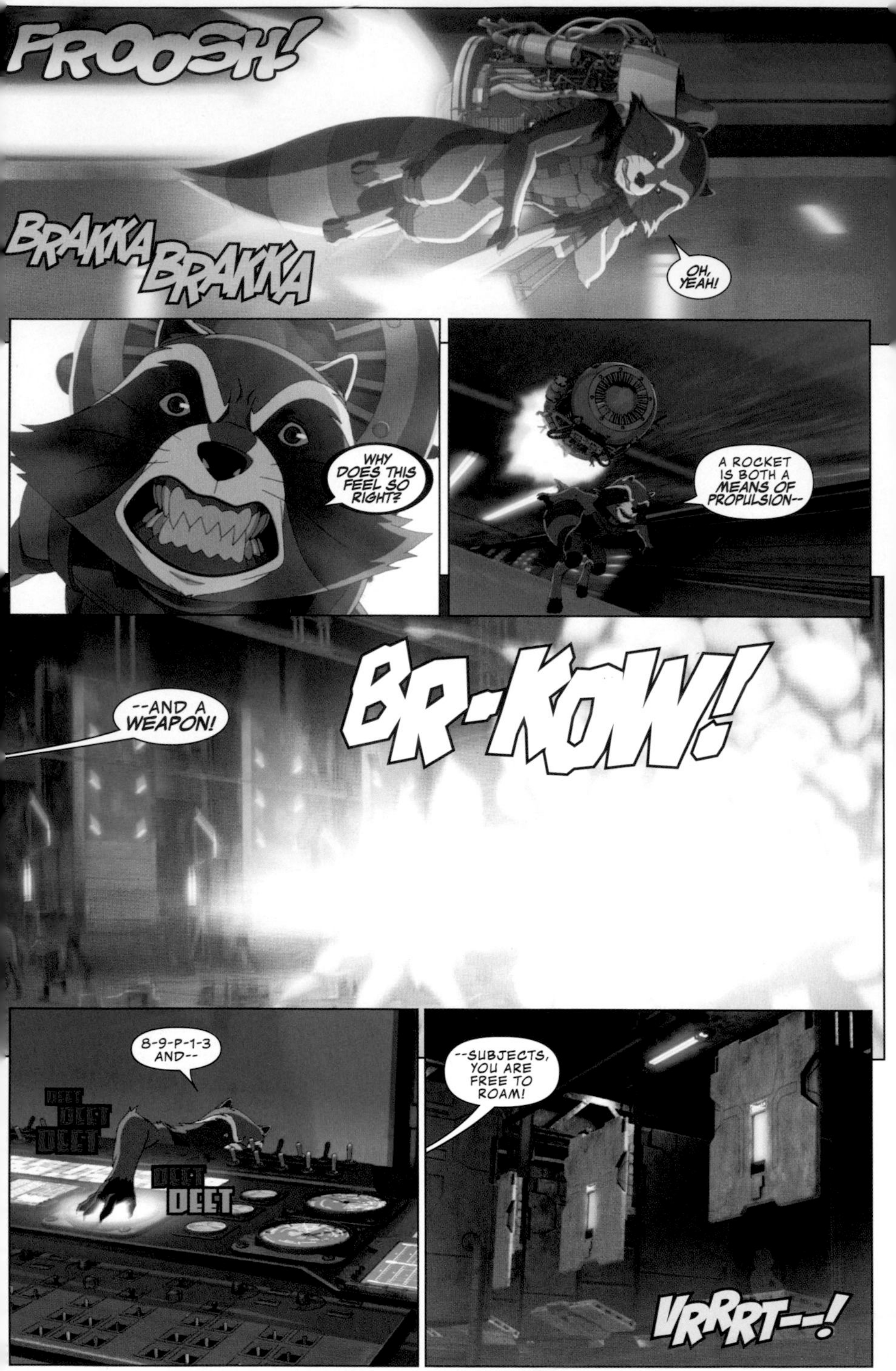
FROOSH!
BRAKKA BRAKKA
OH, YEAH!
WHY DOES THIS FEEL SO RIGHT?
A ROCKET IS BOTH A MEANS OF PROPULSION--
--AND A WEAPON!
BR-KOW!
8-9-P-1-3 AND--
DEET DEET DEET
DEET DEET
--SUBJECTS, YOU ARE FREE TO ROAM!
VRRRT--!

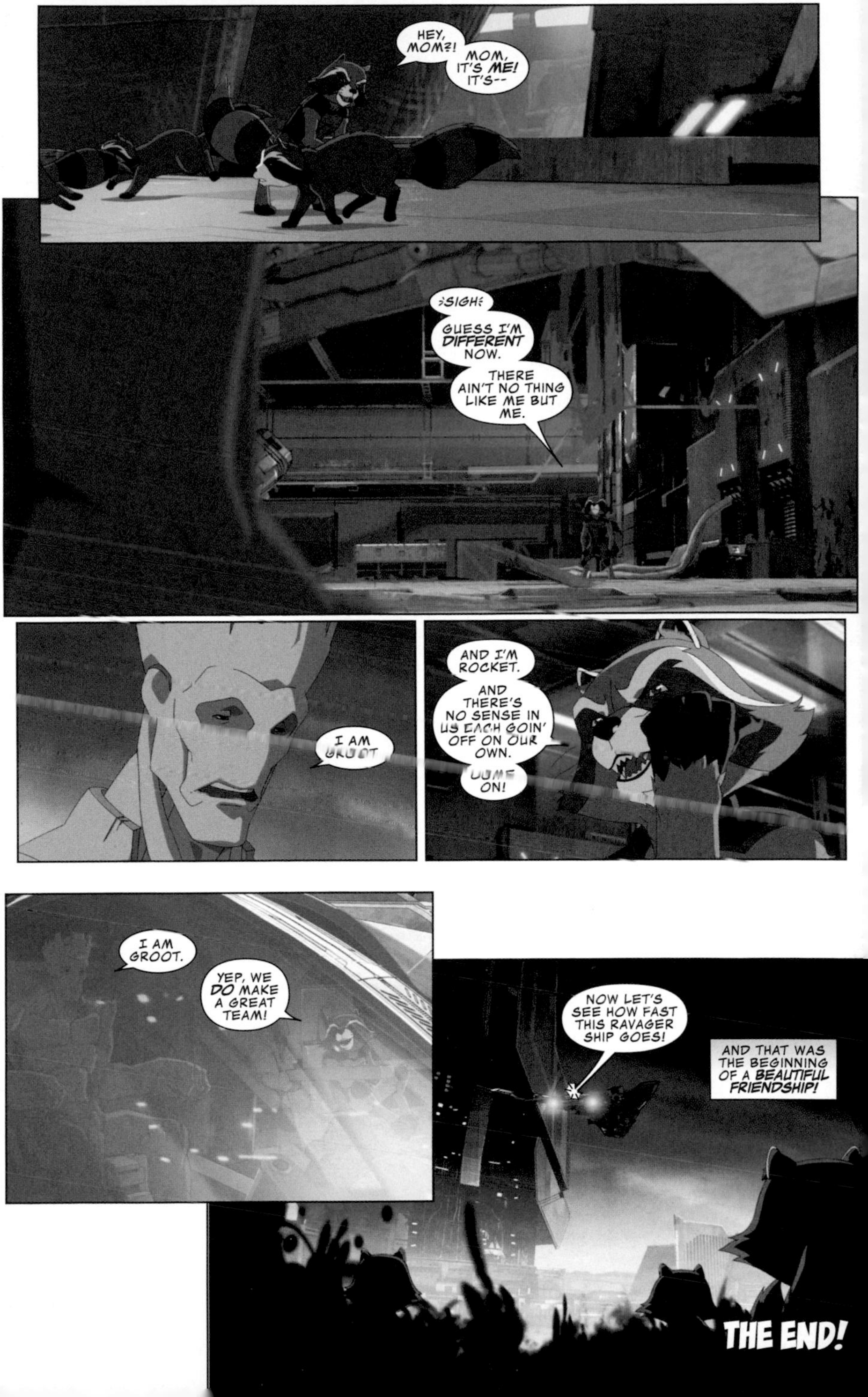
HEY, MOM?!
MOM, IT'S ME! IT'S--
SIGH
GUESS I'M DIFFERENT NOW.
THERE AIN'T NO THING LIKE ME BUT ME.
I AM
AND I'M ROCKET.
AND THERE'S NO SENSE IN US EACH GOIN' OFF ON OUR OWN.
ON!
I AM GROOT.
YEP, WE DO MAKE A GREAT TEAM!
NOW LET'S SEE HOW FAST THIS RAVAGER SHIP GOES!
AND THAT WAS THE BEGINNING OF A BEAUTIFUL FRIENDSHIP!
THE END!

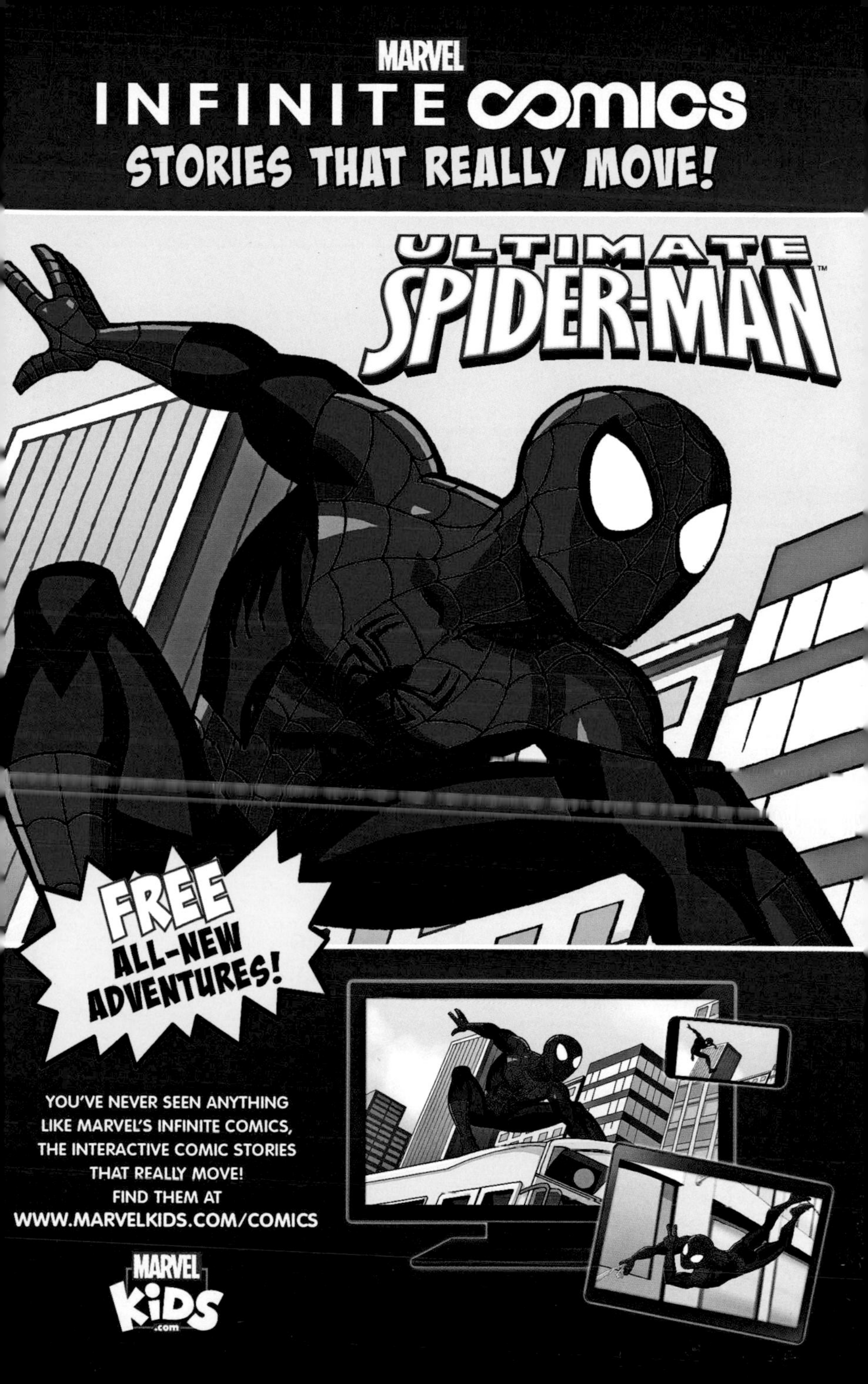
MARVEL
INFINITE COMICS
STORIES THAT REALLY MOVE!
ULTIMATE SPIDER-MAN™
FREE ALL-NEW ADVENTURES!
YOU'VE NEVER SEEN ANYTHING LIKE MARVEL'S INFINITE COMICS, THE INTERACTIVE COMIC STORIES THAT REALLY MOVE!
FIND THEM AT
WWW.MARVELKIDS.COM/COMICS
MARVEL KIDS .com

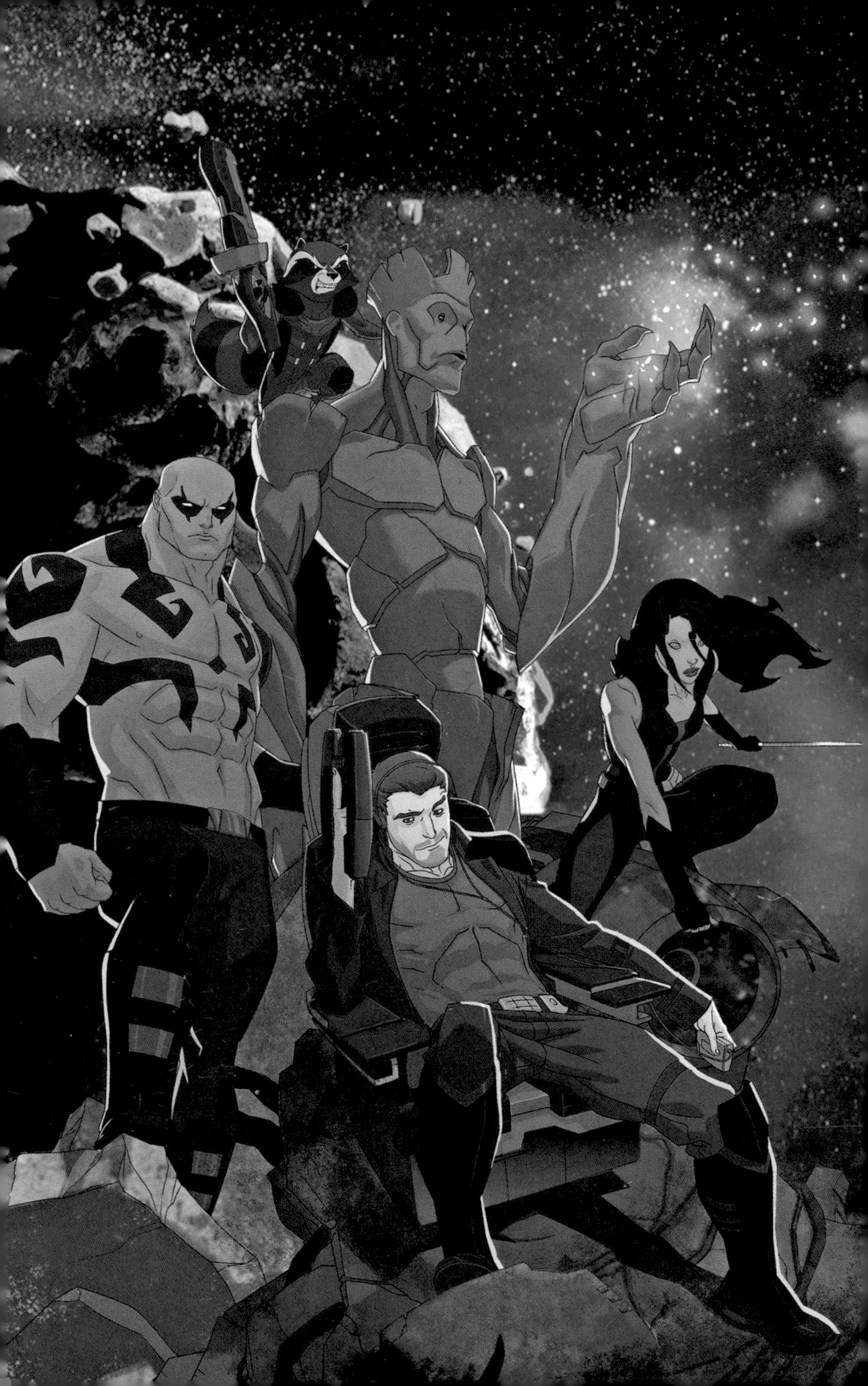

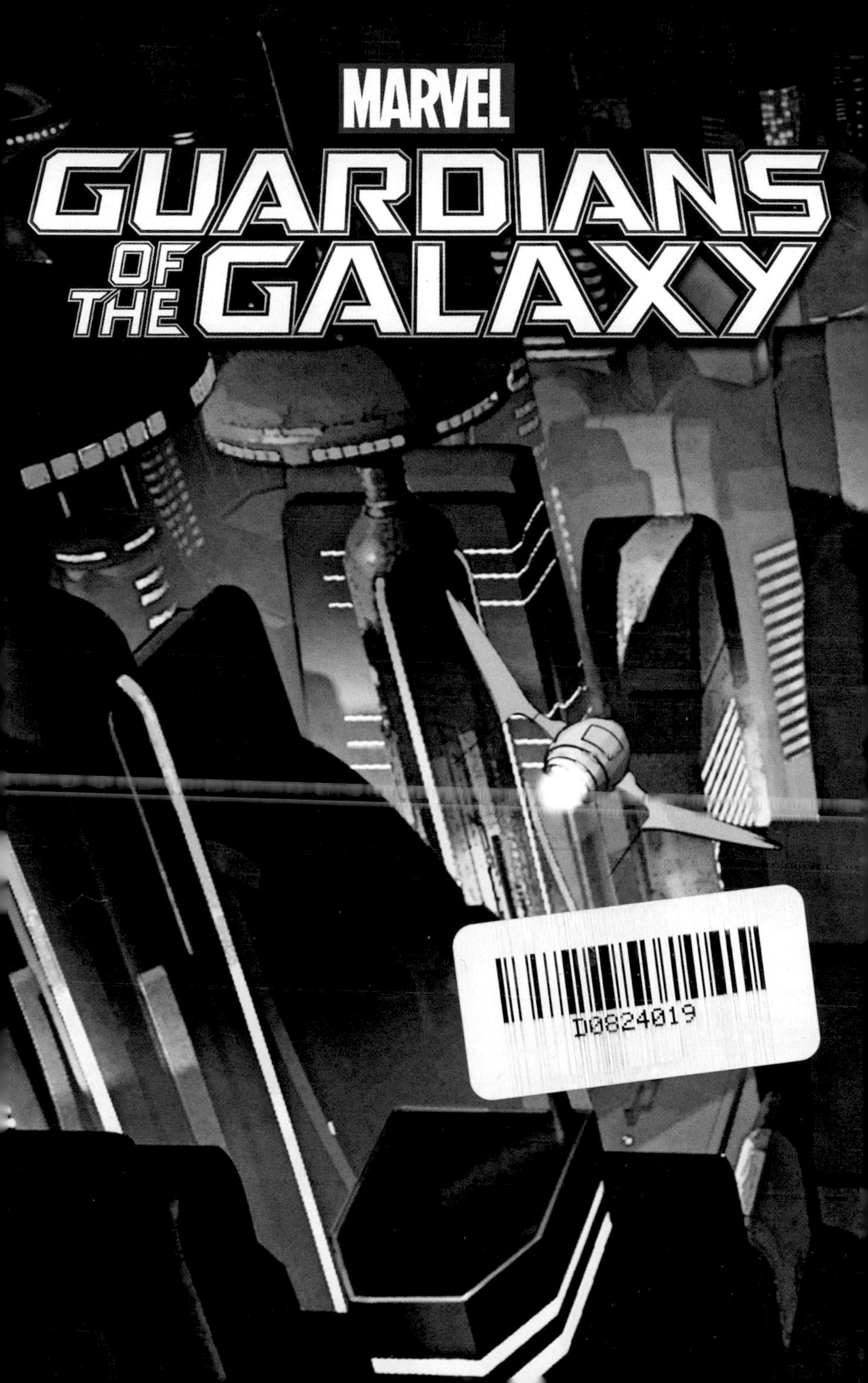
MARVEL
GUARDIANS OF THE GALAXY